Damascus

Damascus
Hidden Treasures of the Old City

Brigid Keenan

Photographs by Tim Beddow

Thames & Hudson

For Alan, who took me there;
for Rabi', who introduced it to me;
for Na'im, who made me a part of it;
and for all who love the old city of Damascus.

Frontispiece: Painted and gilt cupboard doors in the upstairs
reception room at Bait Tibi.

Any copy of this book issued by the publisher as a paperback is sold
subject to the condition that it shall not by way of trade or otherwise
be lent, resold, hired out or otherwise circulated without the publisher's
prior consent in any form of binding or cover other than that in which
it is published and without a similar condition including these words
being imposed on a subsequent purchaser.

© 2000 Safingest International SA

First published in the United Kingdom in 2000 by Thames & Hudson Ltd,
181A High Holborn, London WC1V 7QX

First paperback edition 2001

All Rights Reserved. No part of this publication may be reproduced
or transmitted in any form or by any means, electronic or mechanical,
including photocopy, recording or any other information storage and
retrieval system, without prior permission in writing from the publisher.

British Library Cataloguing-in-Publication Data
A catalogue record for this book is available from the British Library

ISBN 0-500-28299-4

Book design by Adam Hay Design
Printed and bound in Singapore by C.S. Graphics

Contents

Preface	Wafic Rida Saïd	6
Introduction	Brigid Keenan	8
Part 1	Sacred and Secular	13
	Fountains	*30*
	Decorative Tiles	*48*
	Mihrabs and Niches	*76*
Part 2	Palaces and People	81
	Courtyards	*102*
	Ceilings	*122*
	Wall Paintings	*136*
	Coloured Pastework	*148*
	Stonework	*186*
	Windows	*196*
	Doors	*202*
Epilogue		217
Key to the Maps		219
Glossary		220
Bibliography		221
Illustration Credits		222
Index		223

Preface
Wafic Rida Saïd

Opposite: Fairytale Ottoman rococo reception room at Bait Mujallid, before restoration.

I was brought up in an old house in Damascus, a traditional Arab courtyard house like the ones in this book. Looking back, I realize how ingeniously its architect had designed it to cater for the extremes of the Damascene climate. In summer, we lived downstairs, in cool, shady living rooms which opened out into the courtyard garden, allowing the perfume of jasmine and herbs to waft through the house, where it mingled with the scents of coffee and cardamom. The soothing sounds of a waterwheel and fountains enhanced the tranquillity of this private place, a welcome refuge from the harsh summer sun. In winter, our life moved upstairs to the first floor, where the rooms were set out exactly as below, but warmly insulated from the cold by the richly decorated wooden panelling and exquisitely worked carpets. The layout of the house also answered the needs of the family's public and private life. In contrast to the open-plan minimalism fashionable in the West today, unless they were intimate friends, visitors did not pass through the whole house when they came to call. The reception rooms (Al Majlis) had a separate entrance, so that the family could enjoy a great deal of privacy while offering the warm hospitality that is traditional in Syria.

This house where I spent my childhood, which combined the inside and the outside, the hidden and the revealed, the warm and cosy with the cool and airy, inspired in me a lifelong passion for architecture. Nothing has ever seemed to me so beautiful again.

It is a sad fact that people do not know what they have until it has gone. This is true all over the world and many architectural jewels have been bulldozed before people have realized their beauty. In the same way as many European country houses have been lost in the last few decades through neglect or changing tastes, many old houses of Damascus have not survived. Sadly, our family house was knocked down when a subsequent owner obtained planning permission to develop the site. It is a fate which has befallen many other old courtyard houses throughout the Arab world. They do not suit the conveniences, expectations and social structures of the twentieth, let alone the twenty-first, century. As a result, and unless new uses can be found for the courtyard house, all those old cities which are made up of such houses and which owe their beauty to them are endangered.

Brigid Keenan makes a compelling case in these pages for the preservation of one of these splendid cities, the one closest to my heart, Damascus. As she so evocatively shows, Damascus is a city full of fascination, no less for those who live there than for the traveller. Damascus is a city of souks and historic trade routes, of brocade and craftsmen of all kinds, of the mountains and the desert, of an oasis and the Barada river, of the city gates and the Umayyad Mosque, of spices and perfumes carried on the breeze. But most of all, the old city of Damascus is one of family houses. They are its hidden treasures. Tim Beddow's superb photographs reveal to us the Arab courtyard house for what it is: a masterpiece of domestic architecture.

These houses in Damascus, the world's oldest continuously inhabited capital city, deserve a better fate than to lie forgotten. I urge the authorities to take action to list and preserve our architectural heritage and prevent its wanton destruction. These houses also need new owners to preserve, restore and cherish them. It is my hope that, by bringing them and their history to a wider audience, this book will help stimulate interest in finding ways of enabling these glorious houses to survive and flourish in the future.

Introduction
Brigid Keenan

Below: One of the many shops in which herbs and flowers are sold for medicinal potions and teas.

Opposite: The magnificent 19th-century dining room at Bait Mujallid, before restoration.

My husband, a diplomat, was posted to Syria in 1993, and I went with him. Very soon, like Isabel, wife of the famous British Consul Richard Burton a hundred and twenty-odd years before me, I found myself in love with Damascus. (Long after she left Syria, Mrs Burton was often asked if she had liked Damascus, to which her response was: '*Like* it! My eyes fill and my heart throbs even at the question …'. She described an afternoon spent picnicking on Qasyun mountain shortly before she and her husband were obliged to leave the country, as 'my last happy day'.)

I can pinpoint the moment my passion began – it was the first time I went inside one of the great courtyard houses of the old city. The house was Bait Mujallid and I was completely unprepared for what I was going to see, and utterly overwhelmed by its magnificence. Then, when I realized what a poor state the building was in, I was filled with anxiety and rushed back to try and persuade my husband that we should sell our home in England and rescue a Damascene palace instead. Luckily, someone else stepped in to save Bait Mujallid, and I decided to concentrate my efforts on writing this book instead – in the hope that it will convince others of the uniqueness of old Damascus and of the necessity to preserve it.

A traditional way of life continues in the narrow alleyways and crowded souks within the ancient walls of the old city. Heating oil is delivered by horses in beaded bridles and ostrich feathers; earnest small boys dodge and weave through the crowds carrying trays of food from restaurants for their employers; men wheel carts loaded with plants growing in old tins – damask roses, vines – to tempt the owners of the courtyard houses. In the old city, you can drink freshly squeezed mulberry or pomegranate juice; buy handfuls of dried violets or rose-buds to make a *tisane*; pick at Aleppo pistachios (every Syrian will tell you how much more delicious they are than those from Iran); eat piping-hot Arab bread fresh from a cavernous red oven; find a cure for a bad stomach at one of the medicine shops whose shelves are stacked with herbs and powders and potions – and jars of dried baby crocodiles. In winter you can buy the truffles that grow, seemingly miraculously, in the barren desert, and which are said to be the original manna from heaven.

You can watch craftsmen carving wood, or inlaying it with slivers of mother-of-pearl to make exquisite iridescent patterns; see men being shaved with cut-throat razors; or glimpse, through the door of a *hammam* (bathhouse), a scene like an Orientalist painting of men wrapped in towels, lolling on divans smoking hubble-bubble pipes. In the antique shops you might find practically anything – old flower-painted plates from Holland (which came as ballast in ships to Lebanon a hundred years ago), an elaborate Turkish medal, a Russian teapot, a ravishing Persian rug, a Bohemian glass lamp. The goods traded in the souk still come to Damascus from all over the world – one day I came across an old man who had travelled by bus and train from Afghanistan with a haversack of lapis lazuli to sell. The most curious import is a fairly new one (since Syrians emigrated to South America) – this is *yerba maté* from Argentina: the chopped dried leaves of a plant which, when stewed in boiling water, make a bitter tea which is supposed to be good for you. (It is drunk through a curious sieve-straw.) The trade is apparently worth an unbelievable ten million dollars a year.

I am neither a historian nor a scholar, and this book does not pretend to be an academic work; rather, it is intended to give those who do not know the old city of Damascus or its houses a glimpse of the wonders that lie hidden behind the featureless walls, together with a brief background to set the scene.

Before I acknowledge the many people who have been so generous to me with their expertise and time, I would like, first and foremost, to thank Mr Wafic Rida Saïd for his sponsorship and support; truly, this book would not have been possible without him.

I am most grateful to Dr Najah Attar, former Minister of Culture in Syria, for her encouragement.

I am enormously indebted to Mr Ross Burns, author of *Monuments of Syria* (a book that was rarely out of our hands during our five-and-a-half years in Syria), for volunteering to do the maps on pages 73–75. Mr Burns was Australian Ambassador to Syria in the 1980s when he embarked on his brilliant gazetteer of the country, completing it in Canberra between postings. I owe another huge debt to Stefan Weber of the German Institute of Archaeology in Damascus, who shared much of his original research with me and patiently guided me through my own. I would like to thank Dr Sultan Muhesen, former Director-General of Antiquities and Museums in Syria, and his staff; Mme Sarab Atassi and Michel Niéto of the Institut Français d'Études Arabes de Damas, who provided me with so much information. I am very grateful to Dr Peter Clark, OBE, formerly of the British Council in Damascus, for translating Nizar Kabbani's poem 'Letter to My Mother' and for much other help and advice. My thanks also to Professor Talal Akili, Dean of the Architectural Faculty of Damascus University; to As'ad Muhenna, Director of the Commission of the Old City; to Na'im Zabita, architect and expert on the restoration of old houses; to Jeff Spurr of the Fine Arts Library at Harvard University, who spared me so much time and patience; to Peder and Inge Mortensen of the Danish Institute in Damascus; to Fatie Darwish, who first took me to Bait Mujallid; to Mary S. Lovell, for pictures of the Burtons and of 'Abd al-Qadir; to Dr Sabah Kabbani, Dr Geoffrey King, Dr Philip Mansel, Dr Julian Raby, Dr Nadia Khost, Marwan Musselmani, Dr Umm al-Khair al-Azem, Mr Ziyad al-Azem and Amira Amal al-Jaza'iri; to Michael F. Price; to Kate Crowe of the British Foreign Office; to Sir James Craig and Sir Richard Beaumont; to Jehan Tareq, Professor John Carswell, Professor Thomas Philipp, Colin Thubron, Jason Goodwin and Edward Gibbs; to Dr Glenn Markoe of Cincinnati Art Museum; to E. Maxine Bruhns of the University of Pittsburgh; to Joan Aruz of The Metropolitan Museum of Art, New York; to Eileen Powell of Associated Press; to the late Dr Nassib Saliby; to Bassam Ghraoui, Dr Rana Kabbani, Karma Kabbani, Patrick Seale and Hassana Mardam Bey; to Antoine Touma, Carol Ross, Sonia Cachechou, Rabi' al-Darra, Alex Craster, Hana Nahas, Nazih Kawakibi, Marieke Bosman, Catherine Roe and Maya Mamarbachi; and to Khinlyn Fern of the Lawrence Information Service.

I would like to thank all the many house owners who allowed us to invade their privacy, in particular Nora Jumblatt, Sheikha Hussah al-Sabah, 'Ali Shirazi, Hikmat Shatta and the Mardam Bey family.

Finally, I would like to thank my husband for his love and encouragement throughout this project.

Opposite: In the narrow lanes of the old city, the houses almost touch each other across the street.

Part 1
Sacred and Secular

... no recorded event has occurred in the world but Damascus was in existence to receive the news of it. Go back as far as you will into the vague past, there was always a Damascus. To Damascus years are only moments, decades are only flitting trifles of time. She measures time not by days, months and years, but by the empires she has seen rise and prosper and crumble to ruin. She is a type of immortality. She saw Greece rise and flourish two thousand years, and die. In her old age she saw Rome built, she saw it overshadow the world with its power; she saw it perish.... She has looked upon the dry bones of a thousand empires and will see the tombs of a thousand more before she dies.

Mark Twain, The Innocents Abroad, 1869

They say that Damascus is the oldest continuously inhabited city on earth – which makes it, perhaps, the largest unexcavated archaeological site in the world. No-one has ever been able to explore what lies underneath the town because there have always been people living in it. Its mysteries are buried under two-and-a-half metres (eight feet) of earth and debris, to which each ruler, each civilization, has contributed a layer. Almost every time a workman swings his pick and digs a hole in the street to mend a cable or a drain, some antique block or wall is found. When underground repairs were carried out in Straight Street in the 1940s, they came upon a Roman triple arch, which was raised and re-erected where it can be seen today. When, nearby, the foundations of a new house were being dug in the 1960s, four pillars of the Roman colonnade were discovered. Almost the only 'planned' dig that has ever been possible is currently taking place on the site of the old Gold Souk that was burned to the ground in 1960: there the archaeologists have uncovered, under a criss-crossing of later walls, the base of a Roman nymphaeum.

Opposite: The Umayyad Mosque. Minaret of the Bride and mosaics on the Treasury dome.

Above: A reception room at Bait al-Yusuf, dramatically painted, carved and gilt, but needing restoration.

Damascus is sandwiched between the Anti-Lebanon mountains on one side and a desert that extends for thousands of miles, all the way to the Indian Ocean, on the other. Ross Burns, author of *Monuments of Syria*, describes the city as a port: 'It is the natural first landing

Left: View of Damascus drawn in 1668 showing the walls of the city and the river flowing through the town.

Above: 19th-century engraving of a group of travellers approaching Damascus.

for the desert traveller.' The town grew here because this is the spot where the Barada river, gushing out of the mountains eleven kilometres (seven miles) from the city, seeps into the plain, creating a huge oasis: the Ghuta it is called, a patch of vivid green about fifty kilometres (thirty miles) wide in the yellow desert. There are *tells* (*tals* or mounds) left by many prehistoric settlements in the Ghuta, but Damascus is the only one that developed, presumably because of the Barada river. 'It could not die', wrote Mark Twain, visiting Damascus in 1867, 'So long as its waters remain to it – so long will Damascus live …'. From the earliest times, the inhabitants of the town – Arameans, Greeks, Romans – tamed this river, channelling it into streams and canals to feed not only the gardens that were cultivated in the oasis, but the houses of the city itself. Every traveller to Damascus marvelled at the sophistication of its water supply. Al-Maqdisi, an Arab geographer, writing in AD 985, remarked: 'Damascus is a city intersected by streams and begirt with trees. Here prices are moderate, fruits and snow abound and the products of both hot and cold climes are found. Nowhere else will be seen such magnificent hot baths, nor such beautiful fountains …'.

Some eight hundred and fifty years later, Alexander Kinglake, an English historian and traveller, put the same idea in more elaborate terms: 'The juice of her life is the gushing and ice-cold torrent that tumbles from the snowy sides of Anti-Lebanon. Close along on the river's edge through seven sweet miles of rustling boughs and deepest shade, the city spreads out her whole length; as a man falls flat, face forward on the brook that he may drink and drink again: so Damascus,

Below: Two 19th-century engravings showing travellers approaching the city on the road across the Anti-Lebanon mountains. Damascus shimmers like a mirage in the distance.

Right: Map of Damascus drawn in 1572. It was probably the inspiration for the bird's-eye view on pages 14–15.

thirsting for ever, lies down with her lips to the stream and clings to its rushing waters.'

Until the 20th century, travellers to Damascus approached the city by a track over the mountains, and their first sight of it was from above. That view of the shimmering white city in its green oasis, with the dry desert beyond extending to the horizon, was breathtaking, almost mirage-like. According to legend, the Prophet Mohammed travelled to Damascus along this mountain road, but when he saw the enchanting vista of the city at his feet he decided not to continue his journey because 'man should only enter Paradise once'.

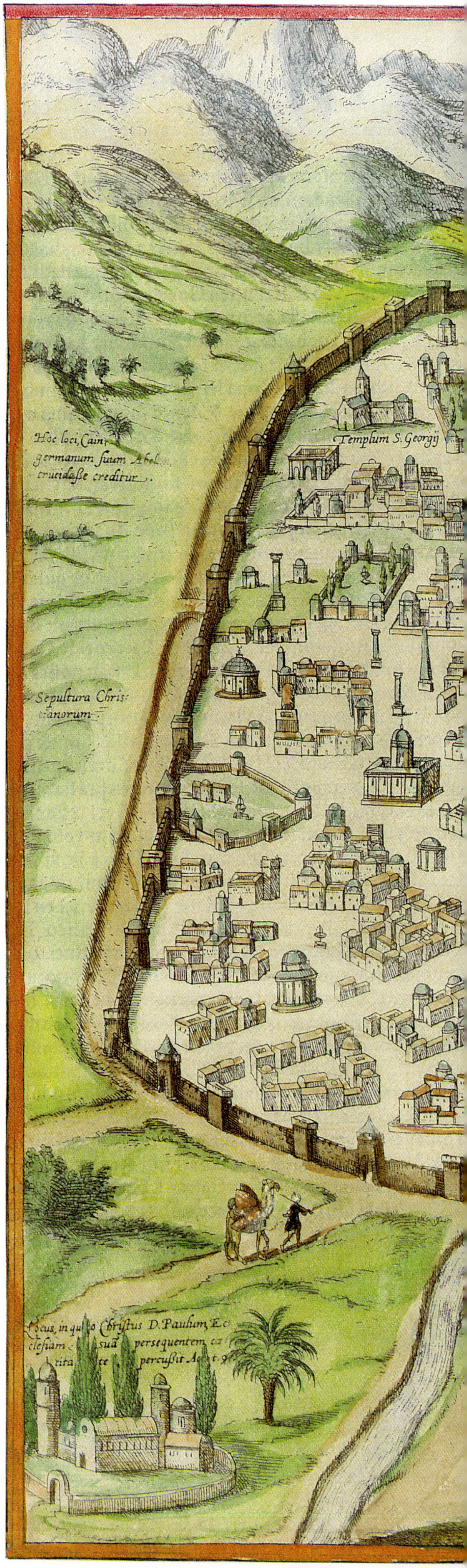

Miss M. E. Rogers, an Englishwoman who visited Syria in 1865 when her brother was Consul there, was told a different story: that, although Mohammed turned away, his guide, bewitched by the spectacular view, cried 'Here let me die!' – and that a little domed shrine on the hill is his tomb. (There is yet another version of the legend, in which the Prophet approached Damascus from the southern suburb of Qadam and turned away, not because of the view, but because he stumbled in the road and took this as a sign not to continue his journey. Qadam means 'foot' in Arabic, and in the old mosque there, a piece of marble with a footprint-shaped impression on it is venerated. In ancient times it was said that the print was made by Moses, but today it is revered as Mohammed's.)

In April 1833, the French poet, statesman and traveller Alphonse de Lamartine came along the hill road towards Damascus, when suddenly, 'through a gap in the rocks, my eye fell on the strangest and most fantastic sight which man has ever seen: it was Damascus and its boundless desert, a few hundred feet below my path ... first the town, surrounded by its walls ... a forest of minarets of all shapes, watered by the seven branches of its river, and streams without number, until the view is lost in a labyrinth of flower gardens and trees.... We stopped walking, we were pressed to the opening in the rock contemplating this magic sight which had unfolded so complete, and so abruptly, under our eyes.'

Perhaps this is the key to Damascus. That it is, if not a magic place, certainly a spiritual one, where religion has played a major part in history. Curious events have happened there. The most famous, of course, and the one which put Damascus on the map for the Christian world, is the story of Saul, the young tent maker, so fanatically anti-Christian that he was riding to the city on the instructions of the Jewish high priests in order to harass the disciples there. 'And as he journeyed,' says the Acts of the Apostles, 'he came near Damascus: and suddenly there shined round about him a light from heaven: And he fell to the earth, and heard a voice saying unto him, Saul, Saul, why persecutest thou me?' A Damascene Christian, Ananias, was instructed in a dream to go to 'the street which is called Straight' and take care of the poor blind, bewildered man; Saul was baptized Paul in the Barada river and 'immediately there fell from his eyes as it had been scales'. ('The road to Damascus', 'seeing the light' and 'the scales fell from his eyes' – Damascus and the conversion of St Paul have given the world at least three phrases in common use.) Eventually, Paul had to be smuggled out of the city because of the vengeful fury of his new enemies, the Jews; and since they were watching the gates, he was let down over the outer wall, in a basket, and escaped.

Today, in the Christian area of Damascus called Sufaniyya, there is a young woman, Mirna, who claims to have had messages from God and visions of the Virgin Mary. When the Virgin appeared on the roof of Mirna and her husband's house – where normally the washing was hung out – Mirna knelt in front of her. 'I put my hands on her feet', she says, 'and they were warm.' A mysterious pool of oil left a stain where the Virgin had stood – which can be seen to this day.

The divine message to Mirna was as simple as the one to St Paul: to pray for the unification of the Christian churches. A very understandable request when you read the section on Syria in the Librairie Hachette guide *Orient, Syrie, Palestine* of 1890. It lists the population of Damascus like this:

Muslims	74,464
Druses	500
Christians, Greek	5,945
Christians, Greek Catholics	6,191
Christians, Syrians	260
Christians, Syrian Catholics	460
Christians, Armenians and Chaldeans	405
Christians, Armenian Catholics	235
Christians, Maronites	406
Christians, Latins	110
Christians, Protestants	70
Strangers, Soldiers	15,000
Jews	4,680

Some of these divisions were caused by the work of missionaries from the Western churches, who began to come to Syria as long ago as the 16th century. Since they were not allowed to preach Christianity to Muslims, they worked on the local Greek Orthodox and Maronites, many of whom were converted to Roman Catholicism or to one or other of the Protestant sects.

Pilgrims come from all over the world to pray with Mirna (and she has her own website on the Internet).

Opposite: The Saddle Souk (Suq Sarujiyya) with the minaret of the Sanjaqdar Mosque.

The north side of the Umayyad Mosque and the Minaret of the Bride photographed in the 1870s by Bonfils.

But pilgrims have been coming to Damascus, 'the land of prophets', the fourth holiest city of Islam (Mecca, Medina and Jerusalem are the first three) and an assembly point for the *hajj* – the great annual pilgrimage to Mecca – for more than a thousand years. In ancient times, they visited the many holy caves on the Qasyun mountain: the cave of Adam; the cave where, according to local legend, Abraham was born; the cave of blood where Cain killed Abel (and the rocks still weep for sorrow); the cave of the seven sleepers – holy men who hid there at a time of persecution and miraculously 'woke' three hundred years later when it was all over; the cave of forty martyrs who died of hunger at another time of trouble, and so on.

These days, Damascus receives between one and two hundred thousand Iranian pilgrims each year on a different mission. Mostly women, they bustle through the narrow lanes of the old city in their all-enveloping *chadors* to visit the tombs of Zainab, Mohammed's granddaughter, and Ruqayya, his great-granddaughter, and the sanctuary of Husain, his grandson, at the Umayyad Mosque. (It is often said that Husain's head is buried in this sanctuary, but in fact it is in the mosque that bears his name in Cairo. It was probably kept in the Umayyad Mosque for a time after his death, so giving rise to this belief.)

The great Umayyad Mosque is the whole religious history of Damascus told in stone. It was constructed within the walls of the Roman temple of Jupiter, part of which had previously been used as a Christian church; the Roman temple had, in turn, been built on the site of an Aramean temple. The Aramean temple was important enough to be mentioned in the Bible, which tells the story of a conquering king who found the altar of the Great Temple in Damascus so impressive that he ordered his own priests to make a copy of it. Since the Aramean temple lies directly under today's mosque, nothing of it can be seen, apart from the statue of a sphinx which was found in the north wall of the mosque during some repairs in 1948, and which is now in the National Museum.

The Roman temple complex spread over a huge area – bigger than that of the Temple of Bel in Palmyra – and pillars and blocks belonging to its outer wall can be found in the houses and lanes of the old city, which have long since encroached into the outer temple area. Indeed, the whole of the old city is a mishmash of recycled stone: high on the south wall of the mosque, for instance, opposite the Gold Souk and the public lavatories (which themselves date from the 14th century), there is a worn Roman bust re-used as a building block. The Roman entrance to the temple, a massive colonnaded gateway, stood at the back of the present-day mosque. In the British missionary Josias Porter's time in Damascus (1850–55) five columns were still standing, but little of it remains today.

The Roman Emperor Julian (AD 361–363), known as 'the Apostate' because he tried to reverse the tide of Christianity that was overwhelming the Eastern Roman Empire, wrote of 'great and sacred Damascus' with its beautiful temples and magnificent shrines; he called it 'Jupiter's city, and the eye of all the East'.

But at the end of the 4th century, when Christianity was proclaimed the official religion of the region and the Byzantine Empire came into being, the inner part of the Jupiter temple, the *cella*, was adapted into the Christian church of St John the Baptist and a great carved stone gateway was opened in the south wall. This entrance is now half-buried in the ground, but its brave inscription – which reads somewhat ironically today – is still there, proclaiming in Greek: 'Thy Kingdom, O Christ, is an everlasting Kingdom and Thy dominion endureth throughout all generations.'

The Kingdom of the Lord was safe in the temple of Jupiter for the three hundred years of Byzantine rule – until Damascus was captured by the Arabs in AD 635. Even then, a deal was worked out by which the Christians and Muslims shared the sacred space: on entering the basilica by the Christian gate, Muslims turned to the right to pray in their mosque of the Companions of the Prophet, while Christians turned to the left to pray in their church. This happy situation lasted for more than fifty years.

The man appointed by the invading Arabs to be Governor of Syria, Mu'awiyya, became a key figure in the world of Islam. On the death of the Third Caliph ('*Khalifa*' was the title of Mohammed's successors), a bitter power struggle began for the leadership of the Muslim world. On one hand was 'Ali, Mohammed's cousin and son-in-law, claiming it as his hereditary right, and on the other was Mu'awiyya, more distantly related to the Prophet, but with stronger support. The Muslim world split into two groups: those who backed 'Ali (and, after his murder, his son Husain) are known as *Shi'a* and those who supported Mu'awiyya are called *Sunni*.

Mu'awiyya prevailed and established the Umayyad dynasty in Damascus, which became the capital of the Muslim world instead of Medina, where the previous caliphs had been based. After his death (he was buried in the cemetery at Bab al-Saghir in Damascus), his son, Yazid, reinforced this Sunni dynasty by killing 'Ali's son, Husain, and bringing his family as prisoners to Damascus (which is why the tombs of his sister and daughter are in the city today).

Above: Iranian pilgrims inside the new mosque built over the tomb of Ruqayya, Mohammed's great-granddaughter.

Opposite: Photograph of the western gate of the Roman temple, before the souk around it was cleared in the 1980s.

The Umayyad period was a glorious one for Damascus, epitomized by the Great Mosque which was built by al-Walid, one of Mu'awiyya's successors, in AD 705. Scholars have argued about whether al-Walid converted the Christian church into the mosque or whether he pulled it down and began again; opinion nowadays is that he built the mosque from scratch within the walls of the Roman temple.

Arab historians write that, when al-Walid asked the Christians to give up their share of the building so that he could build his mosque, they refused. Furious, he threatened that he would pull down the biggest of their churches unless they agreed to leave, so reluctantly they did. Al-Walid, it is said, took a pick in his own hands and began to demolish what is now known as the Minaret of Jesus on the southeast corner, in which a Christian hermit was living.

Before al-Walid began work on the construction of his mosque, according to the Andalusian/Arab traveller Ibn Jubair, writing in 1194, 'He applied to the King at Constantinople to send him twelve thousand of the artificers of his country, at the same time threatening him with chastisement if he delayed. But the King of the Greeks did as he was commanded with all docility …'. The mosque took eight years to complete, with craftsmen coming not only from the Byzantine Empire,

Opposite: An elderly man reads the Qur'an at the eastern door of the great Umayyad Mosque.

Above: A minaret of the Umayyad Mosque seen through the Roman arches that were part of the western entrance.

Overleaf: A glimpse of the courtyard of the Umayyad Mosque through the northern entrance.

but from Persia, India and North Africa as well. According to al-Maqdisi, the mosque cost al-Walid the whole of Syria's revenues for seven years, 'and this does not include what the Emperor of Byzantium and the Amirs of the Muslims gave to him in the matter of precious stones and other materials for the mosaics'. Yaqut, a Greek slave who became one of the great Muslim geographers, wrote in 1225 that just the cost of the cabbages that the workmen ate during the construction of the mosque came to 6,000 dinars (which an ardent English scholar, in the 19th century, worked out as £3,000, equivalent to about £130,000 today).

Al-Maqdisi gave a very detailed picture of the mosque. Apart from its great courtyard paved in white marble and its huge dome supported on pillars (two of which, in variegated marble, were reputed to have come from the Queen of Sheba's tabernacle), he described the interior decoration: 'The inner walls of the mosque, for twice the height of a man, are faced with variegated marbles; and above this, even to the very ceiling, are mosaics of various colours and in gold, showing figures of trees and towns and beautiful inscriptions, all most exquisitely and finely worked. The capitals of the columns are covered with gold and the vaulting above the arcades is everywhere ornamented in mosaic.... Both within the Mihrab and around it are set cut agates and turquoises of the size of the finest stones that are used in rings.... But of the most wondrous of the sights worthy of remark is verily the setting of the various coloured marbles, and how the veining of each follows from that of its neighbour; and it is such that, should an artist come daily during a whole year and stand before these mosaics, he might always discover some new pattern and some fresh design ...'.

According to Ibn Batuta, the great Arab traveller from North Africa, writing in 1326, there were seventy muezzins to chant the call to prayer (to this day, the call to prayer from the Umayyad Mosque is a harmony of several voices together). Ya'qubi, a historian, wrote in 874 that the mosque had praying space for twenty thousand men and that there were six hundred lamps suspended on gold chains. During the construction of the mosque, according to Ya'qubi, workmen found a cave in the foundations and called for al-Walid to come and see. 'By night the Khalif descended thereinto and, behold, it was a beautiful chapel ... and within lay a chest, inside of which was a basket, on which

Overleaf: The famous mosaics of the Umayyad Mosque date back to the 8th century and supposedly show Damascus as it was then: a city of trees and rivers and grand houses.

was written: "This is the Head of John, the son of Zacharias".' Al-Walid ordered the basket to be buried under one of the pillars in the prayer hall and he built a shrine to St John nearby. Ya'qubi finishes with a nice gruesome touch: 'At the time the head was laid here, Zaid (the overseer) states that he saw the same, and that the hair and flesh thereon had nowise suffered decay.'

All sorts of legends grew up around the mosque – that one prayer here was worth thirty thousand prayers said anywhere else; that no spider ever wove its web in the mosque and no swallow built its nest there; that Jesus will descend to earth on Judgment Day at the Minaret of Jesus. On a more practical note, most of the historians mentioned the fact that the mosque could easily be cleaned by flooding the court with water, which then drained away through another outlet.

Al-Walid died in AD 715 and his cousin, 'Umar, became Caliph. 'Umar was the opposite of his predecessor; he was a holy and austere man who felt guilty about the extravagance lavished on the mosque and the fact that it had been taken from the Christians (who lost no time in complaining to him about it). He was tempted to sell its treasures and return the mosque to the Christians, but the people of Damascus objected, and so he gave the Christians 'a great sum' and they built the Church of St John in Bab Tuma. According to Yaqut, what changed the Caliph's mind was a conversation overheard in the mosque between two 'ambassadors of the Greeks'. One said to the other, 'I had told the assemblies of the people of Byzantium that the Arabs and their power would remain but a brief space; but now, when I see what they have built, I know that of a surety their dominion will reach to lengths of days.' Indeed, al-Walid's glorious mosque, uniting as it did the skills of designers and craftsmen from many different cultures into one harmonious and magnificent whole, is the second great treasure of Islamic art – the first being the Dome of the Rock in Jerusalem.

A terrible fire ravaged the mosque in 1069; Tamerlane burnt it in 1401; and yet another fire gutted it in 1893, after which all the craftsmen in Damascus took a hand in the restoration work. (The strange cart parked in the courtyard, which looks like some kind of battering ram, is in fact a special invention made at that time

Fountains

Damascus houses have both indoor and outdoor fountains. The outdoor fountains were placed in the centre of the courtyard, and were usually quite simple in design – made in plain cut stone – until the fashion for lavishly decorated marble came in during the 19th century. Indoor fountains, on the other hand, were highly ornate in inlaid, carved or mosaic marble, often with a matching marble floor around them. Wall fountains were used inside the houses or in the courtyards.

Opposite: Stone mosaic fountain on which fruits could be cooled, at the Historical Museum of Damascus.

Above: Close-up of the carved stone basin of a fountain at the Historical Museum.

Right: The tranquil courtyard of a house in Qaimariyya with a central fountain.

Fountains

Left: Traditional indoor fountain in marble mosaic with floor to match, at Bait Niyadu (Bait Stambuli).

Above: Carved and inlaid stone wall fountain at the Historical Museum.

Opposite: Exquisite indoor fountain in black, red and white marble at Bait Qasim.

Fountains

Above: Ornate white marble fountain at Bait Shamaiyya in the 1870s.

Opposite: The curious marble 'maze' indoor fountain at the Historical Museum.

The Great Mosque at Córdoba, built during the Umayyad dynasty in Spain.

to drag pillars from the quarries in Mezze.) The mosque was restored again in the early 1990s – a subject of heated debate at the time.

In AD 750, the Umayyad dynasty was overthrown by a new group claiming the right to the Caliphate through Mohammed's uncle, 'Abbas, and, with that, Damascus's happiest days came to an end. The first Abbasid Caliph invited the last of the Umayyad princes to a 'reconciliation' banquet, but when they arrived he treacherously had them all massacred. Then, so it was said, he ordered carpets to be spread over their bodies and ate his dinner sitting on top, declaring that it was the most delicious meal he had ever had. Only one prince escaped the massacre and he fled to Andalusia in Spain, which by that time had been conquered and added to the enormous empire of the Arabs. There, the Umayyad love of building manifested itself in the Great Mosque in Córdoba. This was later converted into a Christian place of worship – ironically, the exact opposite of what had happened in Damascus. (When the Holy Roman Emperor Charles V saw what had been done inside the mosque – where dozens of elegant pillars in the centre had been destroyed in order to accommodate a large cathedral building – he is said to have raged: 'You have built here what you, or anyone, might have built here, or anywhere else: but you have destroyed what was unique in the world.')

Muslim government in Spain lasted for seven hundred years and it was a link through which the Arabs influenced Europe in innumerable ways. Fruits and vegetables – artichokes, aubergines, damsons (from Damascus), bitter oranges – went from the Arab world to Europe; words like 'alcohol', 'algebra', 'alchemy', 'alkali' came into Western languages, for the very good reason that the existence of these things was unknown before the Arabs came, and therefore there were no words for them. The technique of distillation came from the Arabs, and it was they, too, who safeguarded the knowledge of the Greeks and studied chemistry, mathematics, medicine, astronomy and philosophy while Europe was in the Dark Ages. The philosopher and historian Joseph McCabe wrote in *The Splendours of Moorish Spain*: 'In the tenth century, Cordova had a

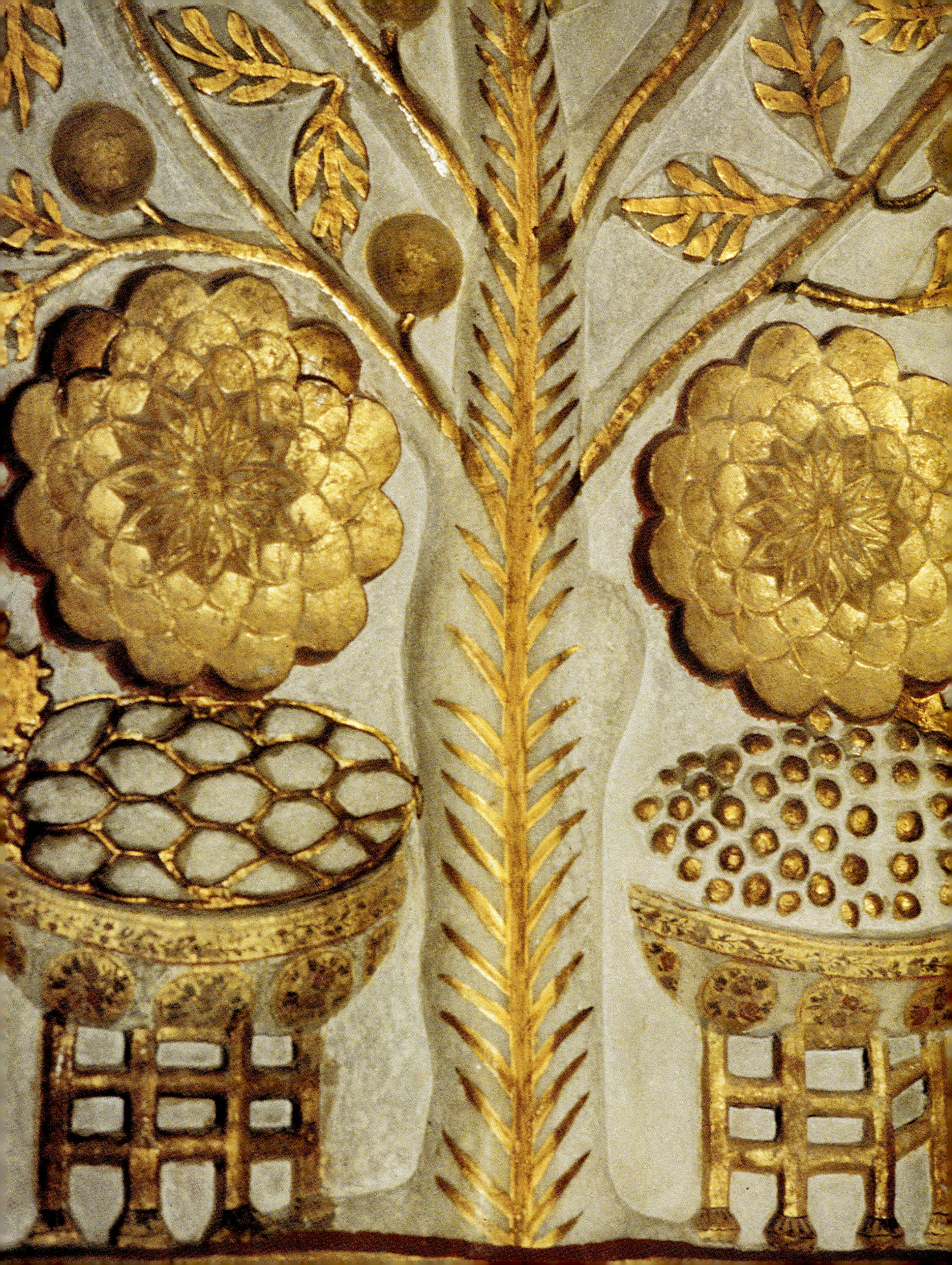

population of a million souls, a lavish supply of pure water and miles of well-paved and lamp-lit streets. There was not anywhere in Europe, outside Arab Spain and Sicily, and there would not be for at least two centuries, a single city with 30,000 people with even the most rudimentary sewerage, with any paved or lamp-lit streets, with a communal supply of pure water …'.

The best-known word in Spanish – '*Olé*' – probably comes from the Arabic '*Allah*' which, in Syria today, you still hear called out by an audience to show its approval of a performer.

After the Abbasids seized power from the Umayyads, they abandoned Damascus and ruled the Muslim world from Baghdad; apart from a brief interlude in the time of Nureddin (see below), Damascus was not to be a capital city again for more than a thousand years. Its fortunes rose and fell under the succeeding dynasties: Damascus prospered when there was peace in the region, and the great camel caravans that brought goods to be traded from all over the world could operate freely without fear of being attacked. At other times, the city suffered from instability caused by warring factions in the region seeking power, or from oppression by those who obtained it. For no dynasty (or Governor representing one) ever ruled Damascus without trying to squeeze the maximum revenue from its people. An example of how much an official could make was As'ad Pasha al-Azem, who governed Damascus for fourteen years: when his fortune was confiscated by the Ottoman Sultan in 1758, it amounted to so much money that the currency of the Empire had to be revalued. (Al-Azem's own Ming porcelain went to the Sultan himself, and now forms part of the Chinese porcelain collection at the Topkapi Palace Museum in Istanbul.)

Over the centuries – in spite of what Ibn Hawqal, a merchant/traveller writing in AD 978, had called 'their violent and insurgent ways' (which he attributed to the fact that Leo is the zodiac sign of the city) – Damascenes learnt the art of survival under their foreign overlords. For security's sake, those who shared a common bond – families, clans, fellow guild members – would live near each other in distinct quarters in the city, sometimes in *haras*, or alleyways, which could be closed with gates at night. Each quarter had its own appointed leader as well as mosques, baths, schools and souks, so that no-one had to venture too far, and the clear-cut Roman

Opposite: Tree of life decoration in gilt marble on the back of a niche in the Historical Museum.

Below: A niche in Saladin's tomb, decorated with stone pastework flowers and Damascus tiles.

grid pattern of streets that had once neatly divided the old city became overlaid with an ants' nest of lanes and passageways. To this day, Damascenes remain private and unfathomable to the outsider. Syrians have a saying: 'A secret must be kept between two', meaning your own two lips. A system of *waqf*, or religious trusts, came into being, by which the revenue from a *khan* (caravanserai) or *hammam* (bathhouse) or *suq* (souk or market) was committed to the construction and upkeep of specific religious buildings, schools or hospitals. This meant, incidentally, that the properties producing the revenue could not be confiscated from their owners at the whim of a Governor or Sultan.

Nature played its own vital part in the well-being, or otherwise, of Damascus. There were years of terrible

Below: Typical late 19th-century Damascus street scene (in the Bahsa quarter) photographed by Bonfils, who wrongly captioned it 'Straight Street'.

Opposite: Straight Street closed on a Friday. The holes in the roof were allegedly made by French gunfire.

drought, when not enough water flowed to turn the wheels of the many mills built along the river. (Some of these old mills are still there today, but none operate with water power.) There were years when half the city was swept away by floods; years when locusts ate the crops; years when earthquakes toppled the buildings; years when the plague all but wiped out the population – one such epidemic was as recent as the 19th century. (John Bowring, a British government official, wrote in his *Report on the Commercial Statistics of Syria* in 1840: 'I have heard the outbreak of plague attributed to the signing of a document with a pen which had come from an infected house; to a thread, which had been bought in a Turkish bazaar, being used for mending a sheet; to a feather in a bed from a fowl which had escaped from the Mohammedan quarter.') Somehow, Damascus always recovered – it had the huge natural advantage of its river and the fertile oasis where almost anything could be grown; and the wheat bowl of Hauran in southern Syria lay on its doorstep. All these made Damascus resilient and, in spite of the ups and downs of its fortunes, it seems to have kept up appearances. At any rate, travellers at most periods of history were impressed.

In 1154, the geographer Ibn Mohammed al-Idrisi wrote: 'The city of Damascus contains all manner of good things, and streets of various craftsmen, with merchants selling all sorts of silk and brocade of exquisite rarity and wonderful workmanship – all this, such that the like exists nowhere else. That which they make here is carried ... to all capital towns both far and near.... The craftsmen of the city are in high renown and its merchandise is sought in all the markets of the earth; while the city itself is the most lovely of the cities ...'. In 1590, a French traveller, Jacques de Villamont, wrote: 'This is a great and powerful city.... The streets are mostly roofed and vaulted so that one can walk without fear of the ardour of the sun or the incommodity of rain; which is something remarkable, as is the lighting at night. Whoever considers the beauty, situation and riches of this town, will judge it to be paradise on earth.' In 1660, the French Consul in Aleppo, Chevalier d'Arvieux, wrote of Damascus: '... the people here are richer, and less exposed to the tyrannies of their rulers. From whatever nation or religion, they like to be well-dressed, well-housed and well-supplied, and they like their freedom. They are the subjects of the Great Sultan, but they are not slaves.'

John Green, an Englishman travelling in Syria in 1736, described Straight Street as it appeared then: 'On both sides of it there are shops, where all the rich merchandises are sold, that are brought every year by the caravans from Europe, Armenia, Africa, Persia and the Indies. The artful manner in which they are ranged tempts people to buy.'

The Abbasid dynasty degenerated, losing power to the Seljuk Turks, one of whose officers, Zangi, rose to become the dominant figure in the region and gave his name to the next dynasty, the Zangids. These were anarchic and confused times: there were the Abbasids in decline; the Seljuk Turks; the Crusaders from Europe; the Assassins in the mountains, with their own violent agenda; a new Shi'a group from Egypt called the Fatimids; Byzantines; and local tribes and chieftains, all jostling for power in the area. Zangi spent his life battling against them all and trying to create some kind of kingdom for himself. His son, Nur al-Din (known to the West as Nureddin) was more successful and managed to secure three decades of comparative peace.

Before Nureddin took power in Damascus, the Crusaders had tried, in 1148, to seize the city. So confident had they been of victory, according to the Syrian writer Ibn Munqidh, that 'They had already bargained amongst themselves for the houses of Damascus, its baths and its

مطبعة
تيسير كروما
واولاده

مشغل عكل

Below: Late 19th-century photograph of Damascus with Saladin's tomb in the foreground.

Opposite: A newly restored section of Damascus Citadel (previously rebuilt by Saladin's brother in the late 13th century), with a modern equestrian statue of Saladin.

bazaars ...'. However, once in front of the city walls, the heat, lack of water and sickness – and the ferocity of the Damascene defenders – brought the siege to an end after only three days. The Crusaders retreated, but made another attempt to take Damascus in 1154: this time Nureddin rode to the rescue with his army and the Crusaders once again abandoned their siege.

Nureddin's reign was a brief golden era for Damascus. Business prospered and an explosion of building work took place. The walls of the old city were restored, the gates reorganized and the towers repaired. (One of these, with the ruler's inscription on it, can be found hidden in the courtyard of a shop near the entrance to Straight Street.) He built the Hammam Nur al-Din in the Suq al-Buzuriyya (Spice Souk), which is the oldest bath still open to the public, and the remarkable hospital, the Maristan Nur al-Din, which has recently been restored, not far from the Suq al-Hamidiyya, using the ransom money of a Crusader prince to pay for it. He did restoration work in the Umayyad Mosque and installed, by the eastern doorway, a wondrously complicated clock which involved brass birds releasing weights into cups to sound the hours. He opened law courts and a dozen schools, the most important of which, the Madrasa al-Nuriyya, he was eventually buried in. The Reverend Josias Porter, writing in 1855, described this as 'among the finest buildings in the city'. Unfortunately, part of it was rebuilt in 1990, but the section where Nureddin's tomb lies remains as it was and is an oasis of tranquillity off the hectic Suq al-Khayyatin (Tailors' Souk).

The great Saladin (Salah al-Din), a Kurd, was one of Nureddin's generals. He had been sent as an emissary to the court of the Fatimids in Egypt, but had ended up taking over that country himself and then, on Nureddin's death in 1174, he defeated all heirs and claimants and took hold of Syria as well, marrying Nureddin's widow to give himself legitimacy.

When in Damascus, Saladin lived in the Citadel, as Nureddin had done, but he was rarely there because of his endless campaigns against the Crusaders; in 1187 he had his finest hour, when he drove them out of Jerusalem. He returned to Damascus in 1192 after yet another campaign, this time against Richard the Lionheart, but he died the following year, aged fifty-five. It was said that, despite all his years of battle and conquest, Saladin's personal fortune on his death was one dinar and thirty-six dirhams, and a contemporary wrote that he was the only ruler of Syria whose death was genuinely mourned.

Saladin was buried in the tomb on the north side of the Umayyad Mosque and next to it his son, al-'Aziz, built a fine *madrasa* (school), of which, sadly, only an empty arch and a pretty fountain in a pleasant garden remain. There are two sarcophagi in the mausoleum; the one carved in wood is the original, which the French orientalist and architect Jean Sauvaget described as being 'among the most beautiful pieces of work that the 12th century has left in Syria'. The other, an ornate marble sarcophagus, is commonly said to have been presented by the German Kaiser Wilhelm II on his visit to Damascus in 1898, but in fact, according to Stefan Weber, an architectural historian currently working at the German Institute of Archaeology in Damascus, it must have been a gift from another donor, since the date inscribed on it is 1878 – twenty years before the Kaiser's visit. Kaiser Wilhelm *did* present Saladin's tomb with a bronze wreath made in Germany, which Lawrence of Arabia was given by King Faisal after their triumphant entry into Damascus together in 1918. Lawrence brought it back to England and gave it to the Imperial War Museum in London, where it is today. (Henry Jessup, an American missionary who worked in Beirut for fifty-three years in the 19th century, wrote that after the wreath had been presented by the Kaiser a devout sheikh was praying in the tomb when he noticed that the wreath was decorated with the cross of the Knights of Malta. 'Take it away!' he cried. 'A Crusader's cross on the tomb of Sultan Saladin! God forbid!') The mausoleum was restored in the early part of the 17th century and decorated with some of the Damascus tiles you can see there today. Saladin was succeeded by his brother, al-Malik al-'Adil, who undertook a major reconstruction of the Citadel. (It is being restored again now and, when finished, will be opened to tourists.) When he died, al-Malik al-'Adil was buried in the attractive Madrasa al-'Adiliyya.

Saladin left seventeen sons to quarrel over their territorial inheritance. The Ayyubids, as this family dynasty is known, did not succeed in keeping Saladin's empire intact – indeed, one of them signed a treaty handing Jerusalem to a new group of Crusaders for several years – nor did they manage to rule it for any longer than sixty-seven years, but their period is rightly famous for its architecture.

There are Ayyubid tombs to be found all around Damascus – that of Saladin's sister, Sitt al-Sham, or Lady of Damascus, was saved at the last minute when the Suq Saruja district was being redeveloped in the 1980s. The watchman who looks after the tomb of one of Saladin's nephews, Furukhshah, in the Zuqaq al-Sakhr quarter (at the back of the garden across the road from the National Museum) says that he often sees ghosts there at night.

The first black-and-white-striped façade in Damascus belongs to an Ayyubid building, the Madrasa al-Qilijiyya (in a narrow lane off the Spice Souk) and the whole popular, busy quarter behind the Umayyad Mosque, known as Qaimariyya, is named after an Ayyubid nobleman who built a school there. (The school still exists, although little of its original Ayyubid architecture is visible today.) But it was in the district of Salihiyya that the Ayyubids put up most of their best buildings, including the Hanbali Mosque, in which they used Roman pillars and capitals. The French writer Gérard Degeorge calls Salihiyya 'a museum of Ayyubid architecture'.

While Saladin's sons and nephews and *their* sons and cousins were fighting each other, two new great powers were looming on the horizon like thunderclouds. In 1260, the Mongols swept in from the east like human locusts, killing and pillaging as they went: first Baghdad and then Aleppo and finally Damascus. In Egypt, the army of slave soldiers, known as Mamluks, which served the ruler (Saladin's nephew), turned on their masters and seized power. The Mamluks were the toughest of soldiers – taken as boys from their families in their native lands of Central Asia or the Caucasus and sold into slavery, their only way to the top was by military prowess. The Mamluks earned a reputation for ruthlessness: 'They would kill a man as easily as others would kill a chicken', wrote a shocked European traveller. But they were just what was needed to face the Mongols. Led by Baibars, who had once been sold cheaply in the Damascus slave-market because he had a cataract in one eye, the Mamluks drove the Mongols back across the Euphrates river and chased the Crusaders out of the Middle East – not surprisingly, it was said that Baibars's seventeen years of rule were seventeen years spent in the saddle. Baibars used Damascus as his base while fighting in Syria, and he built a great palace by the Barada river, where the Takiyya al-Sulaimaniyya stands today. It was called the 'Ablaq Palace and was

Above: 'Mamluk' stripes painted in yellow and black at the Zawiyya Abu Shamat.

Opposite: The genuine Mamluk doorway of the Yalbogha Mosque, now in the garden of the National Museum.

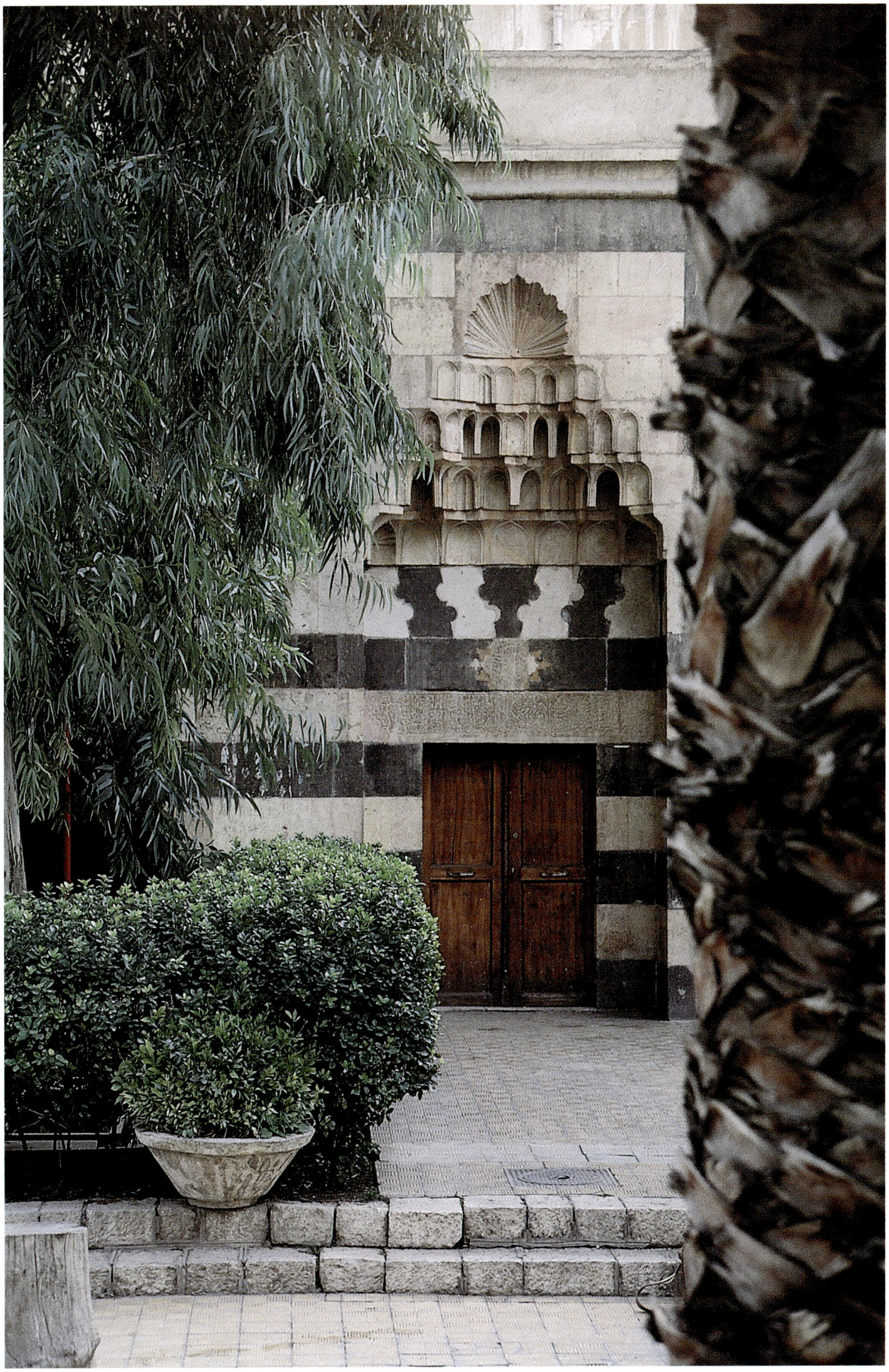

حمام التيروزي
بناه الامير سيف الدين تنكز نائب الشام
٨٢٩ هـ

built in stripes of black and white stone, with marble halls and gilded ceilings. Baibars died there in 1277, having accidentally drunk a poisoned cup intended for one of his nobles. His son bought a house near the Umayyad Mosque that had once been the home of Saladin's father and had it converted into a funeral college called the Madrasa al-Zahiriyya, where Baibars was buried in a handsome mausoleum.

Damascenes suffered under the Mamluks, but even these harsh warriors had to bow in the direction of their religion. Baibars himself gave money to the holy places in Mecca and sank wells and reservoirs along the pilgrim route – in 1269 he made the pilgrimage himself – and he did restoration work in the Umayyad Mosque. (The bronze doors at the back of the mosque are Mamluk and, though some of the decoration on them has disappeared, on the right-hand door the Mamluk emblem, a chalice, can still be seen.)

Another Mamluk Governor or *Wali*, Tengiz, ruled Damascus well. He cleaned and restored the water system, built bridges, did more restoration work in the Umayyad Mosque and is known for his campaign to get rid of stray dogs. Tengiz built a mosque and a Koranic school (opposite the Ayyubid Qilijiyya) and a beautiful mausoleum for his wife, Kukabaye, in the small square off the Suq al-Khayyatin.

Later Mamluk lords built the Yalbogha Mosque (1347) and the Tayruzi Mosque (1423), and all along the Midan road, down which the pilgrims set out on their great journey to Mecca each year, the Mamluks erected tombs and schools and baths and mosques. Indeed, if Salihiyya is a museum of Ayyubid architecture, perhaps Midan is the equivalent Mamluk one. But the Mamluks have been unlucky with their monuments. Only the grand doorway of Tengiz's Qur'anic school remains in good condition; his wife's mausoleum, with its lovely plaster inscriptions, is sadly dilapidated; the monuments in Midan are in a state either of decay or of brutal modernization; and the Yalbogha Mosque, which stood in Marja Square, was demolished in the 1970s to make way for a colossal new version – its giant concrete skeleton stands there today, the work delayed because the new building is subsiding. The doorway of the original mosque has been put in the garden of the National Museum, next to the café. Tengiz's mosque (in Nasser Street) was turned into a military school and the house he built for himself, the Palace of Gold, became the site of the Azem Palace (now the Museum of Popular Arts and Traditions).

Opposite: Typical black-and-white stone stripes for the doorway of the Tayruzi hammam.

However, the Tayruzi Mosque, with its marvellous old tiles, and the hammam next door, are preserved in a reasonable state. Perhaps the earlier monuments suffered too much at the hands of the Mongols, for once again – led by Tamerlane – they had stormed Damascus in 1401 and laid the city to waste. 'Damascus, which was so prosperous, so joyous, so brilliant, so luxurious, so magnificent, was changed into a heap of ruins, a desolate debris, devoid of all her beauty and all her art. Of living beings there were only partially burned bodies, disfigured by dust and covered with flies, which had become prey for dogs', wrote a chronicler of the time. Tamerlane left within three months, taking with him, back to his capital at Samarkand, craftsmen of all sorts: metalworkers who knew how to create the famous Damascene blades, weavers, jewellers, embroiderers, carpet makers, saddlers and many others, as well as more loot than they could find animals to carry – and hundreds of prisoners.

After a civil war between various contenders, the Mamluks came back and re-established their rule until, in 1516, they were finally crushed by a powerful new dynasty: the Ottomans.

The very last Mamluk Governor of Damascus, Siba'i, built a school and a mosque and a tomb (for himself) opposite the entrance to Straight Street. He took so many of the materials used in it from other mosques – marble, stone columns, etc. – that the religious men of Damascus nicknamed it 'The Mosque of Mosques'.

The Ottomans (so called after their first leader, 'Uthman) were originally Turks from Central Asia, but their armies had invaded half of Europe, Egypt and most of North Africa, had gone east to the Caspian Sea and south through the Arabian Peninsula. This vast empire was ruled by the Sultan in Constantinople, but his officials, as well as being Turks, came from all the territories: Albania, Serbia, Greece and so on. 'We in Europe, who speak of Turkey as though it were a homogeneous empire, might as well, when we speak of England, intend the word to include India, the Shan

Decorative Tiles

The earliest tiles to be seen in Damascus today were made in the Mamluk period, probably by itinerant workers from Iran. (Lovely examples are at the Tayruzi Mosque.)

The Ottoman Sultan Sulaiman sent tile workers from Turkey to restore the Dome of the Rock in Jerusalem and to work on his new Takiyya in Damascus.

They stayed on to do other commissions and the Damascus tile industry was born. It flowered in the 16th and 17th centuries, and though Damascus tiles never attained the sophistication of those from Iznik in Turkey, they have their own charm. Examples of Syrian tilework can be seen in London at Leighton House and in the Victoria and Albert Museum.

Above: Beautiful blue-and-white tiles in the Tayruzi Mosque, made by the prolific Ghaybi workshop in the 1420s.

Opposite: Stonework and tiles combined for the doorway of the mosque of Sinan Pasha, late 16th century.

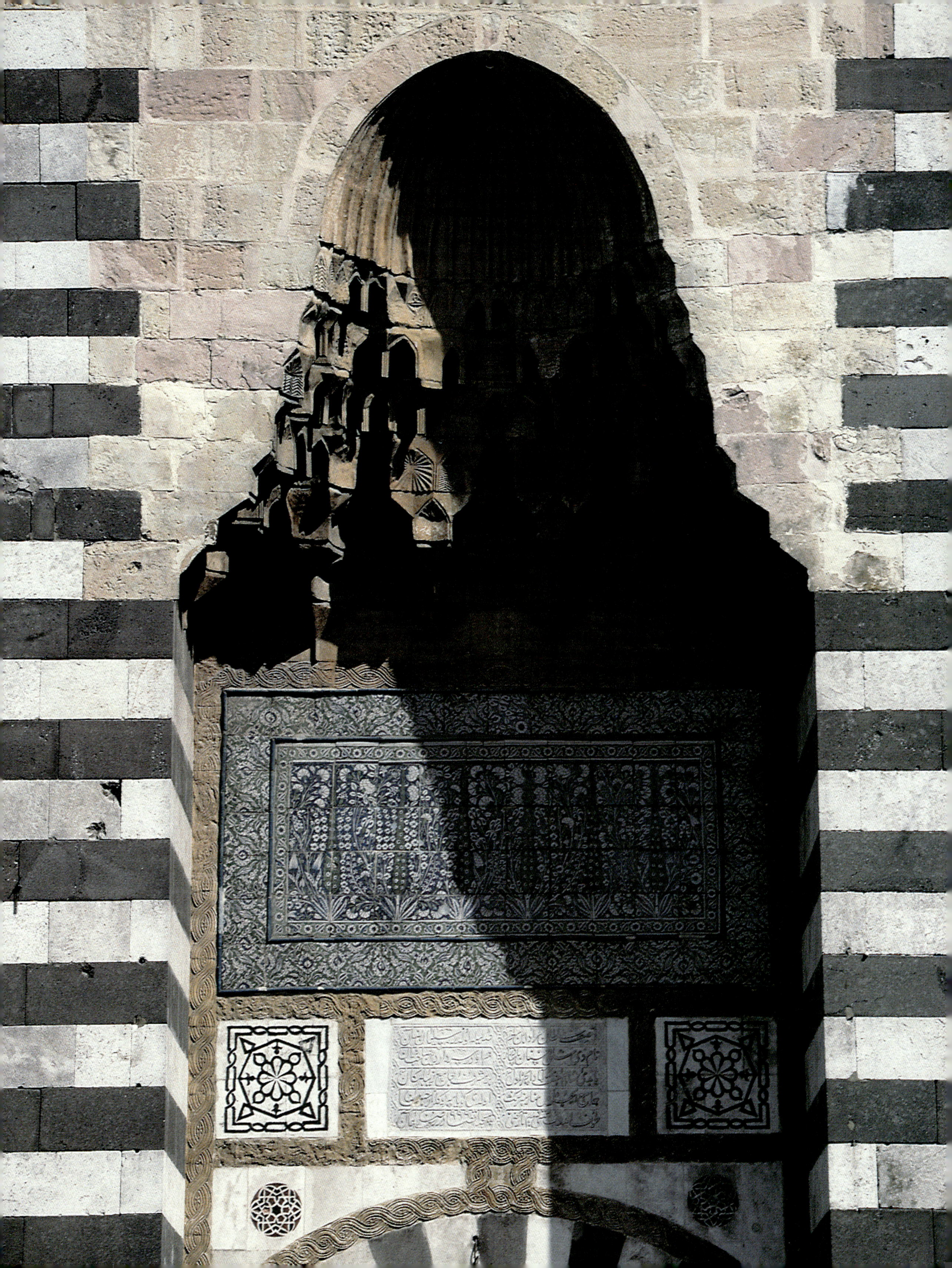

Decorative Tiles

Above: Damascus tiles in the courtyard of the mosque of Darwish Pasha, late 16th century.

Opposite: A magnificent wall of tiles for the tomb of Muhi al-Din Ibn 'Arabi, 16th century.

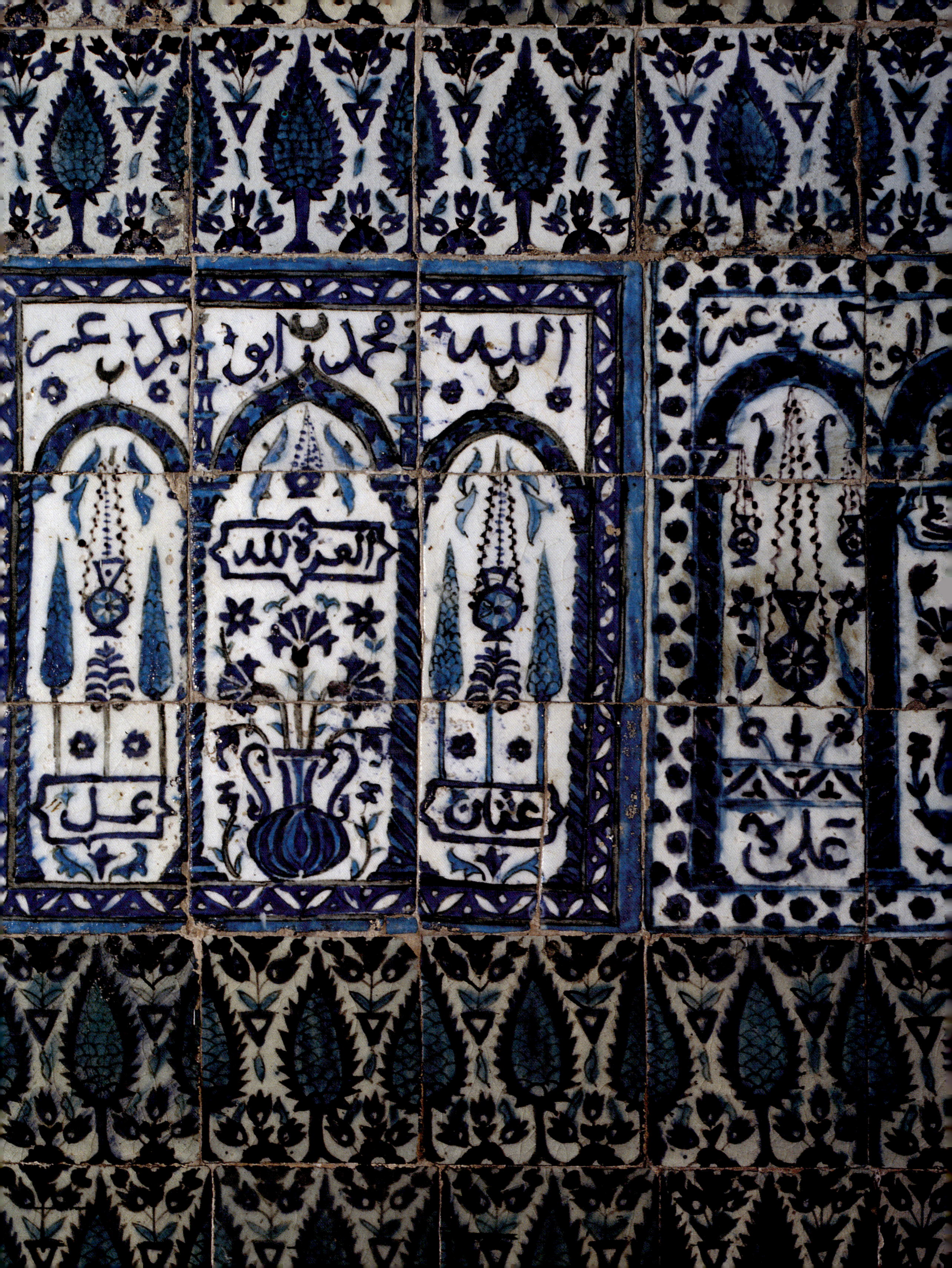
الله
محمد
ابو بكر
عمر
العزة لله
عثمان
على
عمر
على

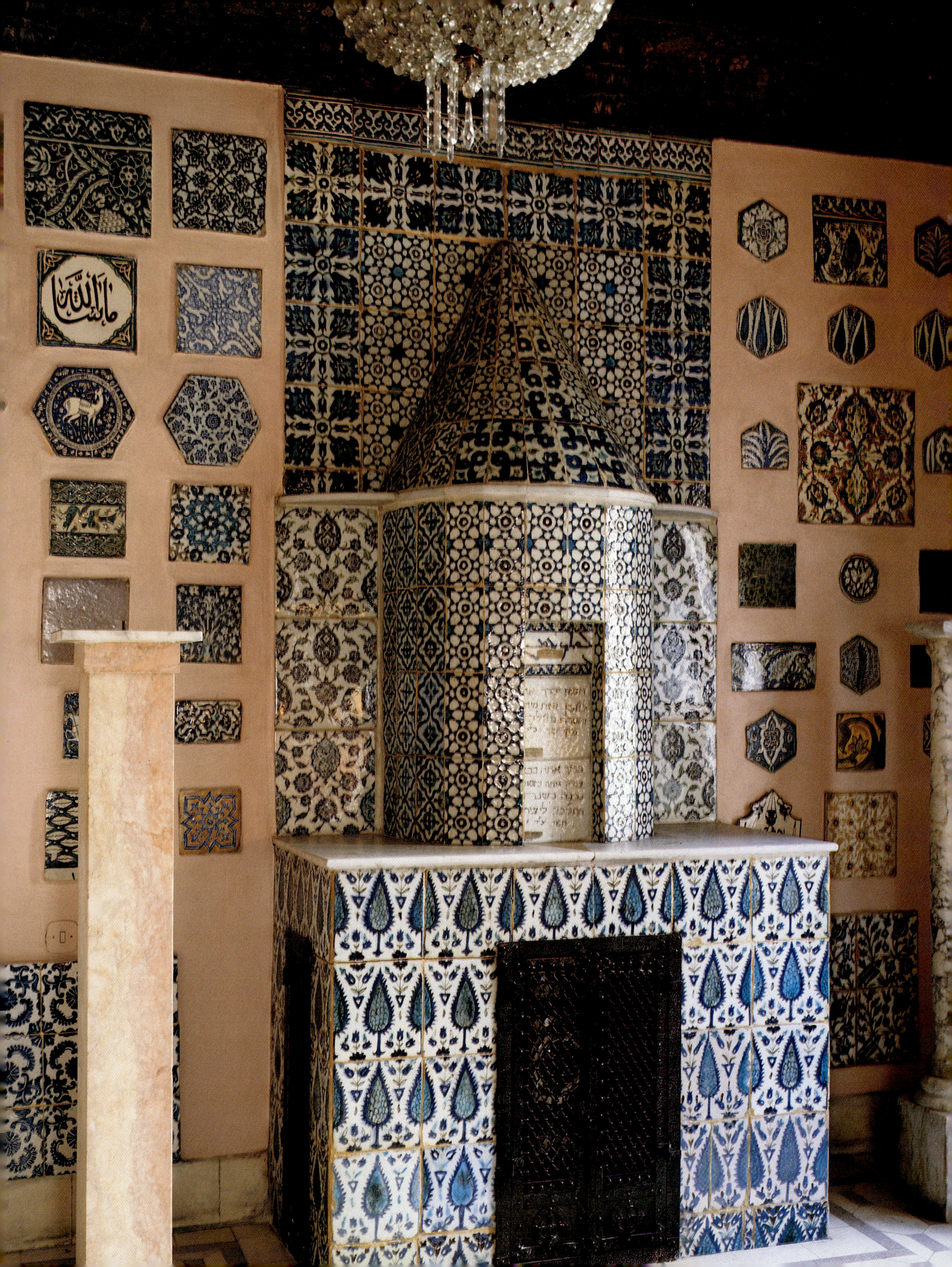

Decorative Tiles

Opposite: Old Damascus tiles and stove re-used in Bait 'Araqtanji in the 1930s.

Above: Damascus tiles in Saladin's tomb dating back to 17th-century restorations.

Decorative Tiles

Above: A mihrab, or niche, of tiles in the mosque of Darwish Pasha.

Opposite: A panel of Damascus tiles imitating a mihrab at the mosque of Darwish Pasha.

يا ناظر المثال النعل نبيه قبل مثال النعل لا تتكبرا
وامسح بوجهك نعلا انتسه قدم النبي وجاوز مسكرا

States, Hongkong and Uganda', wrote the traveller Gertrude Bell in 1905. (It has been worked out that, in the declining days of the Ottoman Empire, even the Sultan's own blood was only one-sixteen-thousandth part Turkish, so diluted had it become with that of the foreign wives and concubines of his forebears.)

The Ottoman Sultan Selim I entered Damascus in the autumn of 1517 and appeared next day at the Friday prayers in the Umayyad Mosque, where the great *qadi* (judge) proclaimed him the victorious servant of the holy cities of Medina and Mecca. These were not idle words; the role of guardian of the holy places of Islam gave the Ottoman Sultans responsibility for the safety of the annual pilgrimage to Mecca, the hajj as it is called, and it gave Damascus pivotal importance in the Islamic world, for, as the last 'port' before the desert, the city became the official assembly point for pilgrims coming from the north and from as far away as China in the east. Future Ottoman Governors of Damascus were to be judged as much, or more, by their ability to ensure a safe hajj than by any other aspect of their rule.

Almost the first thing Selim did was to organize the building of a new mosque over the tomb of the greatly revered Andalusian Sufi sheikh Muhi al-Din (also known as Ibn 'Arabi) in Salihiyya; it was finished in time for him to pray in it before leaving Damascus four months later. The mosque is there today with its mausoleum of beautiful blue-and-white Damascus tiles and the pleasantly busy atmosphere of a place where many pilgrims come to pray. Around it presses the Friday Market – so named because it is one of the few that is open on that day. For tax purposes, Selim ordered a census, which showed that there were approximately 55,000 inhabitants of Damascus at that time. The Sultan returned to Constantinople, leaving Damascus with an

Above: Men performing ablutions in the lovely courtyard of Ottoman Governor Sinan Pasha's mosque before the midday prayer.

Opposite: The Takiyya al-Sulaimaniyya with its Turkish-style pencil minarets, designed by the renowned architect Sinan, built in the mid-16th century.

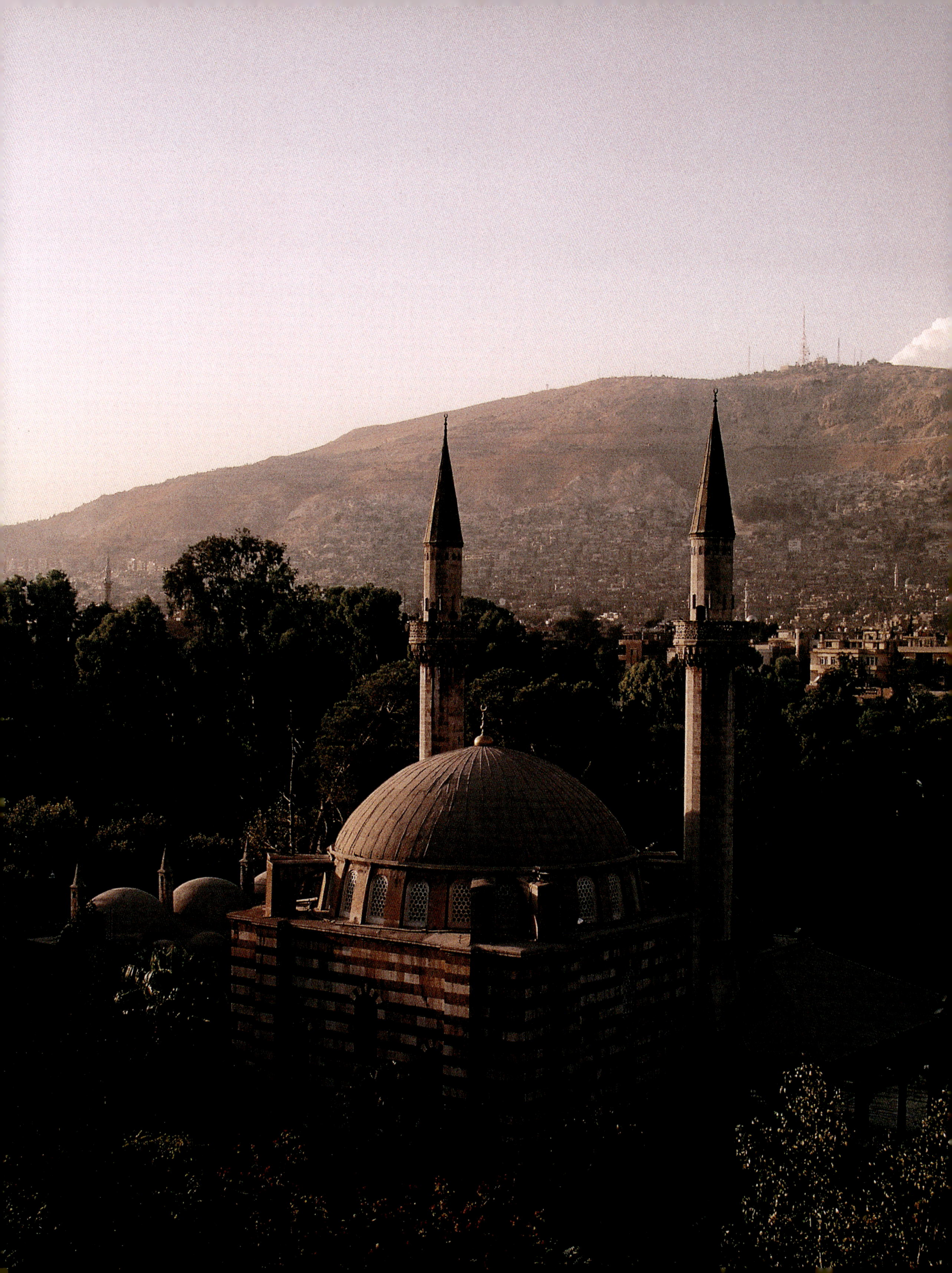

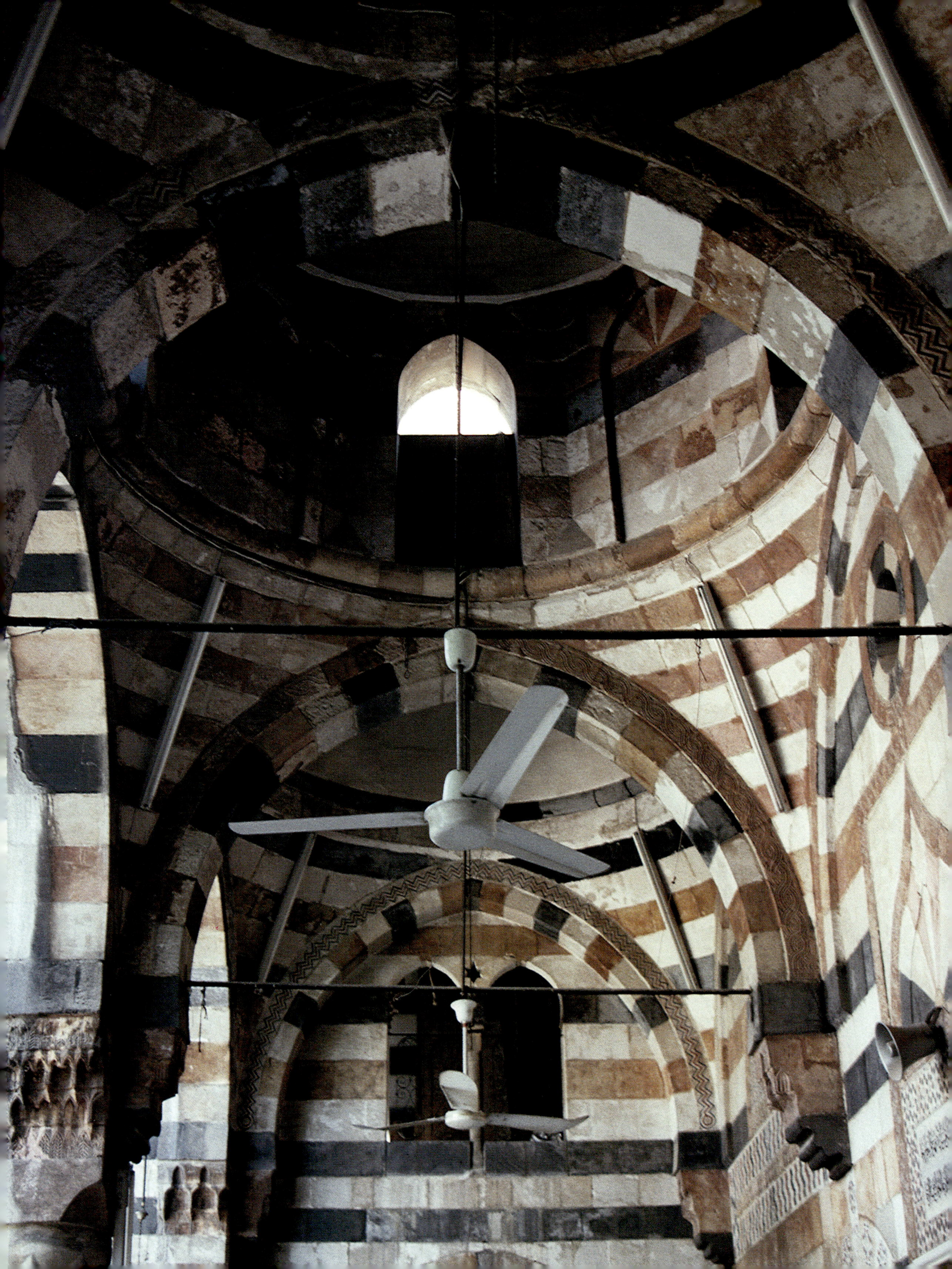

Ottoman Governor, chief judge and treasurer, as well as Ottoman soldiers and some civil servants. These officials were changed frequently, to prevent them becoming too powerful; a Governor usually stayed for only a year or so.

Sultan Selim was succeeded by his son, Sulaiman ('The Magnificent', as he came to be known), and to him Damascus owes what is possibly its most wonderful building: the Takiyya al-Sulaimaniyya. Designed by the great Turkish architect Sinan and built on the site of Baibars's 'Ablaq Palace, which had been destroyed by Tamerlane, it was created for the use of the hajj pilgrims who traditionally camped in the fields alongside the Barada river. ('A beautiful spot', commented Josias Porter in his edition of Murray's *Handbook for Travellers in Syria and Palestine* of 1858, 'and when it is enlivened by the camp of the pilgrim caravans – their horses, camels, tents and various costumes – few places round the old city are more deserving of a visit.')

The Takiyya al-Sulaimaniyya complex gave the pilgrims a place to pray, as well as offering food, lodging and medical treatment. 'A great hospital or inn where the caravans lodge' is how the English traveller John Green described it in 1736. 'It has the air of a monastery. Its first storey consists of long galleries, supported on marble pillars, surrounding a great square court. The chambers are placed as in a dormitory, one after another.... The court is paved with marble of different colours and, in the midst, is a marble basin, supplied with water by the Barada.'

Sulaiman the Magnificent's successor, his son Selim II, added a madrasa to the complex, which has now become an attractive handicraft souk.

In spite of their usually brief postings, the Ottoman Governors built many of the existing mosques, khans and souks to be seen in present-day Damascus. Darwish Pasha, who had been Grand Vizier in Constantinople, was named Governor in 1571; he built the mosque, known for its lovely tiles, that bears his name (across the road from the entrance to Straight Street), and he was buried there when he died. He also constructed the Khan al-Harir (Silk Khan), which is still in existence, though like many of the old khans, it has become overlaid by the shops and clutter of the intervening centuries. Sinan Pasha (nothing to do with Sinan the architect), another ex-Grand Vizier named Governor in 1587, built many things in Damascus, but his most famous achieve-

Opposite: The interior of one of the prettiest buildings in Damascus: the Madrasa al-Fathiyya in Qaimariyya, built in 1743.

Below: The once beautiful façade of the hammam in Midan built by Fathi Falaqinsi Daftardar.

ment is the beautiful mosque with the green-tiled minaret at the entrance to Straight Street. Isabel Burton called this 'the prettiest mosque in the city', but vying for that title is the Madrasa al-Fathiyya in the Qaimariyya area behind the Umayyad Mosque. This charming religious school and mosque was built in 1743 by one of Damascus's most extraordinary characters, Fathi Falaqinsi. A local man from a family of weavers, Fathi became *daftardar*, or treasurer – and so powerful that he was nicknamed the Sultan of Damascus. He had good taste: his mosque is beautiful and the hammam he built in the Midan road still has a handsome façade, though the building has, over many years, fallen into neglect.

Fathi is famous for flaunting his popularity and power in the face of the Governor of the day, Sulaiman Pasha al-Azem, by giving a spectacular wedding party for his daughter only a few days after the Governor had given a more modest one for his son's circumcision. Fathi's party lasted for seven days, with a different group of guests invited for each one: the Governor and his officials; the *'ulama*, or religious leaders; military chiefs; merchants; Christians and Jews; peasants; and, on the last day, prostitutes.

Fathi acted like a Governor, paving roads and repairing mosques, and he had high hopes of becoming one; so much so that he was a thorn in the side of As'ad Pasha al-Azem, Sulaiman's successor, until at last As'ad Pasha received permission from the Sultan to get rid of him (possibly because he promised the Sultan one thousand purses from Fathi's fortune if he was killed).

The Azems were the most famous of all the Ottoman Governors, though the family – which became a mini-dynasty, ruling Damascus on and off for thirty-seven years in the course of the 18th century – was not Ottoman, but Syrian from the town of Ma'arat al-Nu'man, where they first gained favour with the Sultan for controlling the desert tribes. Isma'il al-Azem was the first of the Azems to become Governor of Damascus, where he built a school and a bath in the Suq al-Khayyatin and a coffee shop. The idea of the coffee shop was born in Damascus in the 16th century and flourished there, perhaps not surprisingly, for as the British Consul in Damascus in 1838 remarked: 'The amusements of the Labouring classes are of a simple and tranquil kind, as respects the male it is confined to smoking in the open air …'. The coffee houses of Damascus became famous and almost every visitor wrote about them, particularly the establishments which lay along the Barada river. Henry Maundrell, travelling through Syria in 1697, described 'a coffee house capable of entertaining four or five hundred people … washed all round with a large swift stream and shaded overhead with mats and trees. We found here a multitude of Turks upon the divans, regaling themselves in this pleasant place.' Isabel Burton wrote of a similar coffee house, where she saw the men listening to a traditional storyteller, or *hakawati*, as they sipped their tiny cups of coffee and smoked their *narghilas* (hubble-bubble pipes). In the Nawfara café behind the Umayyad Mosque, the last of the Damascus hakawatis still holds the old men in his audience spellbound on the evenings when he tells the traditional tales. (One of them, the love story of 'Antar and 'Abla, bears an uncanny resemblance to Shakespeare's *Othello*.)

Isma'il al-Azem was followed as Governor of Damascus by his son, Sulaiman, who built the large khan in Straight Street named after him (currently under restoration). This khan was principally used for storing potash, which was a major export from Syria, especially to the soap and glass manufacturers of Marseilles. The potash was made by burning a particular grass that grows in Syria, and Sulaiman, as Governor, held the monopoly.

In 1743, As'ad Pasha, the brother of Sulaiman, entered Damascus as Governor. He was to be in power

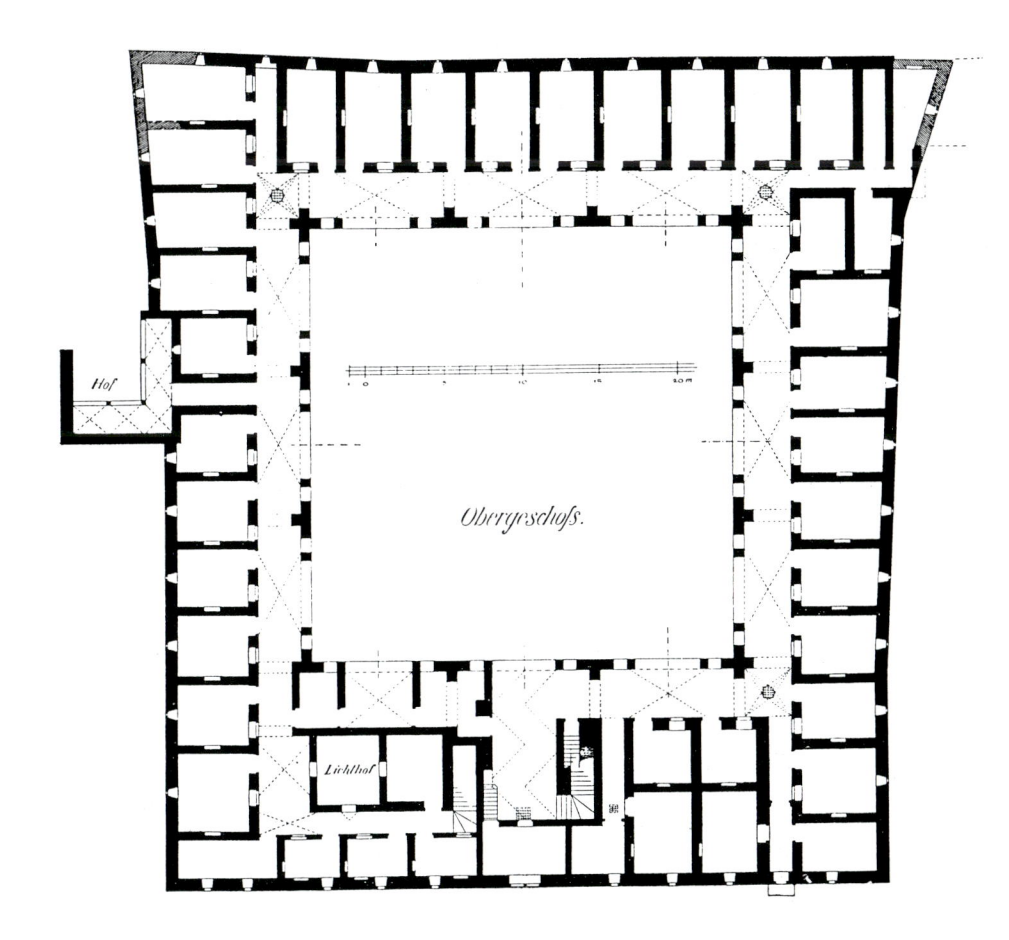

Opposite: Cafés originated in Damascus in the 16th century. A favourite location was along the river bank, as in this 19th-century engraving.

Above: The best-known café today is the Nawfara (on the right), situated behind the Umayyad Mosque, closed in this early-morning picture.

Left: Plan of the upper storey of the Khan As'ad Pasha. The central courtyard is surrounded by rooms, shops and offices.

Overleaf: A dramatic view of the newly restored striped arches and painted domes of the Khan As'ad Pasha.

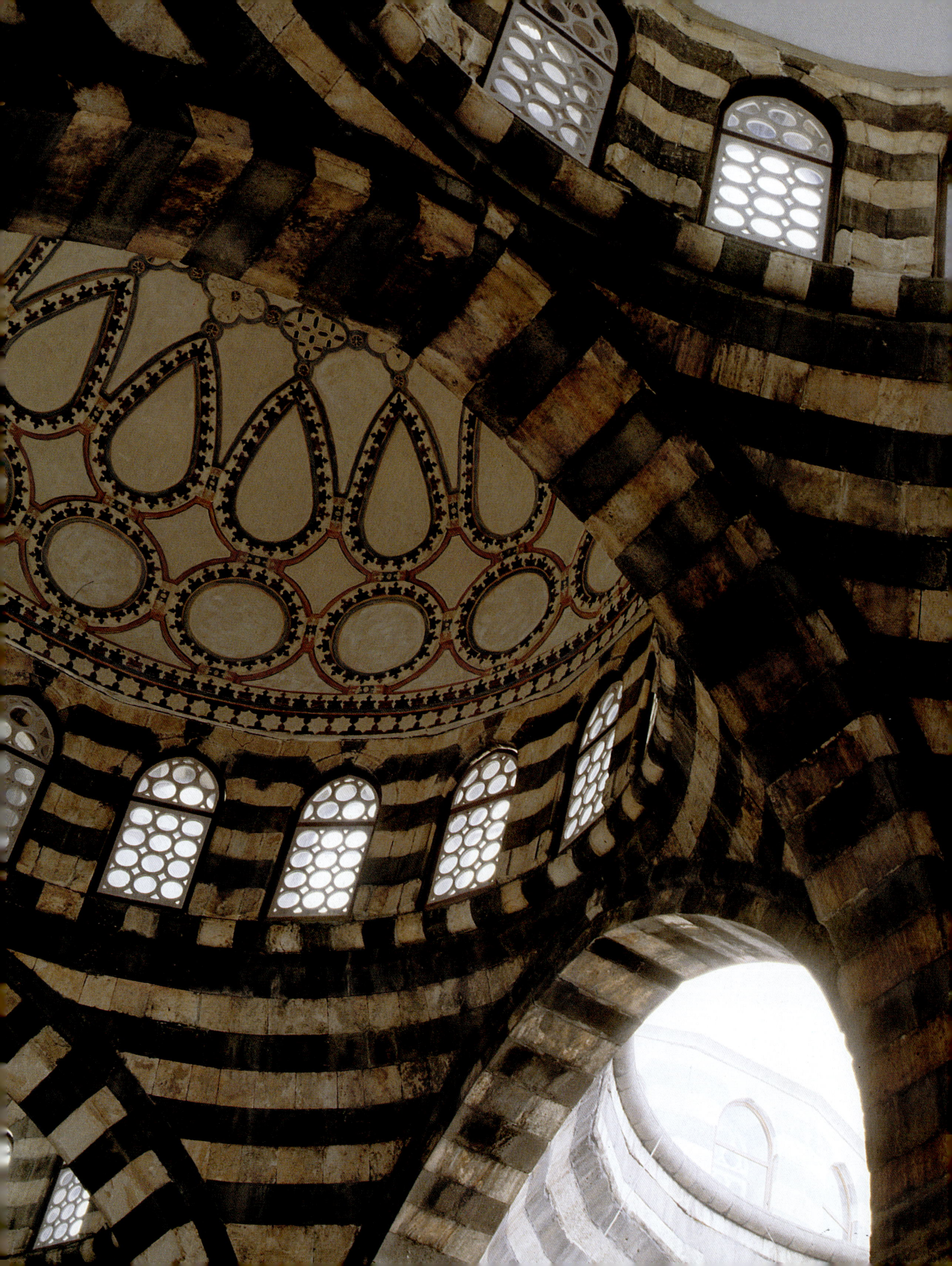

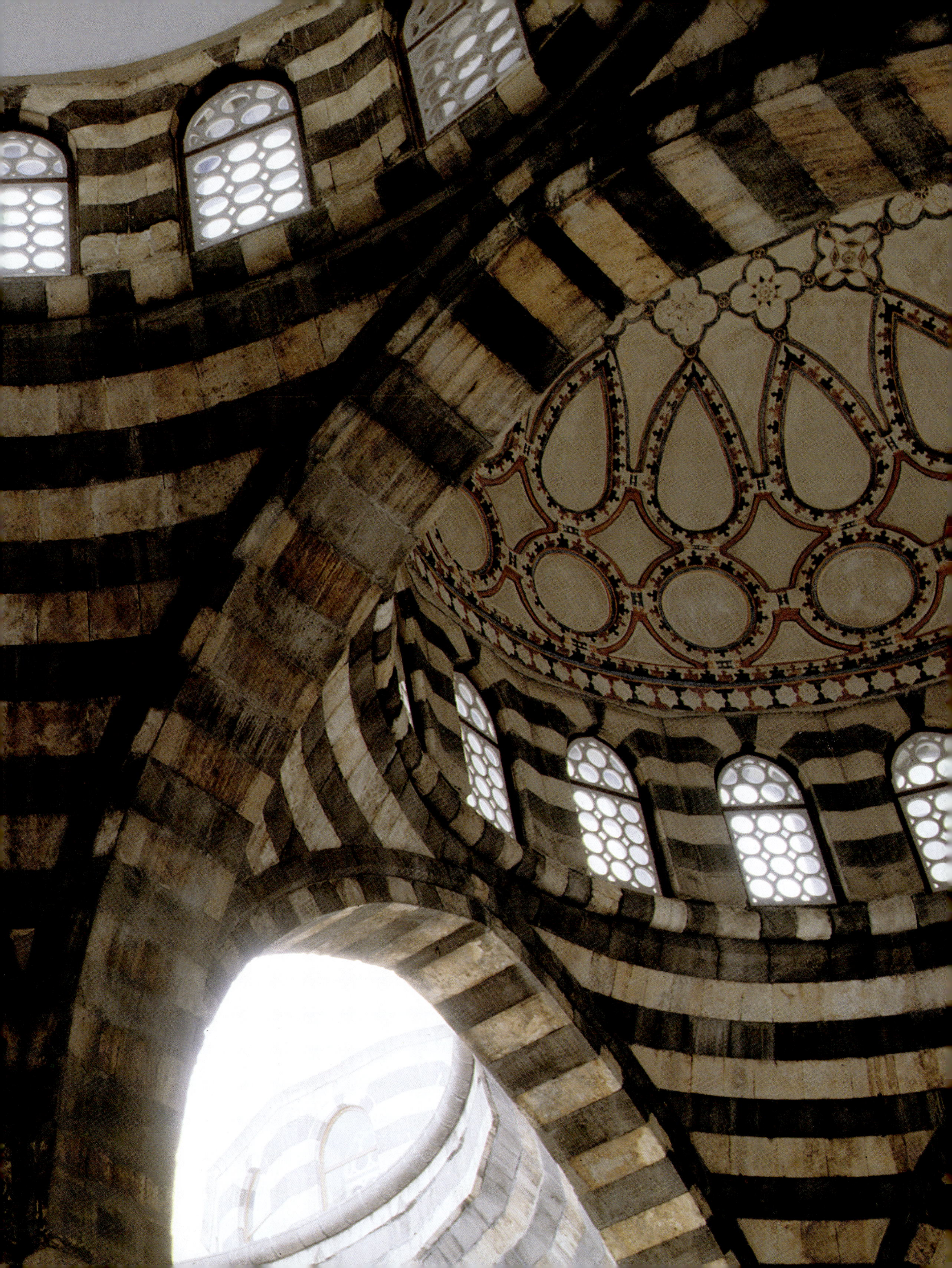

for an unprecedented fourteen years, during which time he was responsible for two of the most important buildings in the city: the Azem Palace, which is described in Part 2, and the Khan As'ad Pasha in the Suq al-Buzuriyya. The khan is breathtaking – its vast space and soaring arches in black-and-white stone stripes are almost surreal. When Alphonse de Lamartine saw it in 1833, he wrote: 'A people whose architects are capable of designing such a monument and whose workers are capable of building it, is not dead to art.' In 1759, only seven years after it was built, a violent earthquake shook down three of the domes, which were then closed over with wood. In its heyday, As'ad Pasha's huge khan acted as a combination of hotel, storage house and centre of commerce, with shops in the rooms off the courtyard on the ground floor, and offices on the first floor. Lamartine reported that every notable businessman in Damascus rented a room there, and Charles Addison, an English traveller in Damascus a couple of years after Lamartine, wrote that 'two English merchants are established in this khan'. The khan survived in its original role into the 20th century; it was restored during the 1990s and its future was widely debated. In 1998, it was finally decided to make it into the Natural History Museum of Damascus (although many would have preferred to see it as a traditional café and shops).

As'ad Pasha's reign in Damascus was allowed to continue for as long as it did because he had managed, every year, to conduct the hajj to Mecca and back without serious disruption – something vitally important to the prestige of the Ottoman Sultan as the leader of the Islamic world. It was also extremely important economically; apart from the fact that every pilgrim took something to sell along the way to help pay for the journey, many merchants accompanied the pilgrimage for safe passage across the desert. They took cereals, olive oil, arms, textiles, soap and dried fruit to Mecca and returned not only with goods, such as coffee, from Arabia, but from India as well: muslin, silk, Kashmir shawls, precious stones, spices, drugs, indigo, camphor, gum arabic, some of which were traded on to the west from Damascus and Istanbul.

The pilgrimage to Mecca is one of the obligations of a Muslim, being one of the five pillars of Islam (the others are *shahada* – acknowledging belief in one God – fasting, prayer and almsgiving). In the words of Guy le Strange, a 19th-century English academic, it 'made every Muslim perforce a traveller once at least during the course of his life'. Since the Arab conquest of the city in AD 635, pilgrims had been assembling in Damascus every year to make the hazardous journey to Mecca together. Many of the accounts of the monuments and life in Damascus in early times come from writers doing this journey themselves: Ibn Jubair came from Spain in 1185, Ibn Batuta from North Africa in 1355.

Under the Ottomans, the hajj became a more and more organized affair. Governors of Damascus were excused from their earlier duty of accompanying the Sultan on his campaigns and, instead, they were appointed *Amir al-Hajj* (commander of the pilgrimage), sometimes travelling with the pilgrims themselves, and with all the responsibility for their safety. This was not easy: the desert was full of rapacious Bedouin, who had to be bought, or fought, off. Unchecked, they could be merciless, blocking the wells so that the pilgrims slowly died of thirst, stripping them of all they possessed and leaving them naked to die in the desert. (It seems that, even as late as 1927, the Bedouin could still be dangerous. William Seabrook, an American traveller who stayed at the Victoria Hotel in Damascus, watched a couple of tourists setting off on an excursion by car. Within hours they were back, as Seabrook described: 'The angry gentleman came afoot, barefoot at that, and naked as a jaybird, except for his linen duster. His lady rode a donkey which they had borrowed on the edge of the city. She had been permitted to retain her skirt and blouse. They only returned at all because they had the good sense to offer no resistance.')

Opposite: The Khan As'ad Pasha in a 19th-century engraving, crowded with merchants and goods.

Above: The Khan Sulaiman Pasha off Straight Street, currently under restoration.

Overleaf: 19th-century engraving of hajj pilgrims camping by the Takiyya al-Sulaimaniyya.

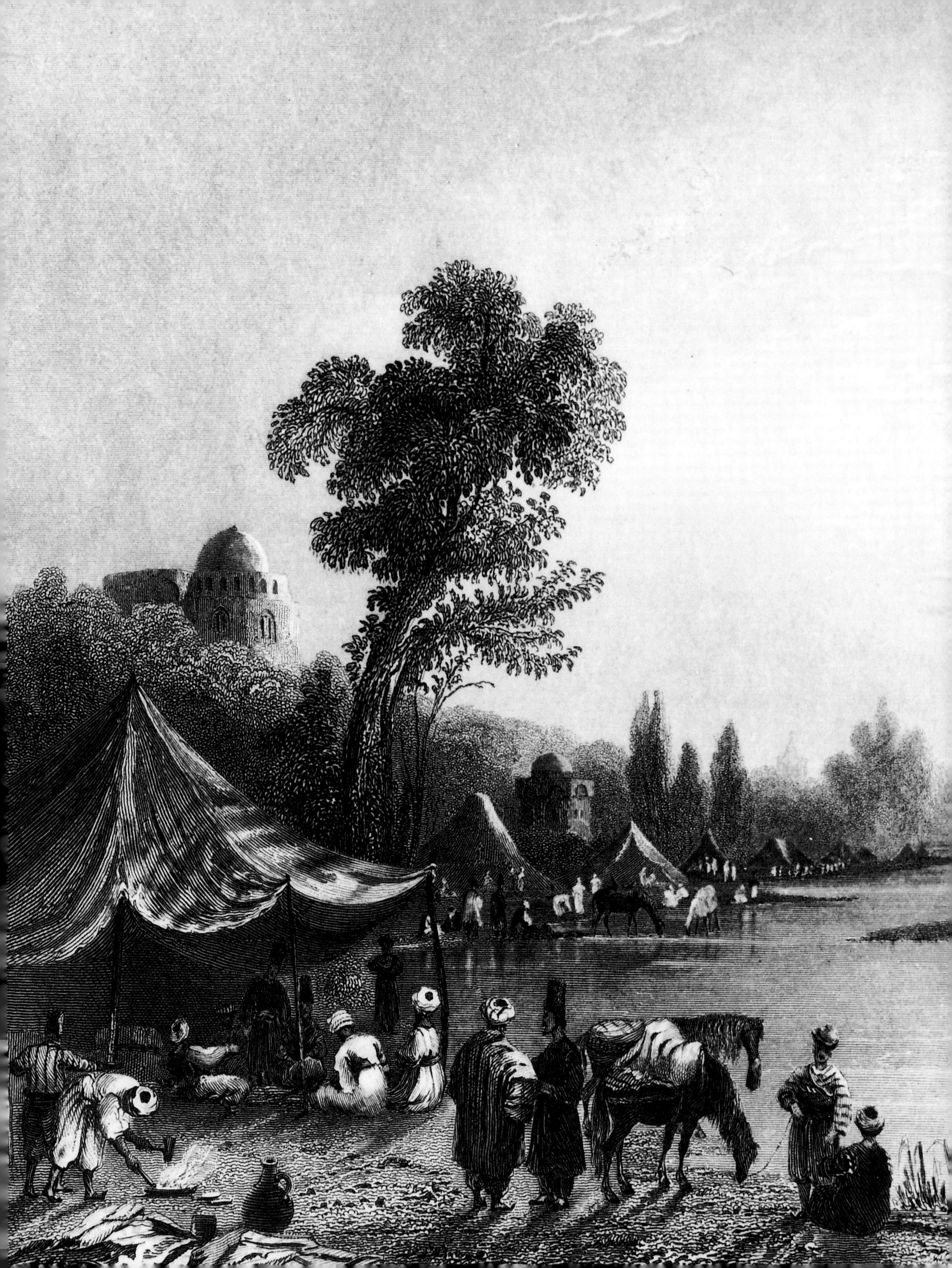

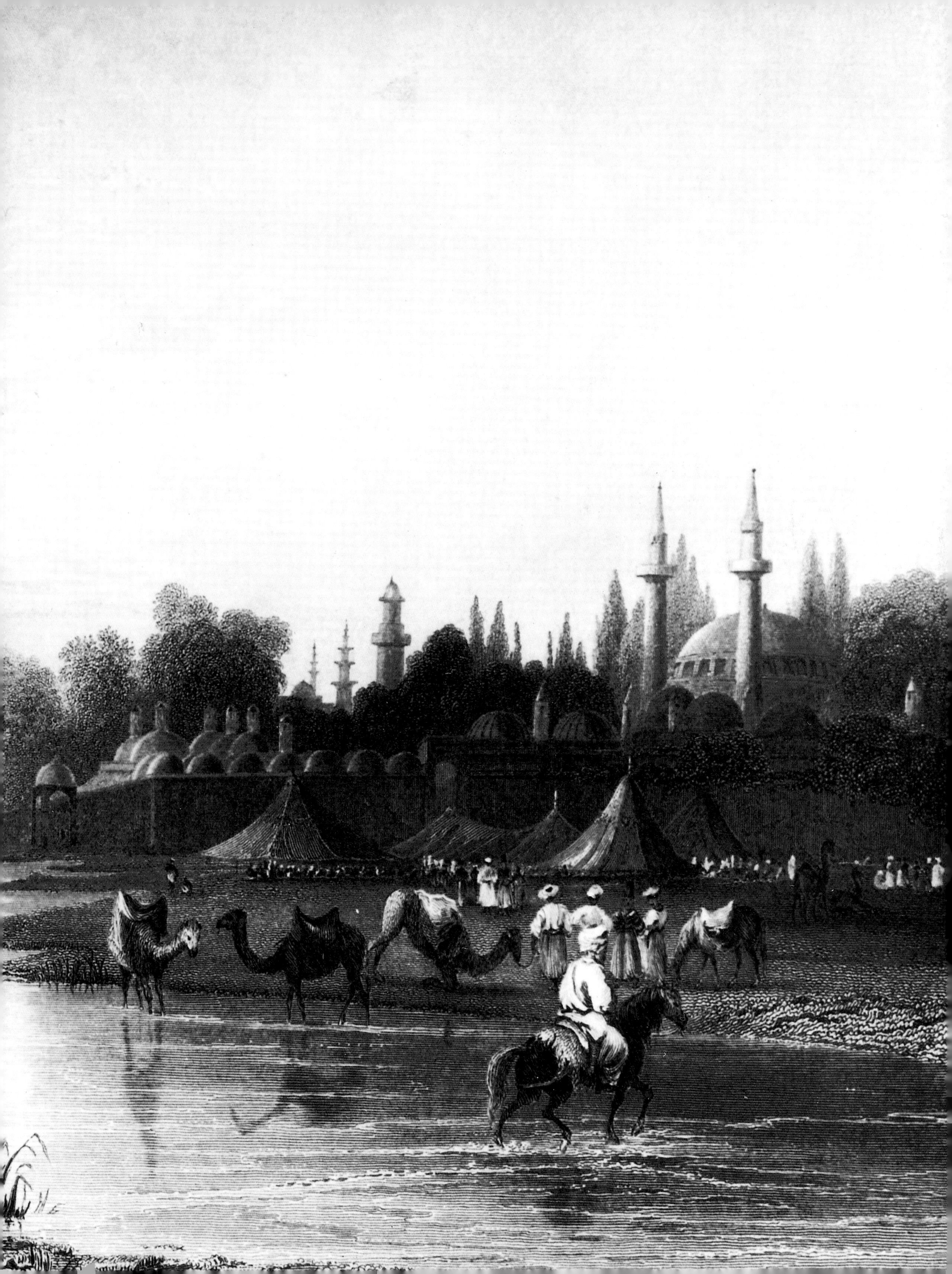

The pilgrims of the hajj were not only at the mercy of the Bedouin, but of nature as well. Flash floods swept them away, snowstorms overwhelmed the caravan, terrible heat parched and exhausted the weary travellers and, sometimes, the caravan lost its way altogether. Many pilgrims never returned home: in 1694, Yusuf al-Nabulsi died one summer night in the arms of his brother, a celebrated Damascene mystic named 'Abd al-Ghani, but the caravan (travelling by night then because of the heat) never stopped for death; bodies were carried along and buried at the next halt.

The hajj was a brave thing to undertake, and each time the caravan left, all Damascus waited with bated breath to hear news of its fate. On the return journey, a special courier was sent ahead to tell the town that the pilgrims were on their way, and the whole population came out to welcome them as heroes.

From Damascus it took thirty-five days to reach Mecca on foot (travelling at two miles [a little over three kilometres] an hour) and thirty-five days back again after a week or so performing the rituals of 'Id al-Kabir. Each year the number of pilgrims varied, but it could be as many as twenty thousand people who set off, together with their thousands of donkeys and horses and camels, trailing across the desert for many miles. At the back came the 'pilgrim brushes' – the men whose job it was to make sure there were no stragglers – and behind them came the scavenging jackals and hyenas. So great were the hazards that, in 1711, when two thousand Persian pilgrims arrived in Damascus to find the caravan had left, they decided to stay and wait for a year until the next departure.

Most pilgrims began to assemble in Damascus a few weeks ahead of time; they camped near the Takiyya al-Sulaimaniyya or lodged in khans or schools or in private houses while they gathered their supplies for the journey. 'In the market there is much taking up in haste of wares for the road', wrote the English scholar and traveller Charles Doughty, who rode with the caravan. There were guide books to tell the pilgrims what to do. According to one of these, the *Kitab al-Munassiq*, Damascus had markets as magnificent as they were numerous, fruits in abundance, public baths with clean running water, enjoyable walks and elegant cafés.

When departure day came, the pilgrims left the city by the Midan road in a carnival-like procession, surrounded by all Damascus on holiday. Dervishes

Opposite: The annual carpet market in Damascus, set up by pilgrims from the Caucasus making the hajj overland.

whirling, vendors selling every imaginable food and drink, sword dancers clashing, drummers drumming – even women of doubtful character made an appearance, 'veils drawn aside ... showing painted cherry cheeks and eyes black-rimmed with *kohl* ...', according to Isabel Burton, who joined the caravan for two days and recorded the order in which it moved. First the chief guide and his men; next the artillery; then the tents of the officials, pilgrims, soldiers, merchants and camp followers; then a group of cavalry, followed by the bazaar and the Sunni pilgrims; then the Amir al-Hajj and his attendants, followed by the *mahmal* (the sacred emblem of every pilgrimage – a decorated tent carried by an enormous camel); after that came the treasurer and his attendants and then a second troop of cavalry, followed by the Shi'a and Persian pilgrims; and, finally, the dromedary riders bringing up the rear. Mrs Burton was fascinated: 'I must say that the *Haj* is by far the most interesting ceremony or spectacle I have ever witnessed and by far the grandest in a wild picturesque point of view.' Murray's *Handbook* agreed: 'The starting of the *Haj* is a sight which should be witnessed by every traveller in Palestine who can arrange to be at Damascus...'.

This was the hajj, the fantastic voyage of faith, which Governor As'ad Pasha al-Azem managed to conduct peacefully for fourteen years. But in 1757 he was deposed, and the very next year, under the new Governor, the caravan was attacked by the Bedouin and nearly wiped out; the sister of the Sultan himself was killed. As'ad Pasha was accused of orchestrating the attack in order to discredit his successor; he was beheaded and his fabulous wealth and vast properties were confiscated by the Sultan. The last Azem Governor in the 18th century, 'Abdullah Pasha, was far less dynamic than As'ad Pasha, but he held on to power for more than ten years, until 1783 – a rare feat, given that the area was in a particularly turbulent state at the time. He built the charming Madrasa 'Abdullah al-Azem, which today is a shop for tourists – and no less attractive for that.

Isabel Burton had worried about the new Suez Canal and the threat of railways. These modern communications, she feared, would put paid to the traditional hajj and all such age-old ceremonies. She was right: in 1908 the Hijaz railway opened in Damascus specifically to take pilgrims to Mecca (Hijaz is the province of Saudi Arabia that contains Mecca and Medina), but the city was still the gathering point for the pilgrims. It was air travel that ended Damascus's role in the hajj – pilgrims from different countries now simply fly direct. With one exception: the collapse of the Soviet Union has meant that the Muslim countries in the Caucasus are free to do their own thing, and suddenly – since 1992 – Damascus has become host to thousands of pilgrims from these mountain states making the hajj overland. About two weeks before they are due in Mecca for the 'Id rituals (the date changes each year according to the lunar calendar), their battered dormitory buses, flying the green flag of Islam, arrive in Damascus and the pilgrims set up an enormous carpet market in front of the Ansari Mosque in Bab Musalla. Strolling among the hundreds of carpets, under the watchful eyes of the Daghestanis or Chechens or Ossetians in their unfamiliar costumes, you feel something of the thrill of what it must all have been like a hundred years ago.

For centuries, Damascus had been a city more or less closed to Westerners, but in 1832 an event occurred which was to change all this: Syria was invaded by the Egyptians and, for eight years, Damascus was governed by an Egyptian Pasha with a much more open approach. Foreigners were welcomed and foreign commerce encouraged. The Egyptians were forced to leave in 1840, but the new order had taken hold and was confirmed by sweeping reforms (*tanzimat*) in the Ottoman Empire. In Damascus, trade with Europe began in earnest and local agents, representing foreign companies, began to grow rich. The trouble was that these agents were, almost to a man, selected from the Christian or Jewish communities. The Muslims grew resentful of this, and of the new laws which gave these communities many advantages. Foreign consulates began to open in Damascus at this time (the British was the first) and, when local men were chosen as honorary consuls, they were invariably Christians or Jews. Even when the Consul was a foreigner (as in the case of the British), the Jews and the Christians were openly favoured and protected. The Bowring *Report* of 1840 was quick to sense the growing communal tension: 'The situation of the Christians has improved.... They are proportionally better off as compared with the Mussulmans who have gained nothing and lost much – higher taxes, greater oppression, more severe conscriptions ... the greater contact with Europeans, both on the part of

Above: Lawrence of Arabia in Damascus on the balcony of the Victoria Hotel (which no longer exists).

Opposite: Amir Faisal, photographed at the Paris Peace Conference, 1919 (probably by the wife of the US President, Woodrow Wilson).

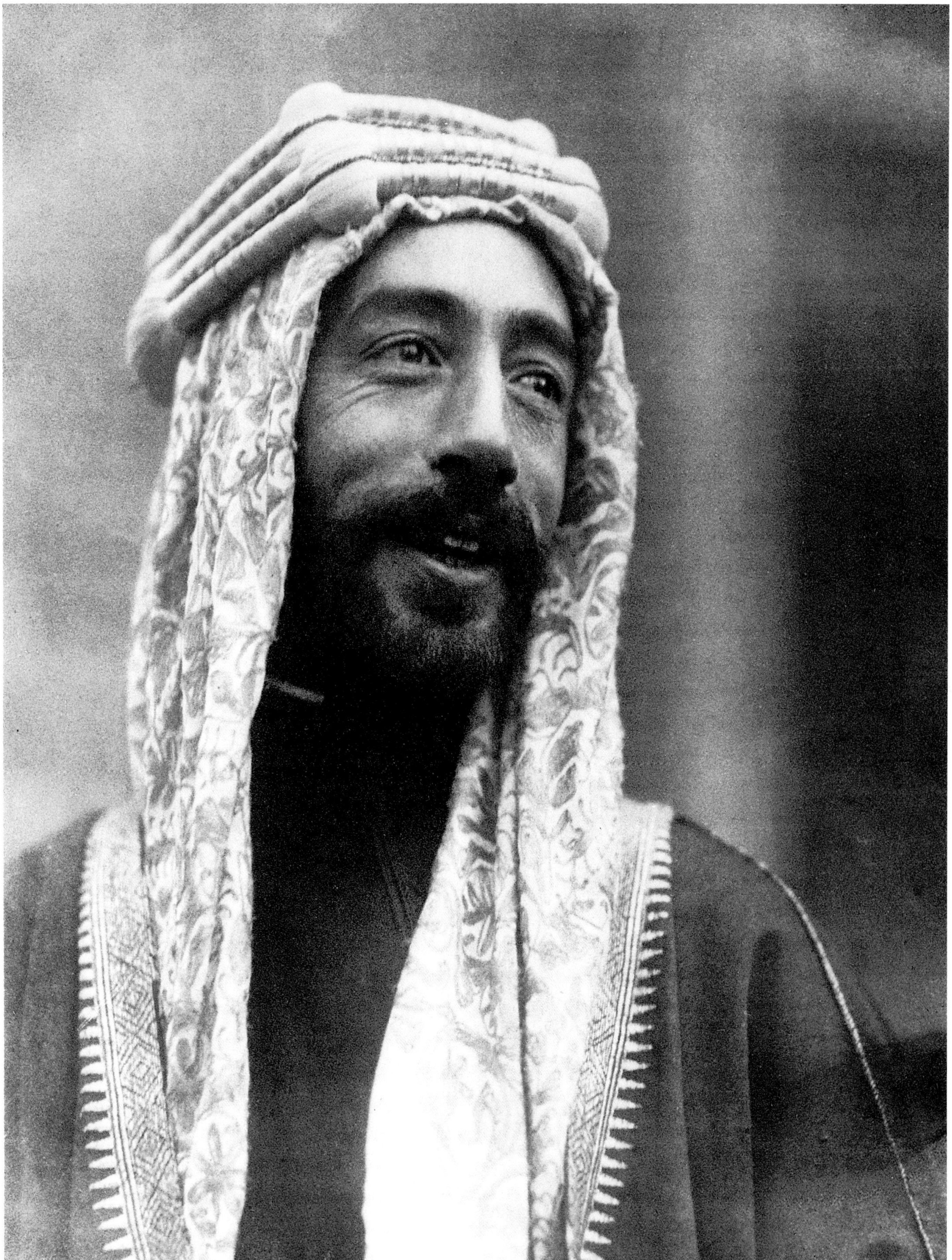

government and people ... have all tended to lower Mussulman pride and confidence.'

In 1860, the resentment suddenly boiled over into rage and violence, and some Muslims in Damascus turned on the Christians, killing thousands and burning their homes. Many Muslims tried to stop the slaughter, and many helped the Christians, but every consulate was ransacked (except the British, which was the only one not in the Christian area) and the whole Christian quarter was laid waste. The European countries were appalled and horrified and demanded reprisals and retribution. The Sultan sent his most important minister to deal with the aftermath; the Ottoman Governor was hanged, along with dozens of others, and many were sent into exile or prison. Henry Jessup, a missionary in Beirut at the time, wrote: 'We watched groups of Moslems, one hundred, two hundred, five hundred, some sons of the highest families, being brought, bound, to Beirut to be sent to various parts of the Ottoman empire.' Restitution was made to the Christians, their devastated area was rebuilt and the Europeans, particularly the French, gained greater access and influence in Syria.

By the beginning of the 20th century, Arabs were becoming increasingly impatient to throw off the Ottoman yoke and gain independence for themselves. Resistance movements began – in Damascus, in May 1916, young nationalists were hanged publicly in Marja Square by the Ottoman Governor, Jamal Pasha. When the First World War broke out, the Ottomans took the side of the Germans, and it was not difficult for the British to persuade the Arabs that this was their chance to revolt, promising them, too, that if Turkey was defeated, they would have independence in their own lands. The Arab Revolt began in what is now Saudi Arabia, and then the Arab army of tribesmen, with Lawrence of Arabia as its adviser, succeeded in pushing their Turkish/German enemy back, all through present-day Saudi Arabia and Jordan until, finally, the Arab army entered Damascus on 1 October 1918.

'Damascus went mad with joy', wrote Lawrence. 'The men tossed up their tarbooshes [fezzes] to cheer; the women tore off their veils. Householders threw flowers, hangings, carpets into the road before us; their wives leaned, screaming with laughter, through the lattices and splashed us with bath-dippers of scent.'

The joy did not last long. The Allies went back on their promises and carved up the lands of the old Ottoman Empire between themselves. King Faisal, who was supposed to rule an independent Syria, was thrown out, and in 1920, the French entered the country. They were there for twenty-six bitterly resented years. In 1925, there was an uprising against them which was brutally crushed. In the course of it, a part of the old city was shelled and destroyed.

During the Second World War, Damascus was the site of a bizarre and nasty battle between the Vichy French ruling Syria (as they did all France's colonies in the war) and the Free French. Fearing that Germany might be allowed to use Syria as a base for operations in the Middle East, the Free French attacked Damascus in 1941, with the support of British, Indian and Australian soldiers. The Vichy French defended the city with North African troops from their colonies. A bitter battle for control of Damascus was fought to the death through the vineyards and orchards of what is now the suburb of Mezze; many were killed and lie in the British and Commonwealth, or French, war cemeteries in Damascus, but the Allies won and the Free French took over from their Vichy countrymen.

Africans and Indians dying in Syria in a battle between Frenchmen – it seems extraordinary, and yet it is somehow just another chapter in the story of an ancient country in which Phoenicians, Arameans, Nabateans, Assyrians, Persians, Greeks, Romans, Byzantines, Crusaders, Turks, Egyptians, Mamluks and Ottomans have fought. Perhaps it is not surprising that the great British historian of the Crusades Sir Steven Runciman once remarked that the history of the region is the history of warfare.

In 1945, on what was almost the eve of their final departure, the French responded to local attacks by shelling the city from their barracks on top of the hill, where the Presidential Palace stands today: many important buildings were damaged or destroyed. The following year they left, and Syria at last became independent, with Damascus as its capital. Today Damascus has more than four million inhabitants. As Murray's *Handbook* put it: 'Perhaps the most remarkable fact connected with the history of this city is that it has flourished under every change of dynasty and under every form of government. It may truly be called the Eternal City.'

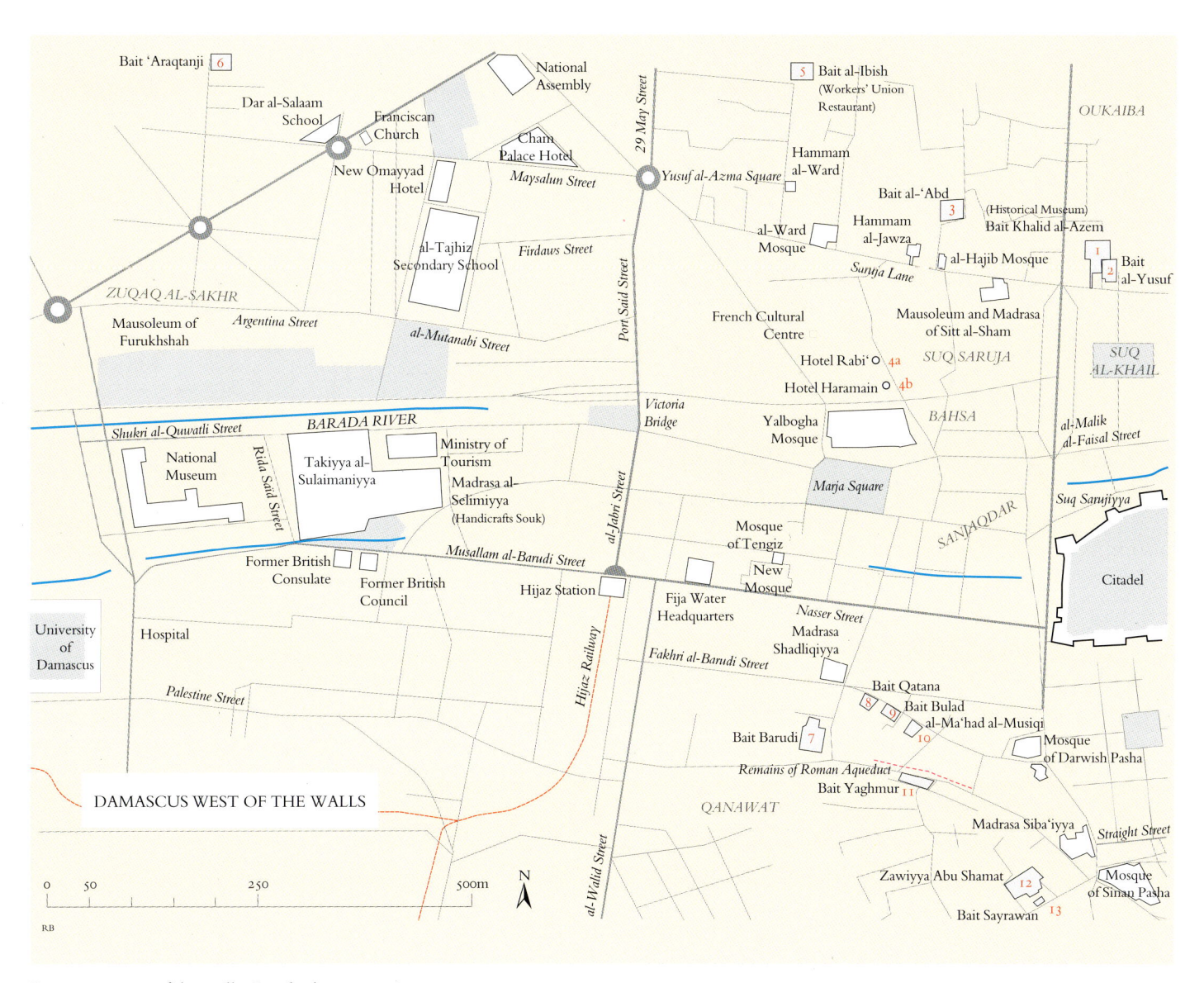

Damascus west of the walls. See the key on page 219.

(Historical Museum)
Bait Khalid al-Azem
Bait al-Yusuf

Jane Digby's House

al-Zainabiyya Mosque

SUQ SARUJA

al-Tawba Mosque

SUQ AL-KHAIL

BARADA RIVER

Bab al-Salam

al-Malik al-Faisal Street

Bab al-Faradis

2

Bait al-Amir al-Jaza'iri
AMARA

Bab al-Faraj

Bait Jaza'iri

5

Suq Sarujiyya

Bait Shirazi

1

Bait Saqqa' Amini

6

Bait Nabulsi

10

Madrasa al-'Adiliyya

Bait Quwatli

7a

Bait al-Sabah

QAIMARIYYA

Citadel

Madrasa al-Zahiriyya

Tomb of Saladin Bait 'Ajlani

9

11a,b Bait Mujallid

3

Roman Gateway

Umayyad Mosque

Nawfara café

11c

Bait al-Sabah

Madrasa al-Fathiyya

Suq al-Hamidiyya

Suq al-Haramain

Bait Quwatli

7b

BAB TUMA (CHRISTIAN QUARTER)

Bait Mardam Bey

38

Madrasa 'Abdullah al-Azem

8 Bait Jabri

Bait Quwatli (destroyed)

7d

Madrasa al-Nuriyya

Bait al-Azem (ruin)

13

Azem Palace

4

Maktab 'Anbar

12

Greek Orthodox Church of St Mary

Mosque of Darwish Pasha

Maristan Nur al-Din

Madrasa al-Qilijiyya

HARIQA

Turba Kukabaye

Hammam Nur al-Din

Dar al-Hadith Tengiz

Roman Arch

Madrasa Siba'iyya

Khan al-Zait

Suq al-Buzuriyya

Khan As'ad Pasha

Straight Street

24

Bait Tuta

HARAT AL-YAHUD (JEWISH QUARTER)

Suq Midhat Pasha

Hammam Suq al-Khayyatin

Zawiyya Abu Shamat

Bait al-'Aqqad

36

Khan Sulaiman Pasha

Bait Qasim

Mosque of Sinan Pasha

37

Bait al-Istwani

Bait Siba'i

30

31

Bait Dahdah

26

Bait Sayrawan

SAGHUR

Bait Quwatli

7c

Bait Nizam

29

SUQ AL-SINANIYYA

27

22

Bait Shamaiyya (ruin)

Bait Niyadu (Bait Stambuli)

35

Bait al-Haffar

Bait Tibi

34

Bait Kabbani

32

BAB AL-JABIYYA

33

Bait Kuzbari

to Midan

Madrasa Sabuniyya

Bab al-Saghir

al-Amin Street

Cemetery of Bab al-Saghir

0 50 100 200 500m

N

RB

Damascus within the walls.
See the key on page 219.

DAMASCUS WITHIN THE WALLS

Mihrabs and Niches

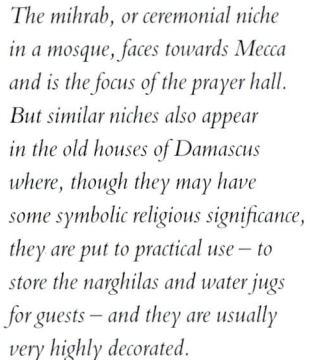

The mihrab, or ceremonial niche in a mosque, faces towards Mecca and is the focus of the prayer hall. But similar niches also appear in the old houses of Damascus where, though they may have some symbolic religious significance, they are put to practical use — to store the narghilas and water jugs for guests — and they are usually very highly decorated.

Above left: Niche at Bait al-Istwani with carved stone muqarnas ('stalactite') arch.

Above right: Marble mosaic and pillars for a niche at Bait Farhi.

Opposite: Painted and gilt wood muqarnas cornice and carved stone muqarnas work for a niche at Bait Bulad, surrounded by coloured paste.

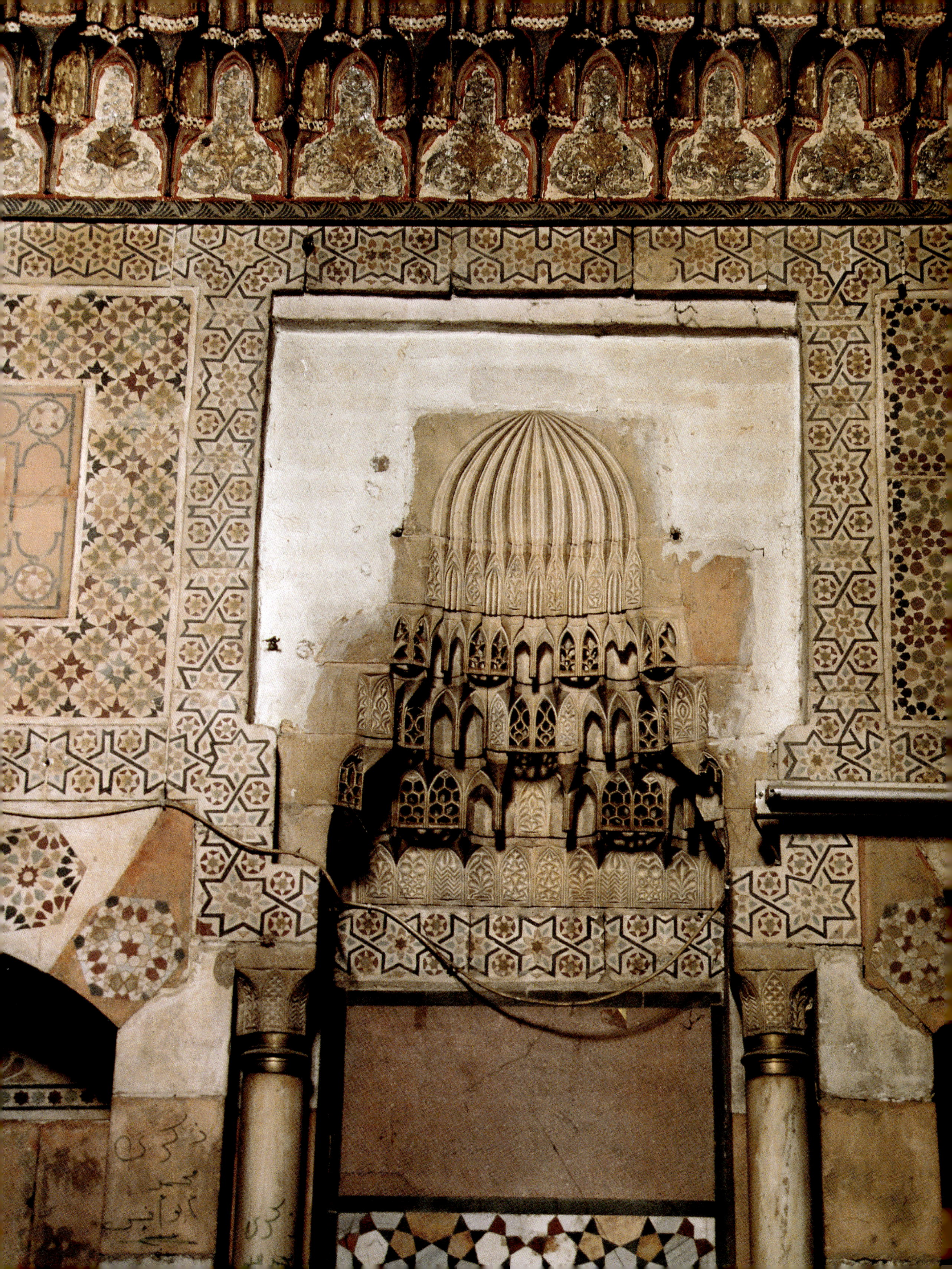

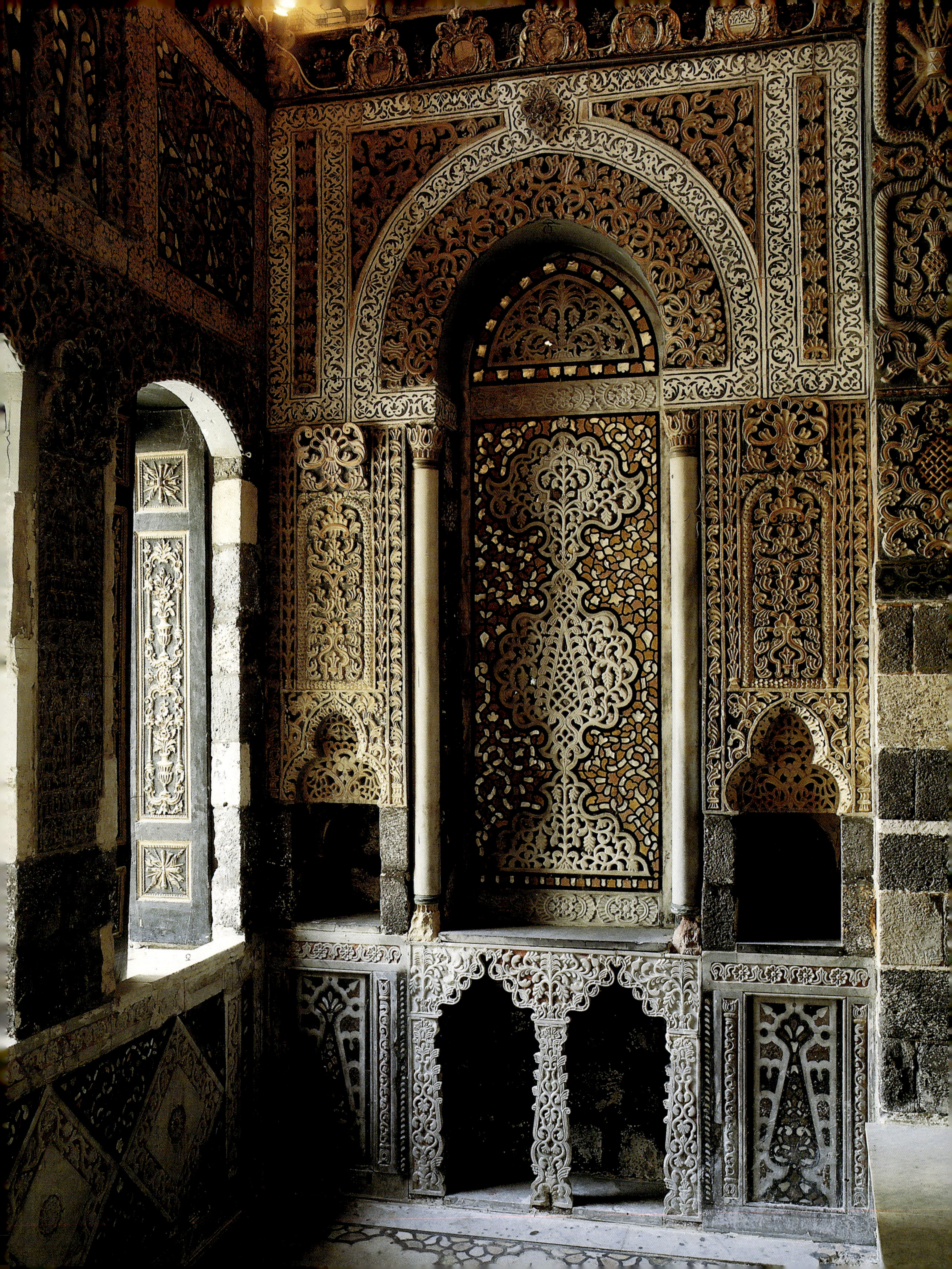

Mihrabs and Niches

Opposite: Mother-of-pearl inlay, marble mosaic and carved stone make an overwhelming decoration for the niche at Bait Nizam.

Below: An elegant example of Mamluk stonework: niche at Baibars's tomb.

Right: A combination of stonework designs for the niche at Bait Shirazi.

Bottom right: Painted wood and carving (late 19th century) at Bait Barudi.

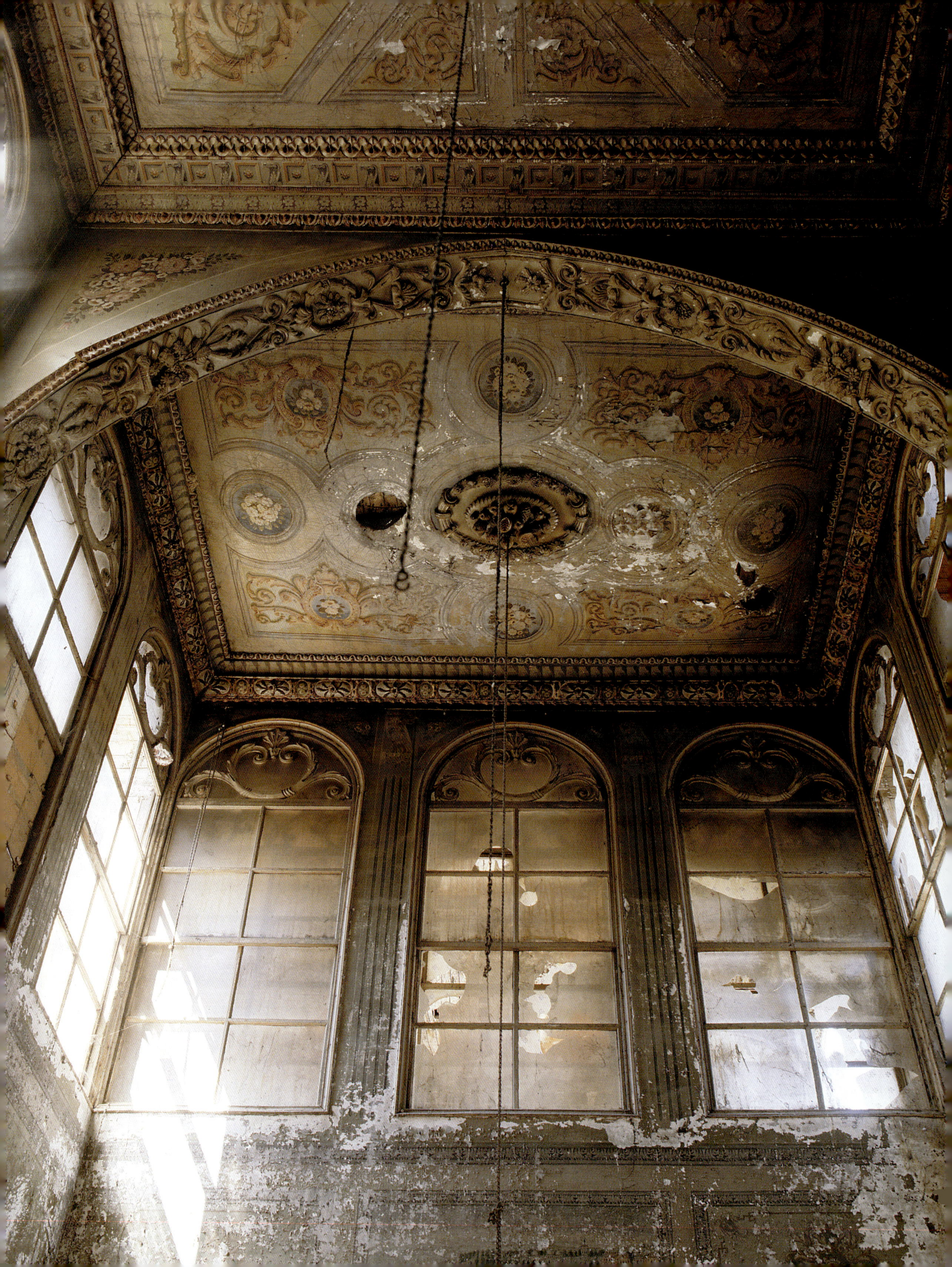

Part 2
Palaces and People

Damascus is like the women I see every morning outside our camp who cover their embroidered dresses with cheap cotton veils; she keeps her treasures hidden and only shows the European visitor who wanders her streets a dull view of windowless walls forming narrow alleyways....
  Anonymous, Extraits du Journal d'un Voyage en Syrie au Printemps de 1860

But the chief glory of Damascus is in the splendour of its private houses.
  The Reverend Josias Leslie Porter, Five Years in Damascus, 1855

Nothing can convey to the English mind a really good Damascus reception room....
  Isabel Burton, The Inner Life of Syria, Palestine, and the Holy Land, 1884

The old city of Damascus has survived for two thousand years – through earthquake, fire, invasion, plunder and pillage, civil war, plague, locusts, drought. None of them ever laid it low for long; after each catastrophe houses were rebuilt, public buildings repaired, the population grew again and the city re-emerged in much the same way as it had been before. But the 20th century has brought with it a new, unexpected, calamity, more devastating than all the others; one that the old city might well not survive in its present form. And yet it is such a harmless-seeming thing: simply that the wealthy and prosperous, the middle and upper classes of Damascene society, have moved out of the old city to apartments and villas in the modern part of the town. In the 1930s, H. V. Morton, a travel writer following the footsteps of St Paul, came to Damascus and wrote: 'The city has suffered a violent collision with the west in the form of French tramcars, telegraph and telephone wires, gramophones, Renault cars and a number of new

Opposite: A glorious painted reception room at Bait Quwatli (c).

Above: Isabel, wife of the British Consul Richard Burton, 1869.

Overleaf left: The highly decorated reception room at Bait Quwatli (a).

Overleaf right: Detail from the reception room at Bait Shirazi.

buildings.' You could equally call it a violent collision with the 20th century which has so dramatically altered the way of life that went with the calm, harmonious courtyard houses of the old city.

Traditionally in Damascus, two or three or even four generations of a family lived together. Each son brought his bride back to his parents' house, where they were allocated their own room off the courtyard. The mother, daughters-in-law, unmarried sisters and aunts all took a

81

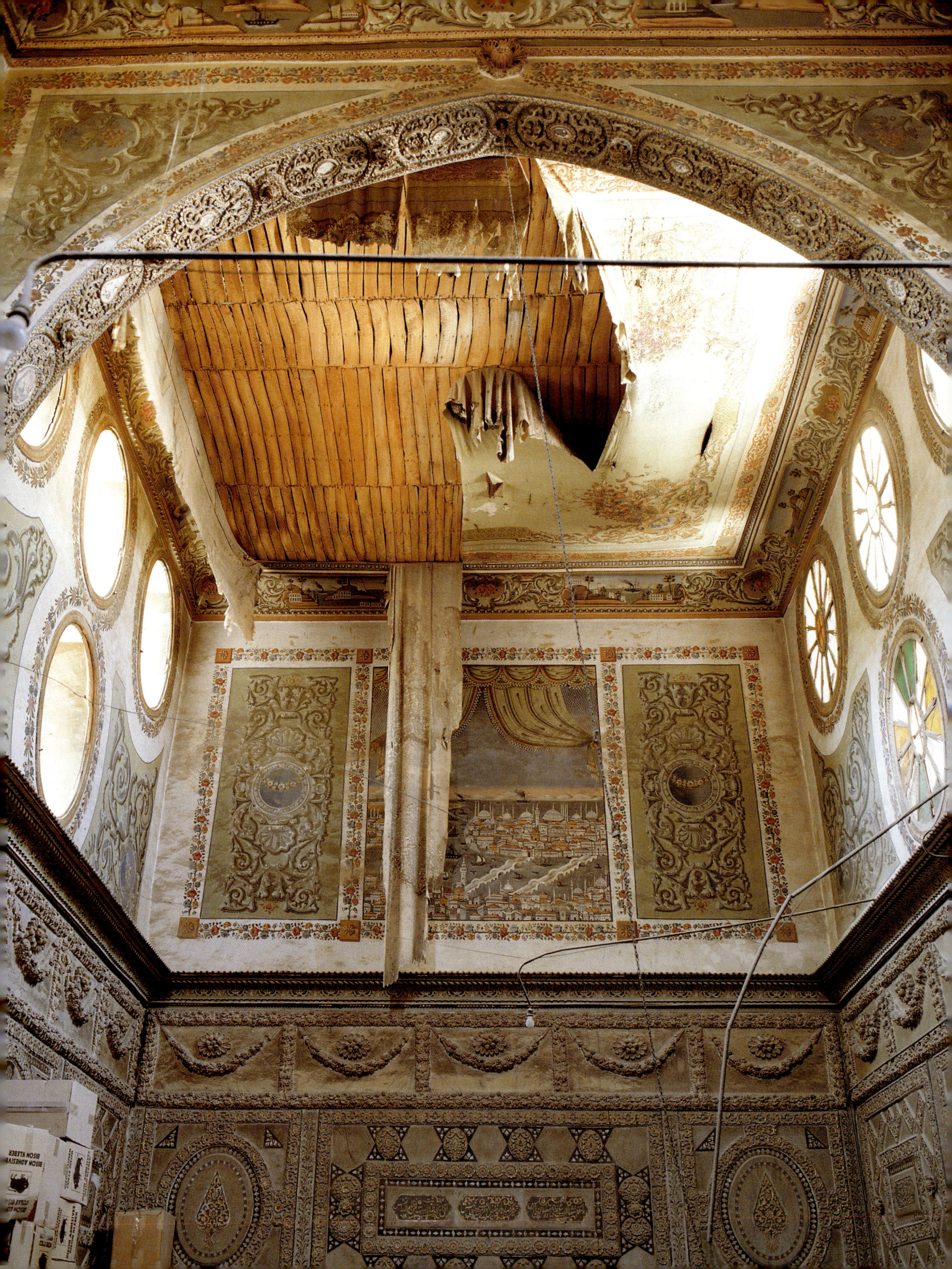

عشق حمایتنا

Left: The painted reception room at Bait Barudi, now under restoration.

Below: Courtyard of the late Nizar Kabbani's original family home.

Opposite: The liwan and paved courtyard of Bait Mardam Bey.

hand with the household chores to a greater or lesser extent, depending on how many servants there were, and they did not often leave the house except on family visiting days or to take a bath in the neighbourhood hammam. In winter, the whole family moved up to the first floor of the house to keep warm, but they usually still had to use the downstairs kitchen and lavatory.

Now, sons and daughters don't want to live with their parents. They prefer to be independent. They want homes that are easy and quick to clean and can be heated and cooled efficiently. The idea of living in a house where you have to cross the courtyard – perhaps in the snow or rain – to get to another room is, in this day and age, just too daunting; and so is the thought of not being able to get a car through the narrow alleyways up to your own front door.

When Richard Burton took up his post as British Consul in Damascus in 1869, his wife, Isabel, had to look for a residence for them to live in, and – like so many others – was torn between whether to move into the old city or not. 'There is a certain sense of imprisonment about Damascus as the gates of the city are shut at sunset; the windows of the Harems are also barred and latticed. On the other hand,' she hesitated, 'the interiors are so grand, so picturesque and Oriental looking, that they make one long to possess "a marble palace".' In the end, she decided on a house outside the city wall, in the Salihiyya quarter, which in those days was a separate village, but has now been overwhelmed by the modern city. (In fact, there were the traditional wooden lattices that she found claustrophobic on the windows of the house there as well, but she ripped them off and made them into a hen-coop in the garden.)

There is a huge nostalgia for the old city of Damascus and its traditional houses. The great Syrian poet Nizar Kabbani said that the beauty of his family's courtyard house had inspired him, and in his poem 'Letter to My Mother' he wrote:

Damascus at night, Damascus jasmine,
Damascus houses
Find a home in our hearts.
Its minarets shed light on our travels

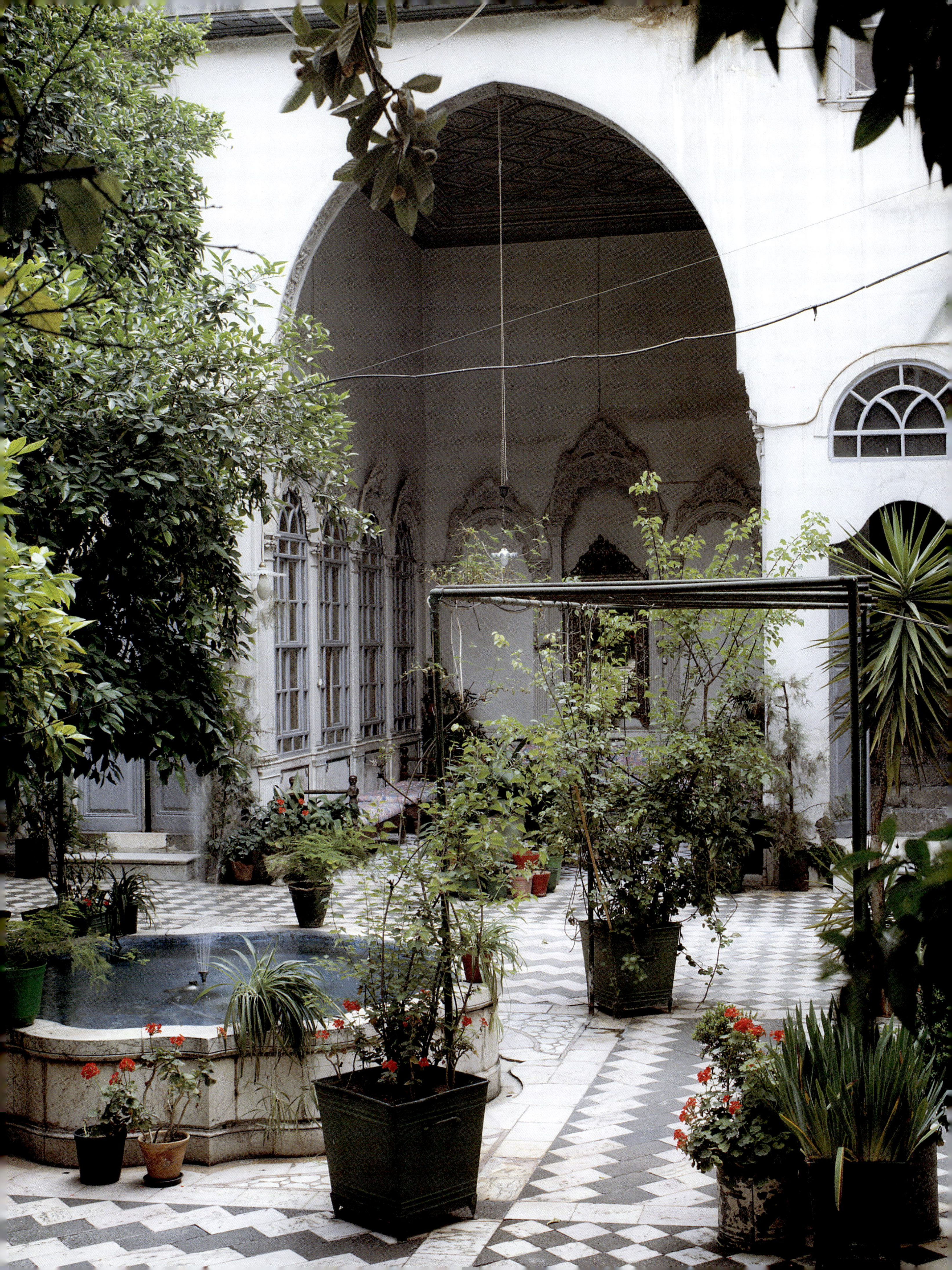

It is as if the Umayyad minarets are implanted within us,
As if the apple orchards linger with fragrance in our minds.
As if the light and the stones
Have come, all of them, with us.

In her novel *Sabriya, Damascus Bitter Sweet*, a well-known Syrian writer, Ulfat Idilbi, wistfully describes the courtyard of her heroine's home: 'Snow-white blossoms pour down the walls in frozen cascades. Red roses climb up the arch of the *liwan*. Yellow jasmine bounds over the trellis … in the pool is reflected the image of the moon, and the spray of the fountain produces a melodious sound …'. Siham Tergeman's book *Daughter of Damascus* is a love-letter to the old city, its pedlars, its donkeys and its charming houses, 'made from mud, water, wood, straw, colours, stones, marble, coloured glass, flowers, poetry and love'. But ironically, these writers, and many others who share the same passion for the old city, all live in the new part of town. Perhaps one should be less surprised at that and more puzzled as to how the

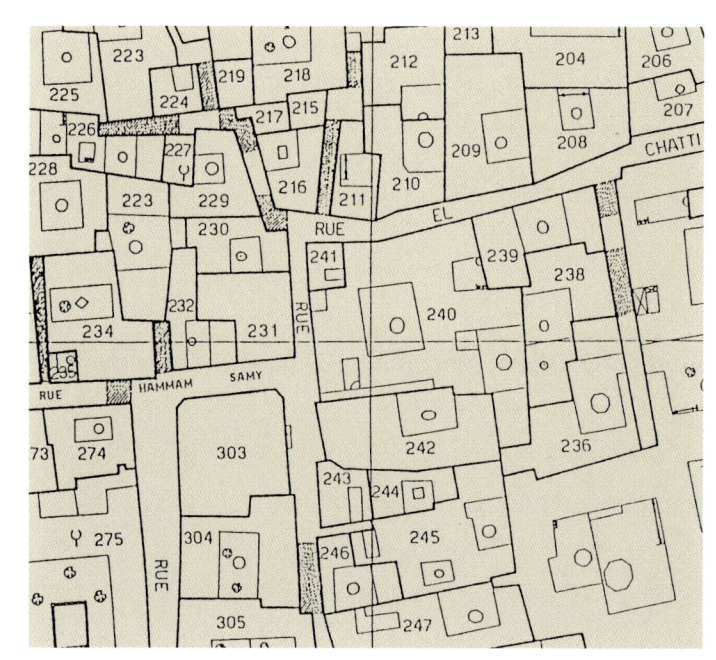

Above: A small section of the French cadastral plan of Damascus.

Below: Early 20th-century photograph across the rooftops of the old city.

Opposite: The houses of old Damascus are traditionally built in stone on the ground floor, and in mud and wood on the floors above.

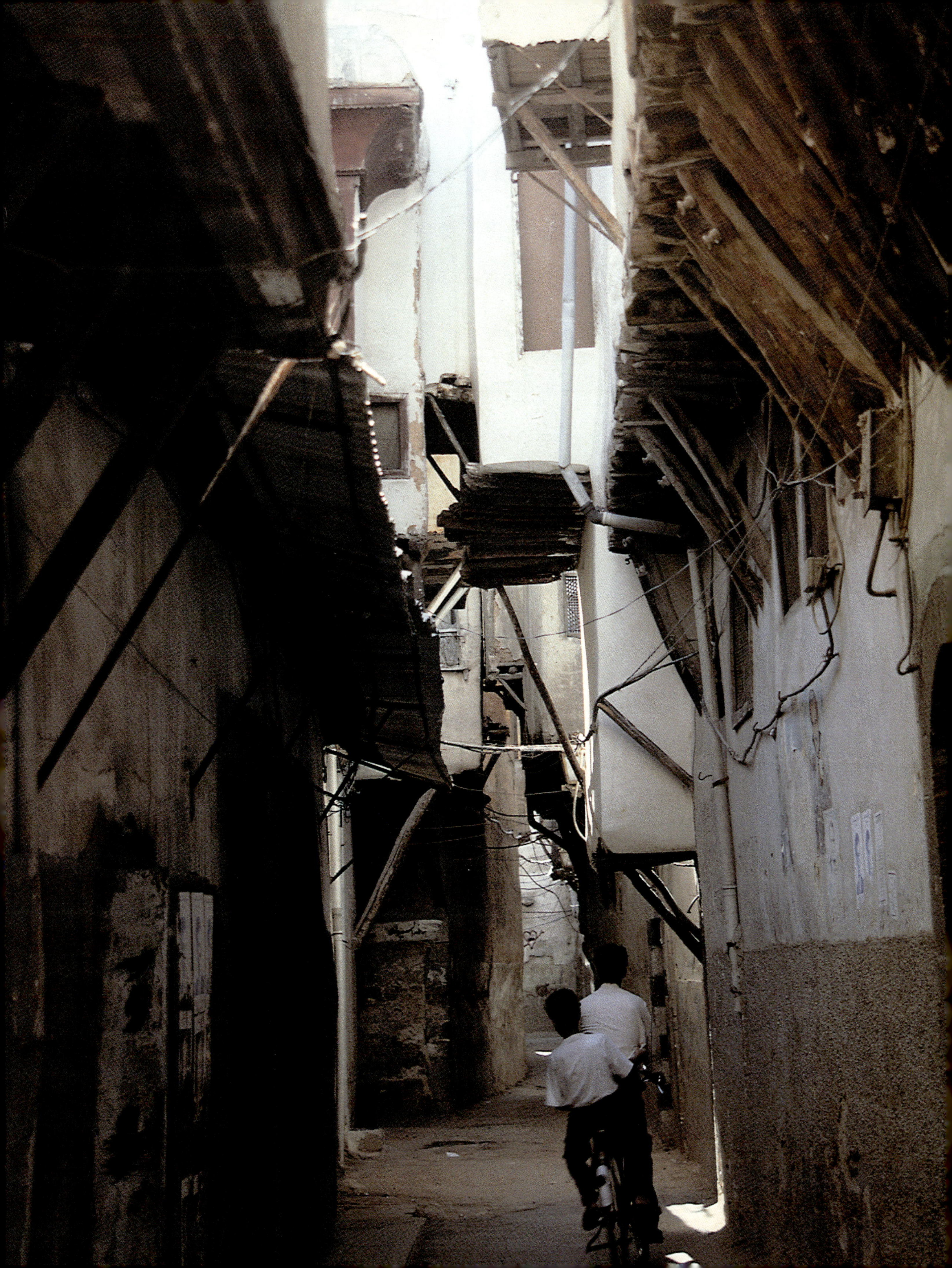

wealthy and powerful put up with the inconveniences of the courtyard houses for so long.

In 1936, when the French ruled Syria, their army engineers made a detailed cadastral plan of the old city – a priceless piece of work, in which every house was mapped with its own courtyard, fountains and trees. It is an astonishing portrait of a city in which there are no parks, no big roads, no open spaces, no roundabouts, views or vistas. Instead, a dense patchwork of squares, large and small, butting up against each other, with the circles of the fountains like extra embroidery. This map, showing that every house has at least one courtyard, and almost every courtyard a fountain, gives you a better idea of what lies within the ancient city wall than exploring on foot through the lanes and alleys.

John Green, the Englishman visiting Damascus in 1736, described the secrecy of the houses: 'Towards the street, no thing is to be seen but great walls with windows. But, as ordinary an appearance as they make outwards, they are within adorned with very rich paintings and gildings.' His description holds good today.

Above: A glimpse into the inner, family, courtyard of the haramlik at Maktab 'Anbar.

Right: Sun streams into the charming courtyard of Bait Shatta.

88

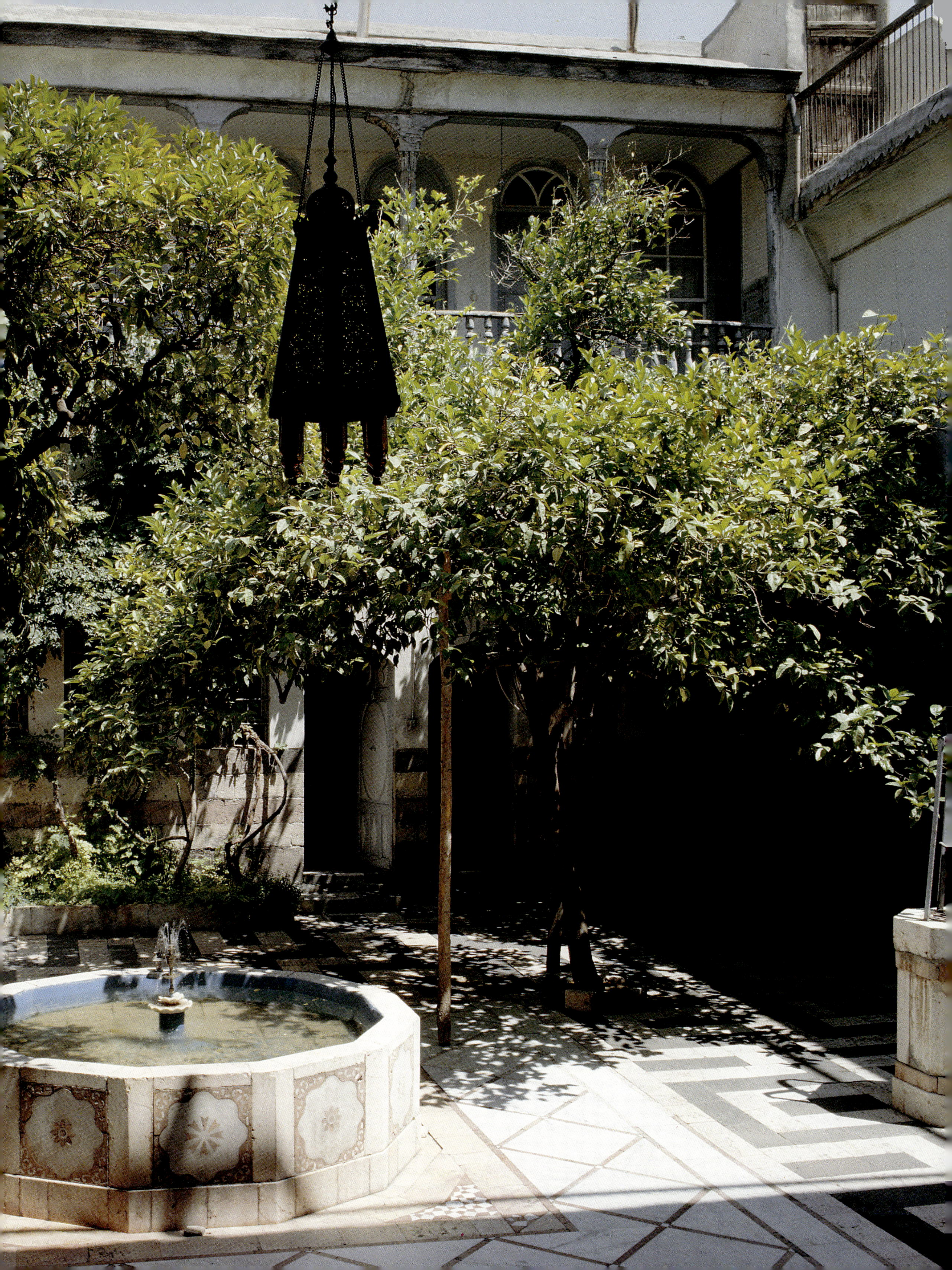

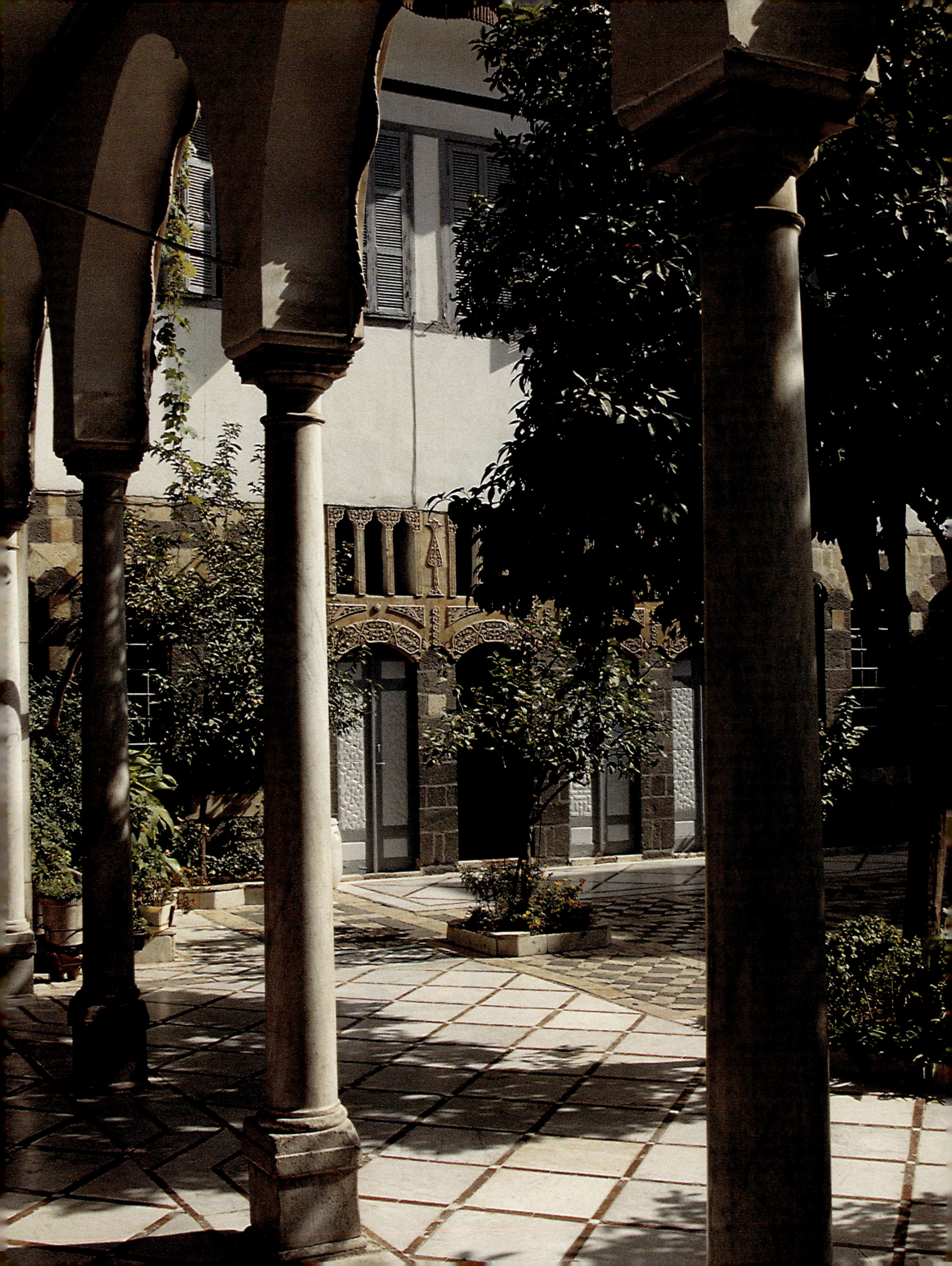

As you wander through the alleyways of the old city, blank walls on either side, there are no clues to tell you that you are passing fairytale palaces with breathtaking decoration inside; and no theatre designer could create a visual impact more intense than when you emerge from the dark streets into the brilliant sunshine of these courtyard houses with their fountains, trees, singing birds, marble paving and lavish ornament.

All through the centuries, travellers have expressed their surprise and delight at this stunning contrast in different words. George William Curtis, an American who visited Damascus in 1852, wrote the most dramatically: 'Are you disappointed, as you tread these streets, by these repulsive walls? Do you tremble lest the dream of Damascus be dissolved by Damascus itself? Oh little faith! Each Damascus house is a paradise.' He goes on to describe the particular house he was taken to see (it belonged to a Jewish merchant): 'A dream palace.... The scene was a poem set to music. The light of the opaline day streamed into the spacious court.... A large marble reservoir occupied the centre of this space into which fountains of fairy device poured humming rills of water. The pavement was tessellated marble, polished to a glow. Huge pots of flowers stood near the walls ... and glistening, trailing, and blossoming plants were ranged along the marble-margined fountain. Roses, lemons and orange-trees, grouped their foliage, clustered their flowers, and perfumed the sun. Gazelles stood and ran in the court ... and among the fragrant trees birds sang. Slightly raised from the level of the court, and entirely open to it, were alcoves loftily-arched, carpeted and divanned with luxurious stuffs. The sides and ceilings of the alcoves were painted in dreamy arabesques. Such a dwelling as you must needs fancy when you look through Lane's illustrated Arabian Nights ...'.

Lamartine, in Damascus in 1833, looked at the lavish reception rooms of a Muslim *agha*'s, or lord's, house, and calculated that the decoration of each must have cost up to 100,000 piastres: 'Europe has nothing more magnificent.' Eugène-Melchior de Vogüé, another French traveller in Damascus, in 1872, described the interiors of the Damascene houses as 'defying the wildest flights of imagination ... all is freshness, silence and delight for the eyes'. (Of course, one must bear in mind that these travellers were seeing the houses in their prime and not as most of them are now: Sleeping Beauty's palaces, untouched and unmaintained for decades.)

The owners of these great palaces were mostly not, as one would be tempted to think, the rich merchants of the city, for the aristocracy of Damascus – the 'notables', as they always seem to be referred to in books – were not the businessmen, but the religious and military leaders. As John Bowring wrote in his *Report on the Commercial Statistics of Syria*: 'The merchant is rarely an honoured being. Those who wield the power of the sword and the authority of the book, the warrior and the *Ulema*, are the two really distinguished faces of society.'

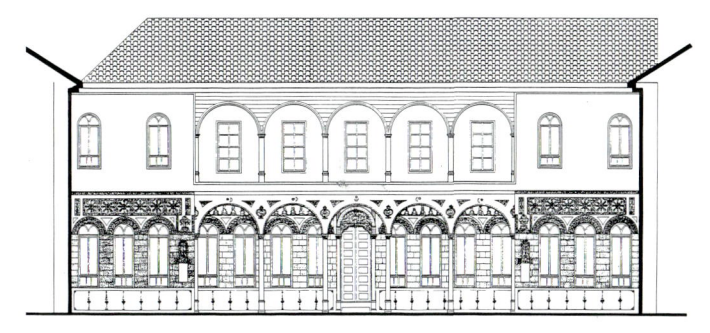

Opposite: View through the carved stone arcade at Maktab 'Anbar.

Above: Architect's drawing of the interior façade of Maktab 'Anbar with the arcade.

Top right: One side of the reception room at Bait Lisbona with its carved and gilt doors, typical of the first half of the 19th century.

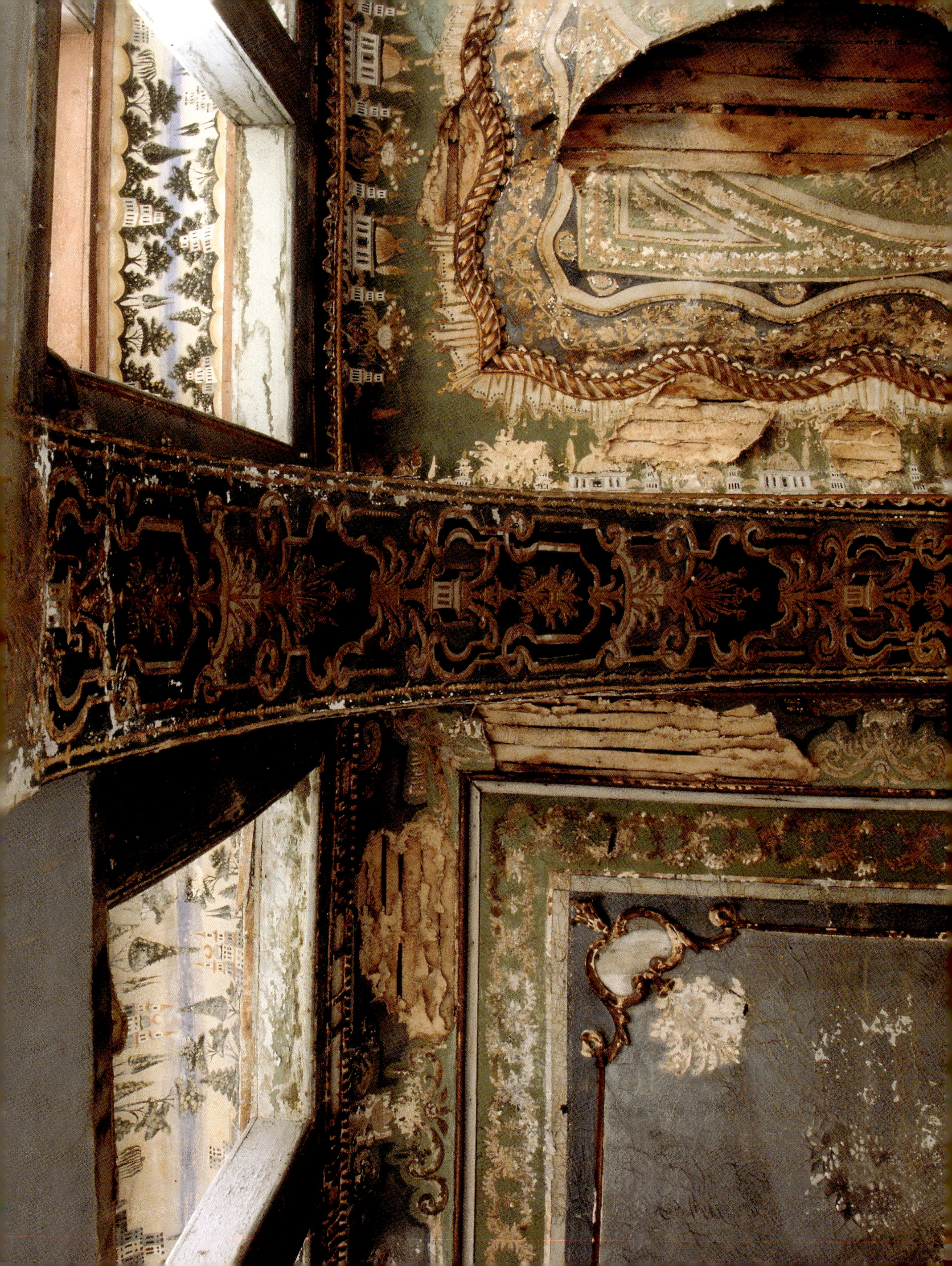

The 'warriors' included the Governors of Damascus and the leaders of the various military groups based there to keep the peace for whoever was currently occupying Syria. The 'ulama were the religious élite: Muslim sheikhs, the judges in the courts, the families acknowledged to be descendants of the Prophet Mohammed (they are called the *ashraf*), and the *sufis* (or mystic religious men). Only then in the hierarchy came the merchants. This did not mean they were poorer – far from it; only less prestigious and powerful. One of the great houses of Damascus is *Bait* (meaning 'house') al-'Aqqad – which the Danish Government has leased from the Syrian Government and restored to become the Danish Institute in Damascus – but the 'Aqqad family appear in no religious histories or historical documents; they were simply successful merchants in textiles. The 'Aqqad house, presumably because of their trade, is in the Wool Souk, whereas many of the houses belonging to the religious leaders were clustered round the Great Mosque, or thereabouts.

Next door to Bait al-'Aqqad in the Wool Souk is another glorious house, Bait al-Istwani. The Istwanis were among the most distinguished of the religious families, but it is known that one member of the family went into trade in the late 18th century, so perhaps this was the home of that successful merchant 'Abdullah al-Istwani.

In his 1840 *Report*, John Bowring names the richest merchants in Damascus – among them a certain Mohammed Sa'id al-Quwatli, who is said to have had capital of between 1½ and 2 million piastres. This is presumably why there were at least four palaces in Damascus called Bait Quwatli (one of which housed the British Consulate 150 years ago). In the 19th century, the Quwatlis had money but not political power, but a century later a member of the family, Shukri Quwatli, rose to become President of Syria. This is one of the interesting aspects of the prominent Damascene families – though the population of Damascus is now four million, and not a mere hundred thousand-odd as it was in Bowring's time, the names that were famous then still crop up among the city's élite.

In the old Damascene Muslim society, there were no class distinctions when it came to where people lived – the rich and the poor dwelt side by side, as they prayed side by side; neighbourhoods or quarters were made up of extended families or clans and their dependants. But the old city as a whole was – is – roughly divided into three parts: the Muslim area to the west, the Christian area to the northeast and the Jewish area to the southeast. The Roman arch half-way down Straight Street more or less marks the boundary between the Muslim quarter and the other two. 'The streets are rarely repaired and never cleaned and they regularly become deep furrows of dark mud and puddles of dirty water', wrote Isabel Burton, adding rather touchingly: 'With

Opposite: View up into the painted ceilings at Bait Lisbona, showing how an arch divides the reception room into two halves.

Right: The other half of the reception room at Bait Lisbona seen on page 91. Here, in the entrance, decoration is in stone rather than wood.

all my love for it, I know that it is not the cleanest city in the world; but there is such a thing as being so much in love as to wish the object unchangeable …'.

At sunset each evening, in the old days, not only were the nine great gates of the main city closed for the night, but other, inside, gates were too: 'By these, Christians, Moslems and Jews are locked into their respective quarters', reported Mrs Burton.

Since the Muslim conquest of Damascus in AD 635, Christians and Jews had held a particular position in society: as 'people of the book' they share many of the same prophets as Muslims, who also hold Mary and Jesus in great reverence. (Indeed, there is a legend that Mary and Jesus lived for a time in the lovely valley of Rabwa, in the suburbs of Damascus.) Christians and Jews did not do military service of any sort, but paid a forfeit – a sort of poll tax – instead; they had the right to freedom of worship, but political power was denied them. However, none of this prevented them from doing well for themselves in their traditional roles as accountants, financial administrators, bankers and money-lenders, though they remained vulnerable to the whims and moods of Governors and other officials, like their Muslim compatriots. Indeed, the richest man in Syria at the beginning of the 19th century was a Jew, Haim Farhi, who was the banker and administrator of the then Ottoman Governor of Sidon and Damascus, the notorious 'Butcher' al-Jazzar. A few years later, a Christian, Hanna al-Bahri, held the same powerful position for the Governor of Damascus during the short period when the Egyptians took over Syria.

When Western trade with Syria opened up in the 19th century, the Christians and Jews benefited enormously, for it was they who were favoured as agents and partners by the Western traders, and not the Muslims. Both communities became richer – the Reverend Josias Porter wrote in 1855: 'The Jews of Damascus are not numerous, but they are very influential on account of the vast wealth of some of the great families.' By then, visitors from the West were coming to Damascus in numbers – usually as part of a tour including the Holy Land. All of them wanted to see the fabled palaces of Damascus and, since the Muslim houses were usually closed to foreigners and impossible to visit, they almost always ended up being shown Christian and Jewish houses. Murray's *Handbook* of 1858 advises travellers that 'Old Abu Ibrahim, the Jew *cicerone* [guide]

Above: The courtyard of Bait Farhi today – a shadow of its former glory. The house is now occupied by many families.

Opposite: *Gathering Citrons*. This is Bait Farhi, painted by Sir Frederic Leighton in 1873. The arches on the right lead to another courtyard.

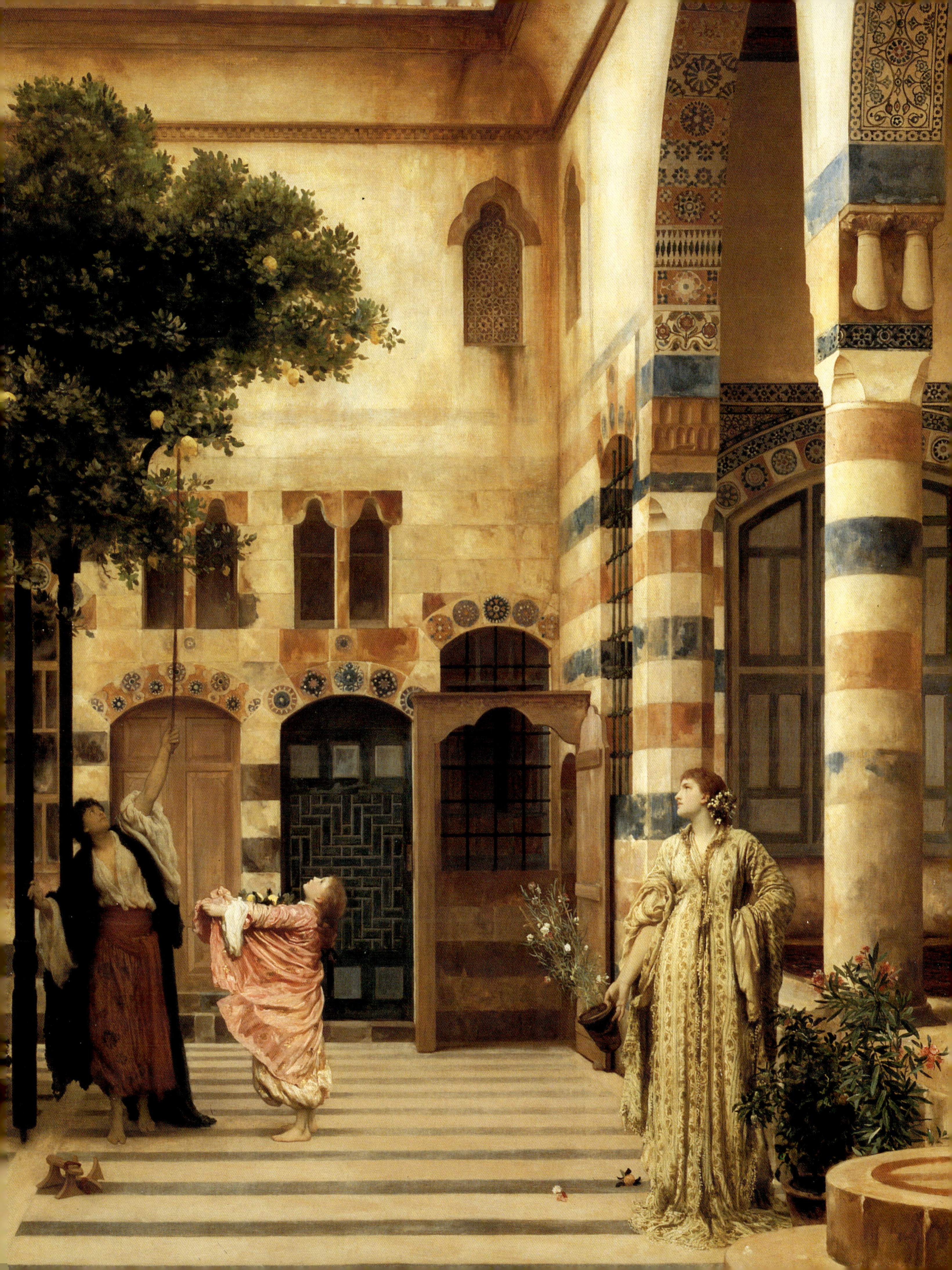

can conduct travellers to the Jewish houses.... If possible they should be visited on Saturday ... they will be found clean and their fair inmates will be seen all blazing with gold and jewels.' On the whole, though, Murray's *Handbook* found the Jewish houses, though clearly decorated at enormous expense, 'sadly wanting in anything like taste!' Nonetheless, it did recommend the Jewish palaces of Lisbona and Farhi as being exceptionally beautiful. The Christian houses, however, 'if inferior to those of the Jews in size, far surpass them in taste and beauty', and it proposed Bait Shamiyya and Bait Fransa as good examples. The *Handbook* warned, though, that visitors wanting to see these Christian houses would need to obtain an introduction from a resident friend.

Lady Hester Stanhope, the English aristocrat and adventurer, visited Damascus in 1812 and, with her long-suffering companion and doctor, Meryon, was taken to see the Farhi house. He wrote: 'On entering, the eye was struck with the glitter of the walls and ceiling, resembling the descriptions of fairy palaces. Mock precious stones, mirrors, gilding and arabesque paintings covered it everywhere, and the floor was of elegant mosaic. The pipes with their amber heads; the coffee cups with a gold stud at the bottom, on which ambergris was stuck to perfume the beverage as it dissolved in it; the embroidered napkins to wipe the mouth with; and the brilliant colours and high flavour of the sherbets corresponded with the grandeur of the house.' Lady Hester herself, who had astonished everyone by defying the rules and riding into the old city unveiled, was not at all pleased with the accommodation she had been allocated in the Christian area (as was usual for any visiting European). She spent only enough time there to decide that she did not want to live surrounded by 'Greeks and Armenians'; she wanted the *real* Orient, so poor Dr Meryon was sent off to persuade the Governor to relocate her in the Muslim area. They found her a beautiful house: 'It opened through a narrow passage into an oblong marble paved court. In the middle was a large basin, shaded by two very lofty lemon trees, in which two brazen serpents poured a constant supply of fresh water.' In her Damascene palace, Lady Hester held court for a while – she had become famous overnight and everyone wanted to see her – before moving on to adventures in Palmyra, and from there to Lebanon, where she spent the rest of her days.

Top and above: Bait Niyadu (Bait Stambuli) as it is today and as photographed by Bonfils in the 1870s.

Opposite: Bait Shamiyya, once one of the grandest of the Christian houses, now a convent. These inlaid doors led to a dining room which is now a chapel.

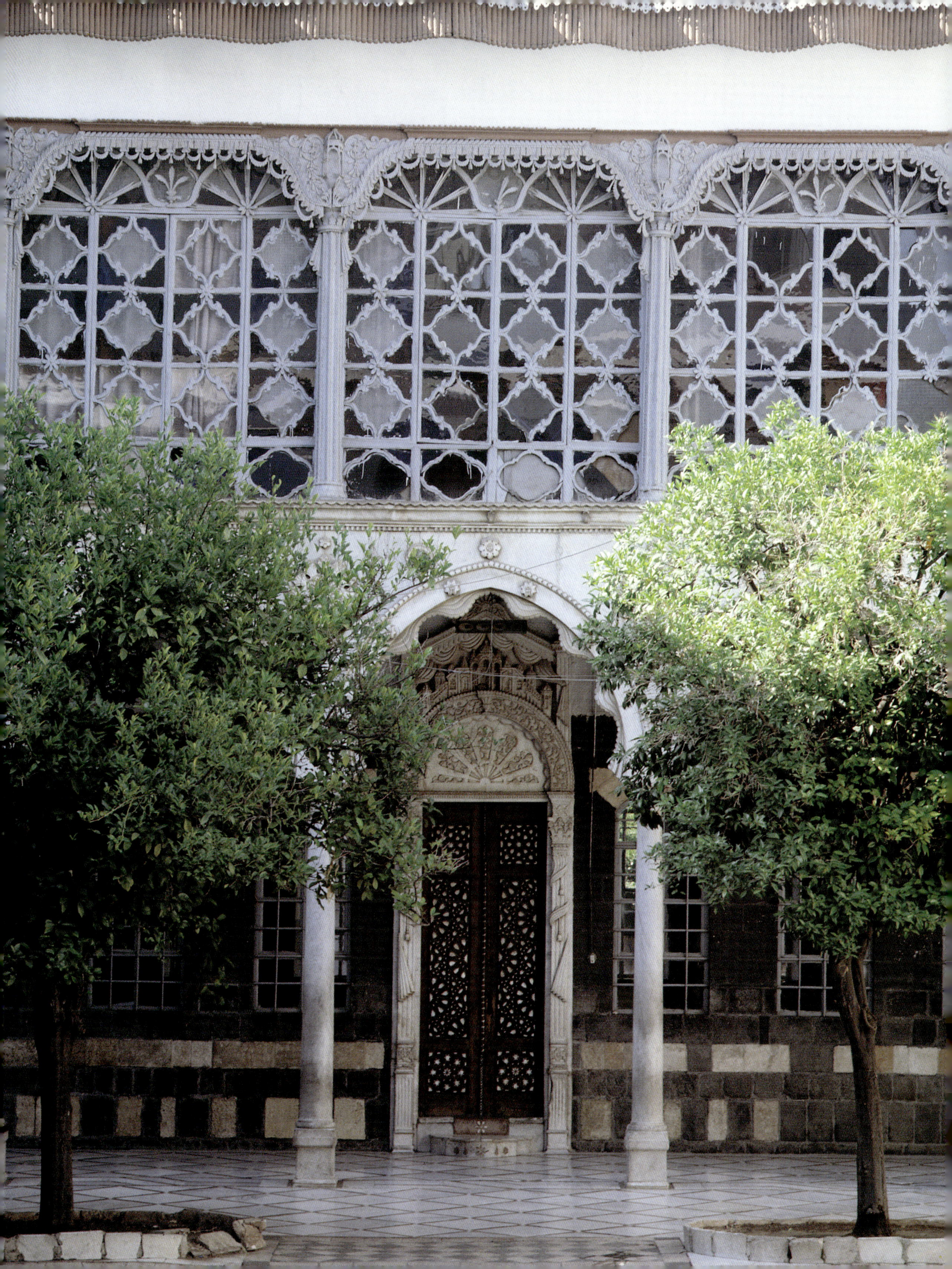

Today, all the houses recommended by Murray's *Handbook* of 1858 still stand. Bait Lisbona – which Isabel Burton thought was the second prettiest house in Damascus (the first being the Azem Palace, which is described later) – is being restored by its new owner (a Christian) and may become a hotel; the four courtyards of Bait Farhi, where Dr Meryon had admired the coffee cups with gold studs, have, over the years, fallen almost into ruin and are divided up between many tenants. Bait Fransa remains a charming, elegant little house with some exquisite panelling in the main reception room, but it, too, has deteriorated over time. Bait Shamiyya (which was rebuilt in even grander style after the destruction of the Christian area in 1860) is now a convent school and its large Western-style dining-room has become a chapel.

At the time of Isabel Burton's stay in Damascus, another great house, now known as Maktab 'Anbar, was being constructed by a newly-rich Jew, Yusuf 'Anbar (the story was that he had gone to India as a servant and come back with diamonds in his fez). 'It is in more modern style', wrote Mrs Burton, 'and therefore less pleasing to me. The fashionable luxury is rich, but too rich. Lisbouna's is tasteful as well as old.' Mrs Burton went on to describe how Yusuf 'Anbar was 'buying up all the old tenements around him to spread his establishment over as much ground as he can; unhappily he is also burning their carved wood and ancient ornaments, in which he sees no grace and beauty, and laughs at me for my heartache.' But at the end of the day, Yusuf 'Anbar was unable to pay his taxes, and so the Ottoman authorities confiscated his house in 1890 and turned it into a school (hence the name '*maktab*', meaning 'school'). Restored by the Syrian Government, it was opened as the offices of the Commission of the Old City in 1986 and is easy to visit.

Until the creation of the state of Israel in 1948, there had never been any particular problem for the Jews of Damascus. They simply lived as one of the religious minorities in a Muslim town – as they did in Cairo, Istanbul or Baghdad. In 1948, a few of the Jewish families went to Israel and their houses were mostly reallocated to Palestinian refugee families. In 1993, the Jews of Syria were all given exit visas by the Syrian Government. Tremendous pressure was then put on them by American Jewish organizations to leave Syria, and,

The liwan of another Christian house: Bait Fransa in the Bab Tuma district.

according to one of their community leaders, large financial incentives were offered. Most of the four-thousand-strong Damascus Jewish community were persuaded to go, leaving behind only a tiny group of about one hundred. Now, it seems, many would like to return, but, having sold their houses and businesses, this is not easily done.

The Jews were famous for their metalwork, particularly the intricate art of inlaying silver or gold into another metal. (The most exquisite examples of this are the Torah cases kept in the oldest Damascus synagogue, in the district of Jobar.) But the last metal craftsmen left in 1998, and the work being done in Damascus now is nowhere near the same standard.

The largely deserted Jewish quarter of Damascus is changing character and losing its boundaries as Muslims and Christians are taking over the old properties. Bait Niyadu, a famous house originally known as Bait Stambuli because its owners were Jews from Istanbul, is now owned by a Shi'a sheikh who loves it passionately. 'Is this not paradise?' he asked, as we sat one summer evening in the vast and elegant courtyard, eating grapes from the vine above our heads, with the fountain playing and the jasmine scenting the air, while his grandchildren wandered in and out.

Damascus seems always to have been known for the opulence of the palaces built by her rulers. The Arameans are supposed to have had a palace so rich that, when they were defeated by the Assyrians in 796 BC, the Assyrian King himself came to Damascus to collect the spoils of victory. In Byzantine times, there was a great palace near Straight Street, called Al-Baris, where visitors are said to have been refreshed with water and wine. The Umayyads built the Green Palace near the mosque, and the Mamluks built the Palace of Gold and the 'Ablaq Palace. But not a stick or a stone of any of these once-renowned buildings remains. Indeed, the oldest complete houses in present-day Damascus go back only to the 18th century. This has much to do with earthquakes and fire, but it is also because of the fragile and impermanent way in which the traditional houses of the city were constructed. For, though the walls on the ground floor of a Damascus house are built in stone – usually black basalt from the south of Syria – the upper storeys are made with a framework of slender poplar trunks filled in with sun-baked mud bricks (which the workmen make on site, using a wooden mould). The mud is strengthened by adding shreds of straw, or fibre from old gunny sacks (to this day, there is a shop, opposite Maktab 'Anbar, where they chop old sacks into tiny shreds just for this purpose). Over the mud bricks goes a layer of more mud, which is finished off with a coating of lime plaster.

The traditional roof in Damascus is made of poplar beams with a layer of wooden slats placed over the top, which are then thickly covered with mud, rolled and re-rolled until it is as hard and impermeable as cement (old roofs sometimes still have their rollers – looking like giant stone rolling-pins – lying around handily). If not maintained regularly, these mud roofs quickly begin to let in the rain, which soaks into the mud walls below, and very soon the house begins to deteriorate.

It's a puzzle to know why, when so much skill and money were lavished on the inside of a Damascus house, the habit of building the outside in mud and wood continued through the ages. Henry Maundrell, writing in 1697, was baffled: 'It may be wondered what should induce the people to build in this manner, when they have in the adjacent mountains such plenty of good stone.' Maundrell's explanation was that the first people to settle in Damascus, 'finding so delicious a situation', were in such a hurry to build their homes that they simply took as their materials the first things that came to hand, which were the poplar trees and the mud of the Ghuta oasis. But he continued to be amazed at their methods: 'In these mud walls you find the gates and doors adorned with marble portals, carved and inlaid with great beauty and variety … it is not a little surprising to see mud and marble, state and sordidness, so mingled together.' 'A golden kernel in a shell of clay' is how Moritz Busch more briefly summed up the Damascus house.

Over the centuries, the mud walls of the houses tumbled down, were repaired, rebuilt and redesigned to suit new fashions – but the lower stone walls and the foundations of the Damascene houses often go back far earlier than the upper floors. What proves this is the fact that, twice in the last few years in Damascus, workers restoring or rebuilding houses have come across buried treasure in the old walls they were repairing: in 1995, a clay jar containing hundreds of gold and silver coins dating from 1576 to 1710; and in 1998, a large Mamluk painted pot with sixteen thousand tiny silver Mamluk coins from the 13th, 14th and 15th centuries, together with some very early Ottoman coins. The recent work done on Bait al-'Aqqad (the house off Straight Street that the Danish Government has restored) has revealed that the unmistakably Roman wall in the entrance courtyard is part of a Roman theatre whose gates were discovered beneath the house. In the restoration of another palace, Bait Mujallid, an ancient fountain was found in the front wall of the house. The architect restoring a house in the street behind the Great Mosque discovered, behind some modern bookshelves, a colossal, heavily carved Roman stone lintel built into the wall. The Damascene houses were recycled and rebuilt so often over the centuries that one house – such as Bait al-'Aqqad – may have Roman remains, a 15th-century courtyard and 18th-, 19th- and 20th-century wooden panelling and wall painting. In Bait Barudi, which has become Damascus University's centre for student architects learning about the old city, restorers have found entirely different wall paintings under the present 20th-century murals. And in Bait al-'Aqqad and Bait Mujallid, architects have discovered, under late 19th-century decor, earlier frescoes.

Dorothée Sack, a German architect whose 1989 book on Damascus is one of the bibles for academics studying the city, says that Damascenes changed their

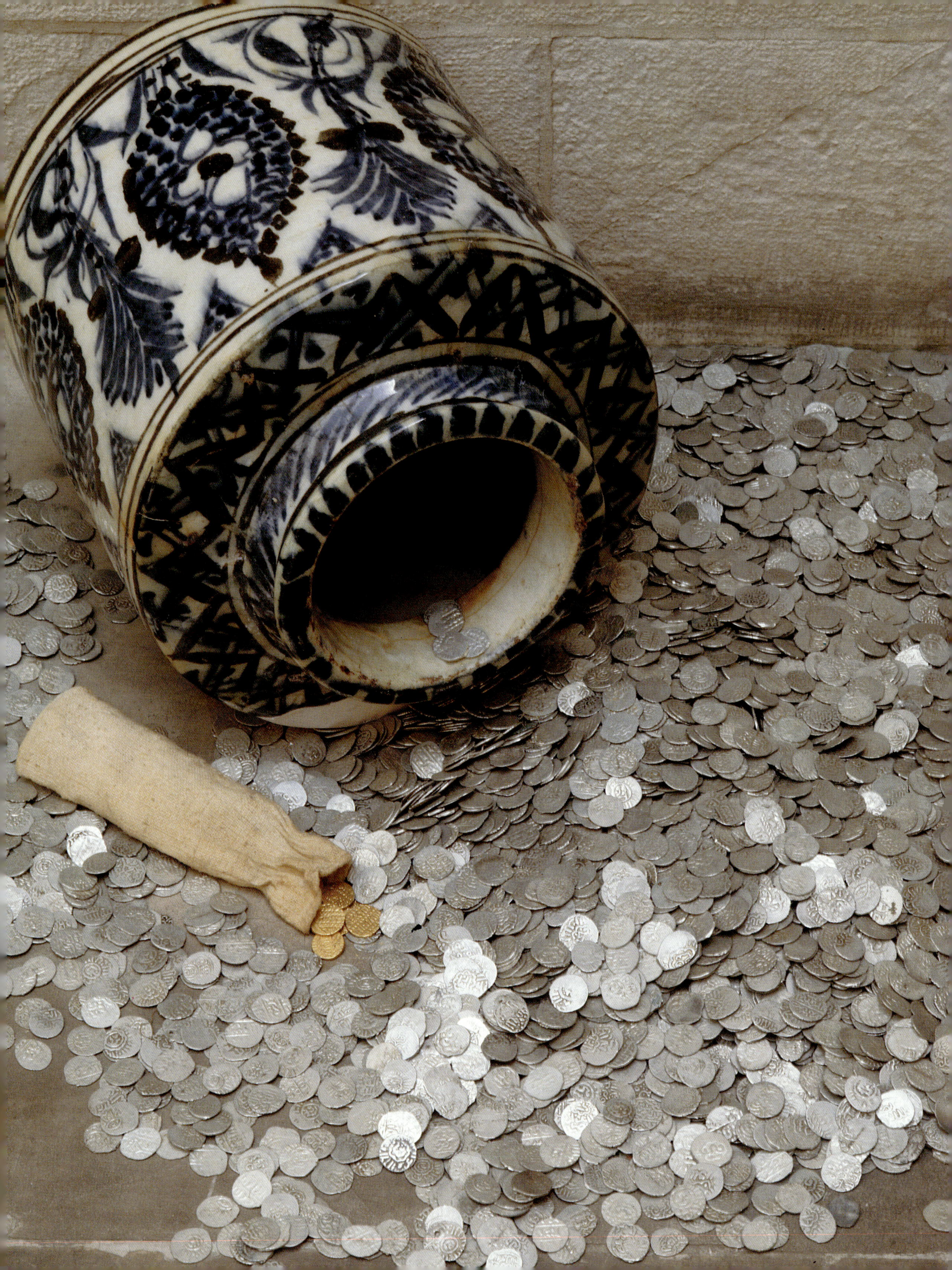

Opposite: Treasure found in Damascus – gold and silver coins in a Mamluk jar.

Below: Cleaning of a wall at Bait al-'Aqqad revealed previous paintings.

houses around as often as Westerners put up new wallpaper. But these alterations and redecorations never fundamentally changedthe basic layout of the traditional Damascene courtyard house. In 1959, when the ground was being prepared for a modern bank building in the Hariqa district of Damascus, the bulldozers uncovered part of a mosaic floor. The Antiquities Department was alerted and ten workers were allowed to dig there for three weeks before the foundations for the new building were laid. They uncovered the remains of a wonderful Byzantine house or palace dating from the end of the 5th century. The whole site was not accessible because there were buildings all around, but the archaeologists found the remains of rooms set around a paved courtyard. They uncovered floors made of variously coloured marble set in geometric patterns, walls which had been decorated with pink marble, and coloured glass fragments and the remnants of plaster. The discoveries were carefully recorded and then the site was reburied and the new bank built on top, but this extraordinary glimpse into the past showed that the ground plan of a Damascus house has been the same for centuries. Further proof is that, when the Mamluk Sultan Baibars died in Damascus in 1277, his tomb was placed in a small palace close to the mosque. Part of the ground floor was adapted for the burial chamber and a new gateway was built, but the rest of the house, as visitors can see today, clearly follows the traditional layout of rooms around a courtyard.

The Damascene house is *always* built around a courtyard (*ard al-diyar*), or two, three or four courtyards. But not all the courtyards of a house were necessarily constructed at the same time – they could be added later, built on a garden, or bought from the house next door;

101

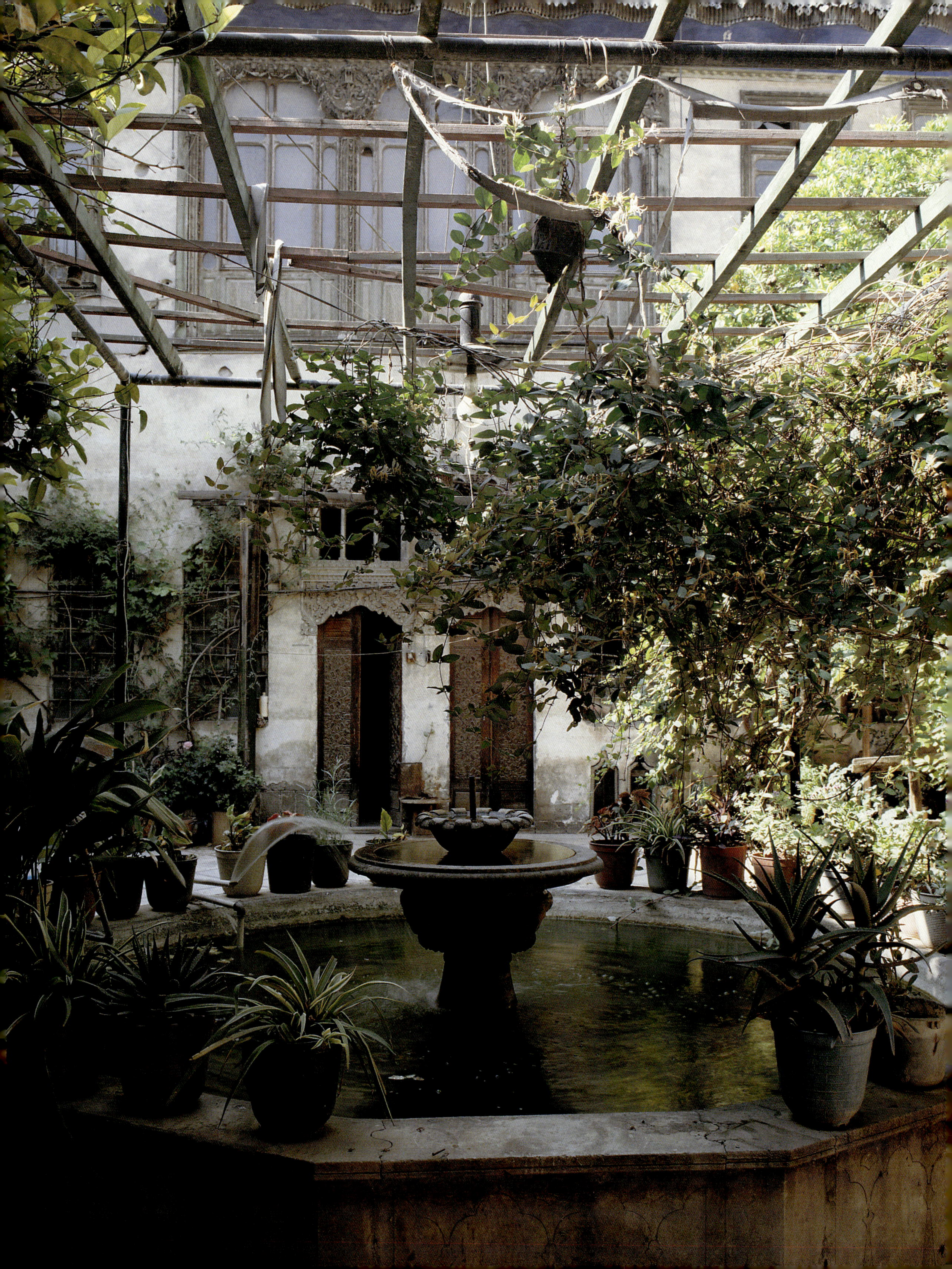

Courtyards

It is a stunning surprise to pass through the dark streets and alleys of the old city into the sunlit courtyards of the Damascus houses with their trees and singing birds. Houses may have one courtyard, shared by all the family, or two: an 'outer' court (salamlik) for entertaining and visitors, and an 'inner' one (haramlik) for the family. An important house might have three, or even four, courtyards, providing necessary space for the servants and services.

Opposite: A trellis over the fountain in the courtyard of the House of the Spanish Crown.

Above: A lovely arcade shelters the liwan in the courtyard at Bait Dahdah.

Overleaf: The secret garden – one of the four courtyards of a grand Damascus house that has fallen into disrepair. Restoration of traditional houses in old Damascus is easier than it might appear.

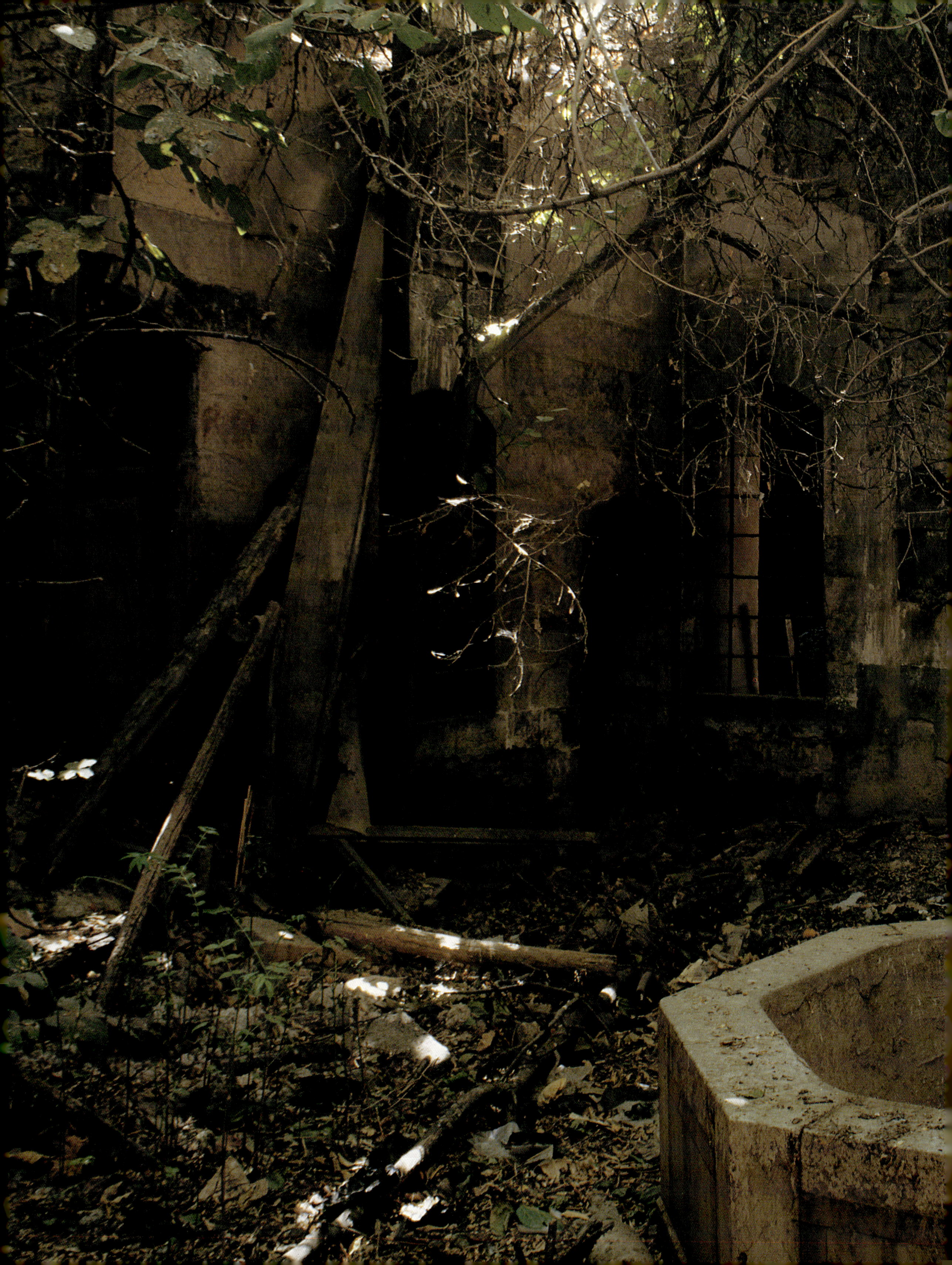

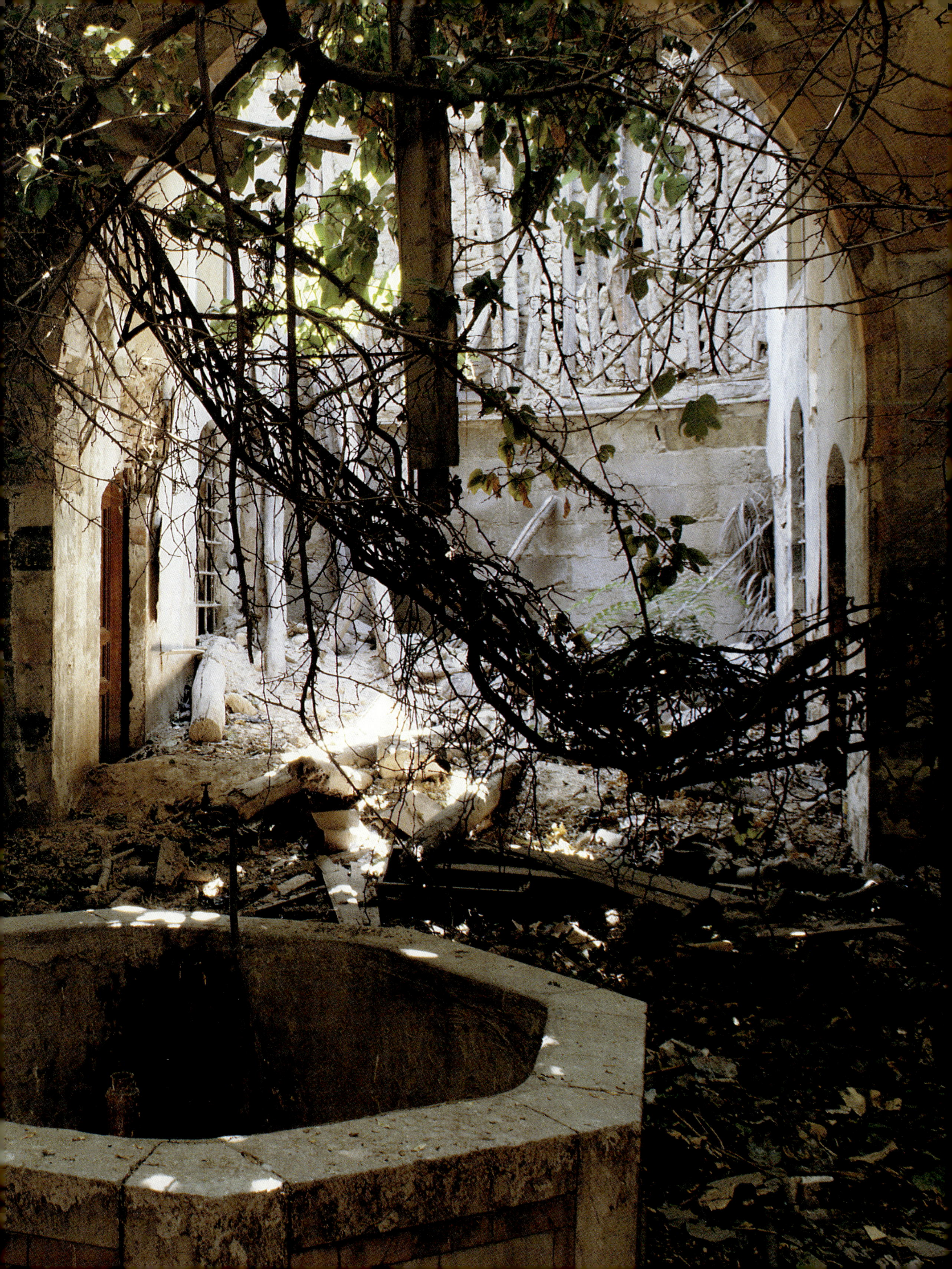

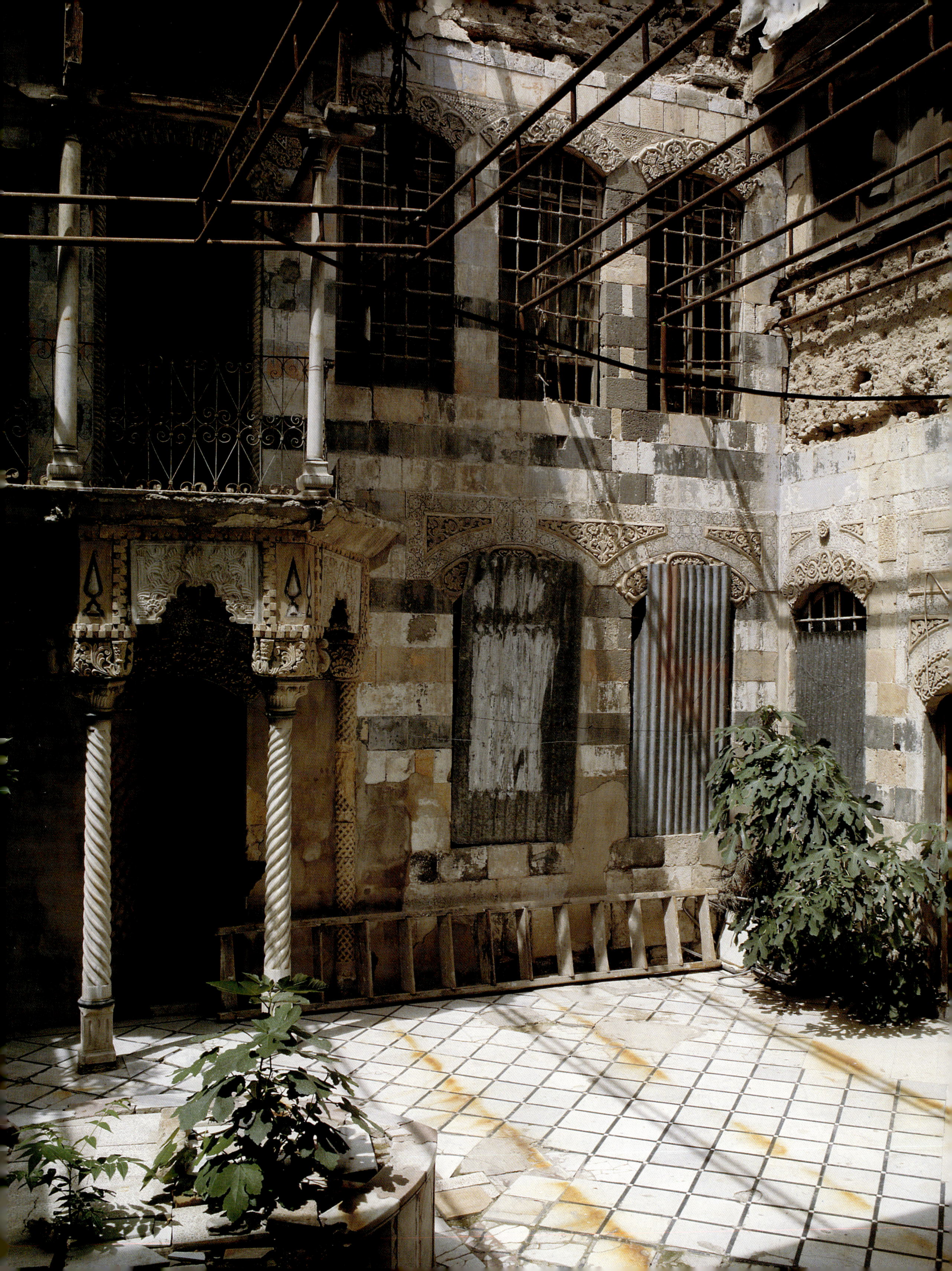

Courtyards

Opposite: The modest courtyard of Bait Tibi, a jewel of a house.

Above: The grand courtyard of Bait Nizam with its magnificent stonework.

Courtyards

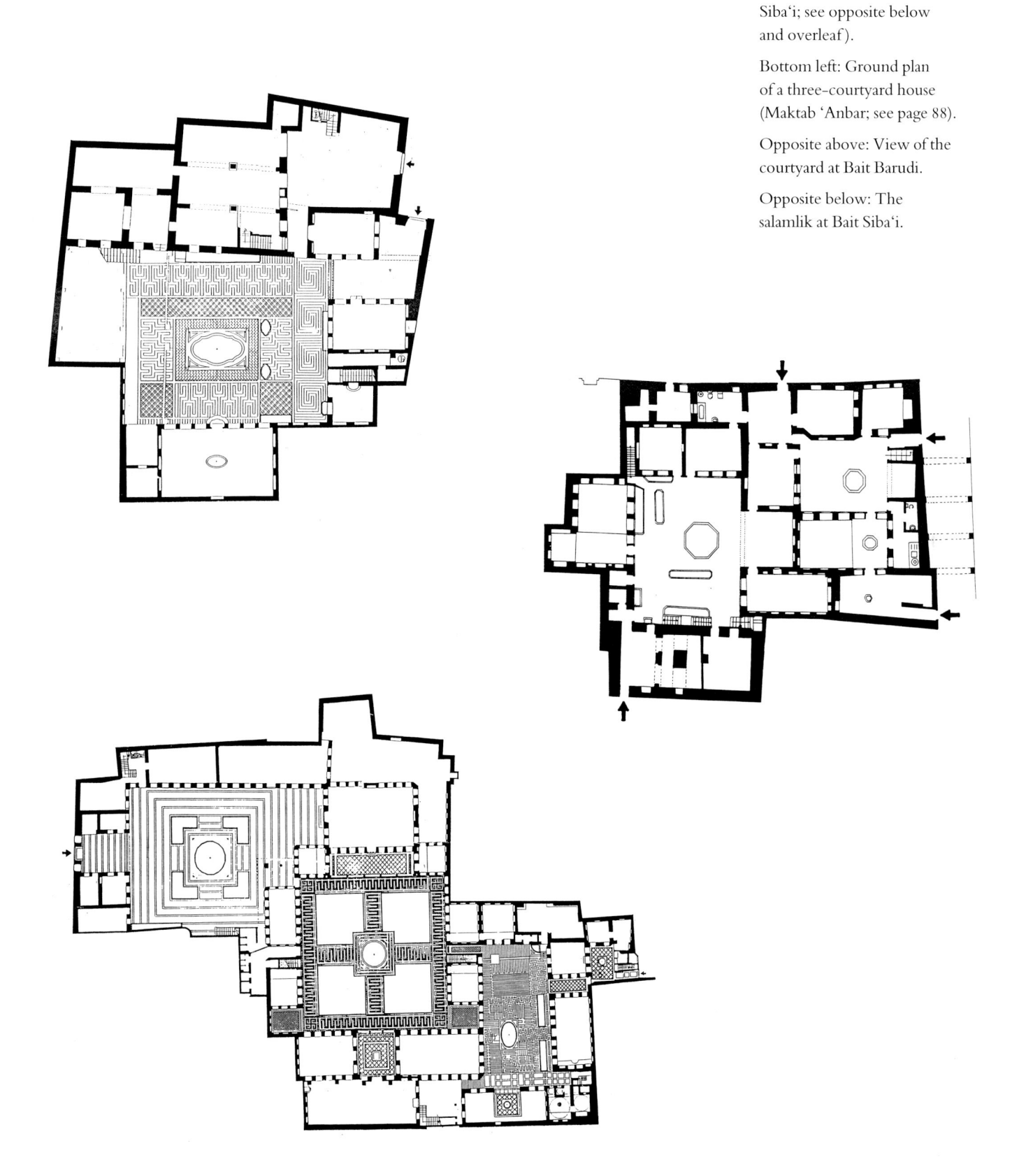

Top left: Ground plan of a one-courtyard house (Bait Barudi; see opposite above).

Below: Ground plan of a two-courtyard house (Bait Siba'i; see opposite below and overleaf).

Bottom left: Ground plan of a three-courtyard house (Maktab 'Anbar; see page 88).

Opposite above: View of the courtyard at Bait Barudi.

Opposite below: The salamlik at Bait Siba'i.

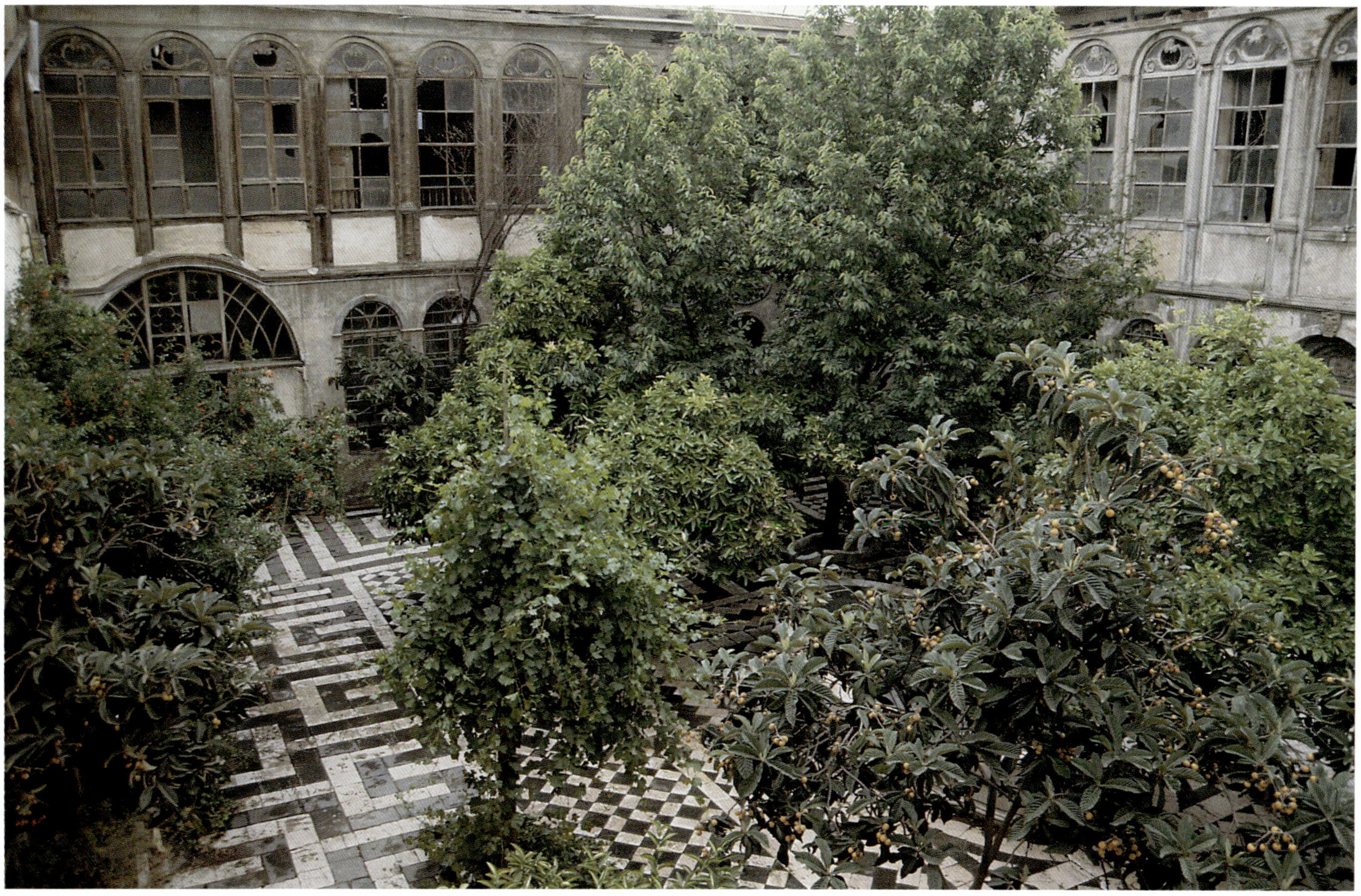

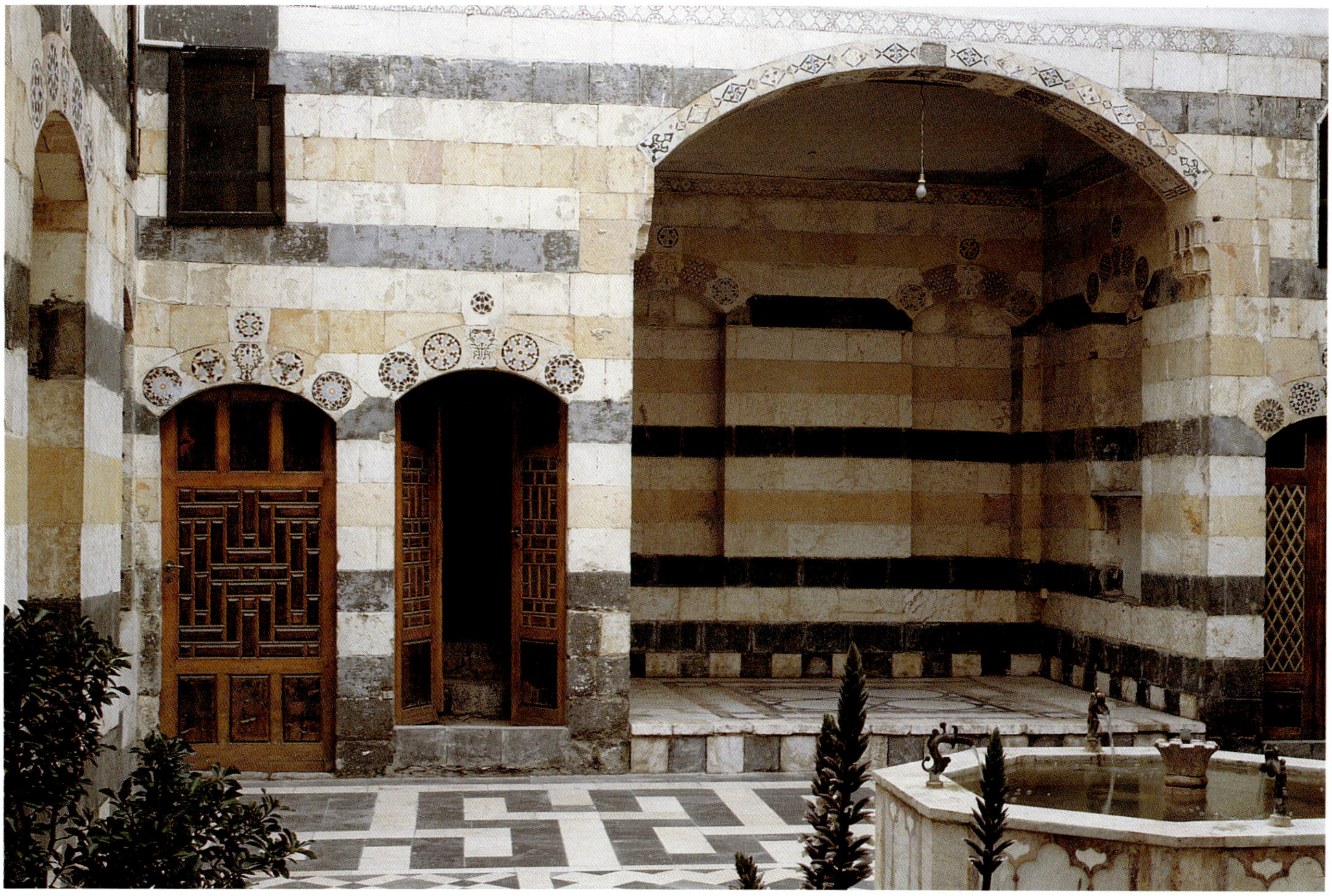

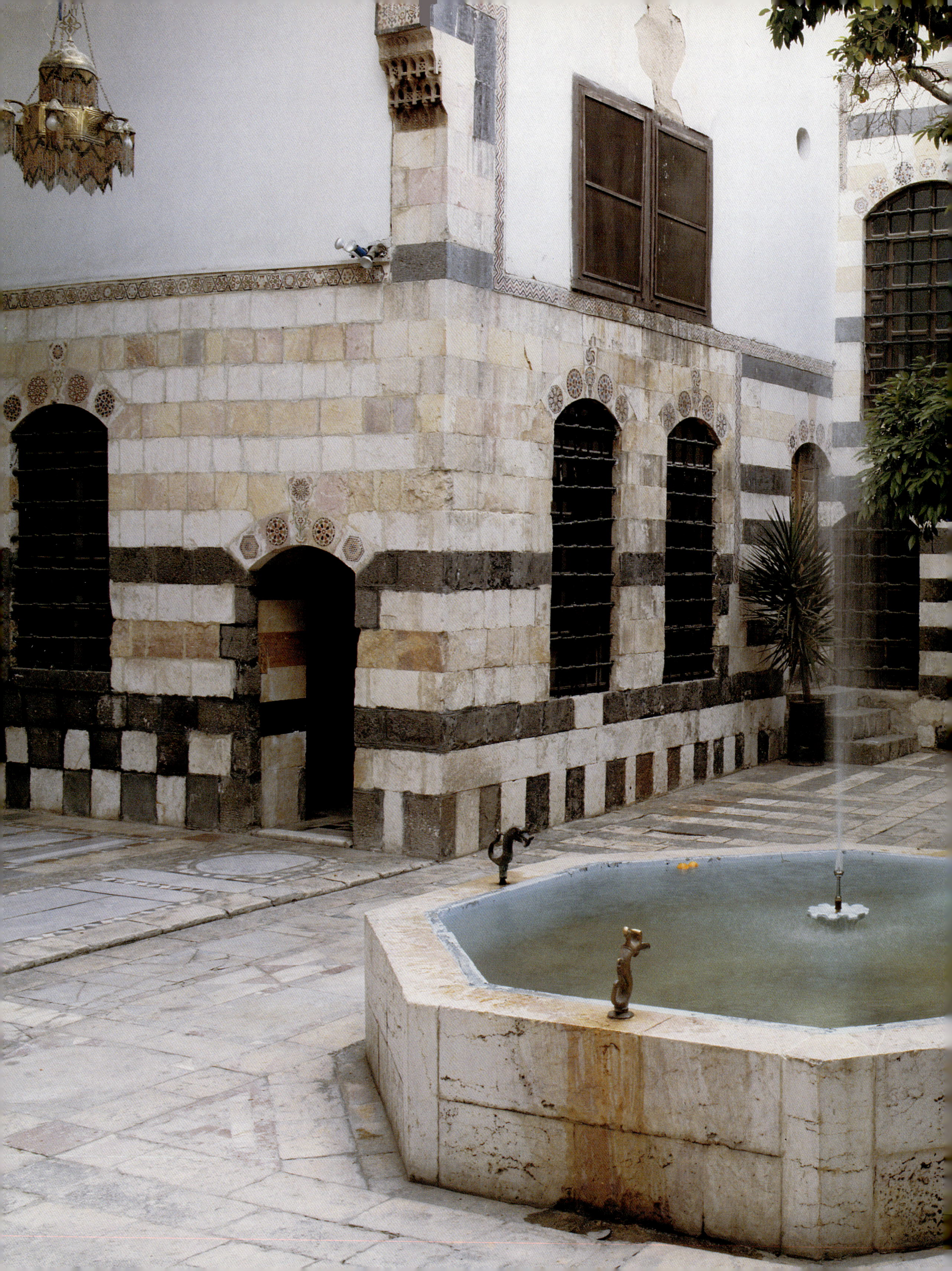

The haramlik, or family quarters, at Bait Siba'i. Steps up to the qa'a, or reception room, can be seen at the back.

configurations could change down the centuries. A one-courtyard house was lived in by all members of the family together, until male visitors or business colleagues entered, at which point the women all went upstairs to the *haramlik*, or private quarters. In a two-courtyard house, one court would be the *salamlik*, or public area where male visitors were entertained, and the second courtyard would be the haramlik for the family. The salamlik was usually decorated more austerely than the haramlik and it was the smaller of the two courtyards (this can be clearly seen in the Azem Palace). A third or a fourth courtyard – *khadamlik* – would be for the servants and the services for the two main courts. A very grand house might have a hammam off the haramlik court and the kitchen might have its own courtyard, as in the House of the Spanish Crown or at Bait Mujallid. There might be a small entrance court or corridor (*dihliz*) as well, to protect the inner courtyard from being seen through the front door. Often, even in the richest houses, the doorway and the entrance hall or corridor would be deliberately kept plain, even neglected and dirty (though there was almost always a stone or marble water basin of some sort for guests to wash off the dust of the city streets). As Isabel Burton wrote: 'A peculiarity is that every house has a mean entrance and approach. This is done purposely to deceive the Government and not to betray what may be within, especially in time of looting and confiscations. You approach an entrance choked with rubbish, with the meanest doorway, and perhaps a winding passage or outer circle of courtyard, and you think with horror, "What people must I be going to visit".'

Above: Beautiful Bait Jabri, entrance to the reception room.

Opposite: The liwan of al-Ma'had al-Musiqi (music school) in Qanawat.

The courtyard of a Damascus house might be as big as a football pitch, or tiny, but either way it was designed to cool and delight in the hot, dry days of Syrian summer. The sun filtered through the leaves of trees, sweet-scented jasmine tumbled in great cascades and water splashed into fountains. There was always a pot of sweet basil somewhere, because it was the plant that the Prophet Mohammed loved, and, of course, the famous damask roses of Damascus. There were traditional trees for the courtyard: a strange kind of lumpy lemon called *kabbad*, ordinary lemons and Seville oranges (*naranj*), which, in fact, went to Seville from Damascus and not the other way around. The pith of the kabbad and the skin of the Seville orange were crystallized into delicious sweets, and the leaves of the lemon trees, soaked in boiling water, made a refreshing tea. And there were grapevines, trained on immensely long stalks all the way from the courtyard to the roof, where they branched out to give fruit and shade.

There were even traditional animals for the courtyards: tortoises and, in the heyday of the houses, gazelles that teetered exotically on the marble paving. It is said that every house in the old city is also inhabited by a special snake that lives for a thousand years and gives off a lovely perfume. These snakes – known as the *alfiyya* or 'thousand-year ones' – are huge, but will never harm you if you leave them in peace. Hassana Mardam Bey, a young woman from a famous Damascus family, was told a story by her great-grandmother. It seems that the great-grandmother unwittingly disturbed the nest of their resident alfiyya, so the snake came and injected venom into the saucer of milk that was always put out for it. The great-grandmother realized her mistake, replaced the nest in the courtyard and the snake came back and tipped over the saucer so that no-one would be harmed by the poison.

Damascus courtyards are full of birdsong, mostly from the caged canaries which almost everyone keeps (songbirds must have been the equivalent of music on the radio in medieval times). High on the rooftops of old Damascus there exists another world involving birds. This is the realm of the pigeon fanciers or *kashash hamam* – all that remains of the days when carrier pigeons were the postal service to Baghdad and Aleppo. Look up to the sky and you can see their flocks flying in neat formation, often dyed pink like flamingoes. The aim of each fancier is to capture birds from rival groups, and since an intrinsic part of the game is lying about whether or not they have kidnapped another man's pigeons, they are, as a group, mistrusted in Damascus, and supposedly their evidence is not allowed in a court. 'Furthermore', wrote Miss M. E. Rogers, the Englishwoman who visited Damascus in 1865, 'it is thought that they yield to the opportunity afforded them of viewing from their lofts the harems of the surrounding homes.'

Older courtyards were paved with blocks of black basalt and red stone (from the quarries in Mezze in the outskirts of Damascus) worked together in intricate and maze-like patterns, but in the 19th century it became fashionable to replace the stone with marble in ever more complex geometric designs. The walls of the house facing into the courtyard were almost always built in stripes of black and white stone and were frequently decorated with coloured pastework in stone. This is a technique first used by the Mamluks in the 14th and 15th centuries, but developed by craftsmen in Damascus to reach the peak of perfection and beauty in the 18th century. It was a complicated process: a stone block was incised with a geometric pattern, which was then filled in with pastes made of different coloured stones that had been ground up. Later, in the 19th century, the paste was sometimes dyed into un-stonelike colours such as blue or green or red (examples of this work can be seen in Maktab 'Anbar) or the effect was imitated by simply painting the pattern on to the stone. The earlier work, when the patterns were finely crafted in earthy shades of brown and terracotta with white and black, is harmonious and beautiful. One of the prettiest examples (though over many years it has become sadly neglected) is the interior façade of Bait al-Istwani in the Wool Souk; Bait Jabri, Bait Siba'i and Bait Dahdah are other palaces decorated with fine pastework. The courtyard of Bait 'Ajlani (which is easier to see since it has become a public area with shops inside) has walls dotted with coloured pastework stones which are, says Stefan Weber, an expert on the subject, 'like sample sheets of designs'.

Since time immemorial, travellers to Damascus have praised its water-supply system – the network of canals

Below: Ceiling of one of the highly decorated reception rooms at Bait al-Yusuf.

Opposite: The 'ataba, or entry threshold, at Bait Siba'i, seen from the raised platform.

and channels from the Barada river that, from Roman times, irrigated the oasis and brought water to the dozens of public baths and water taps and to every delicate fountain spray in every courtyard. Idrisi described the river's source (at 'Ain al-Fija) and how it fed Damascus: 'The waters burst out high in the mountain-flank like a great river, making a frightful noise and a great rushing which you may hear from afar. Before it comes to the city it branches into many canals and water is conducted to all parts of the city, entering the houses and the baths and the markets and the gardens.'

Every house had clean water coming in via this system and dirty water going out through a different channel. (In the Khalid al-Azem and Mardam Bey houses, these old connections can still be seen.) The organization of the water, once inside the houses, was impressive. It would pass efficiently from fountain to fountain, through even the largest palace, because each fountain would be built fractionally lower than the previous one. Finally, having fed all the fountains along the way, the water would end up in the kitchen and lavatory.

There was always a fountain in a Damascus courtyard – sometimes, as at Bait Quwatli, Khalid al-Azem's house and Bait Siba'i, almost big enough to swim in. The older fountains, like the paving they sat on, were in plain dressed stone, but in the 19th century, when houses were often revamped, they were re-created in marble. The indoor fountains of the house were smaller and extremely decorative, in marble mosaic, sometimes inlaid with mother-of-pearl. The most curious type of fountain design can be found in Bait Shirazi and in the house of Khalid al-Azem: this takes the form of a shallow carved marble maze, through which the water finds its way.

The courtyard fountain was always placed directly in line with the dominant room of the house, the *liwan*, which was not really a room at all but a giant arched alcove, enclosed on three sides but open to the courtyard on the fourth. This liwan always faced north for coolness and it was where the owner of the house and his family, or guests or business associates, would sit in the summer, smoking their narghilas.

For maximum air and breeze, the liwan was the loftiest room in the house, taking up two floors in height, and since it was the main place for summer entertaining, it was usually very elaborately decorated with a glorious painted wooden ceiling, coloured pastework, intricately carved and inlaid stone, frescoed walls and a marble floor as complicated in design as a carpet.

Across the courtyard from the liwan was the next most important room in the house – the *qa'a*, or main indoor reception hall. Facing south so as to have the benefit of the sun in winter, this room was the glory of the Damascene house, where decoration ran riot and the Western visitor was transported to the Arabian Nights.

The qa'a had two sections: an entrance area on the same level as the courtyard and paved in stone or marble – this was called 'ataba, or threshold, and very often had a marble fountain in the middle and, possibly, a mihrab-shaped niche (called a *masabb*) in the wall facing the door (not for any religious reason, but for keeping the narghilas, jugs of water and so on). This niche was usually highly ornamental, with marble mosaic work and, sometimes, carved-stone 'stalactite' design (*muqarnas*). The second part of the room was the seating area; this was separated from the 'ataba by a great arch and raised about sixty centimetres (two feet) above the floor of the 'ataba. This platform area had a plain floor which was covered with carpets and rugs and a low seat (*divan*), or cushions, running all around the walls. Guests removed their shoes in the 'ataba and then climbed up to sit on the platform and be served with all sorts of sweetmeats and sherbets, cardamom-flavoured coffee, tea made of wild flowers and, of course, the ubiquitous hubble-bubble pipes. In a Damascene house, there was no such thing as a dining room, sitting room and so on – each room, including the qa'a, could

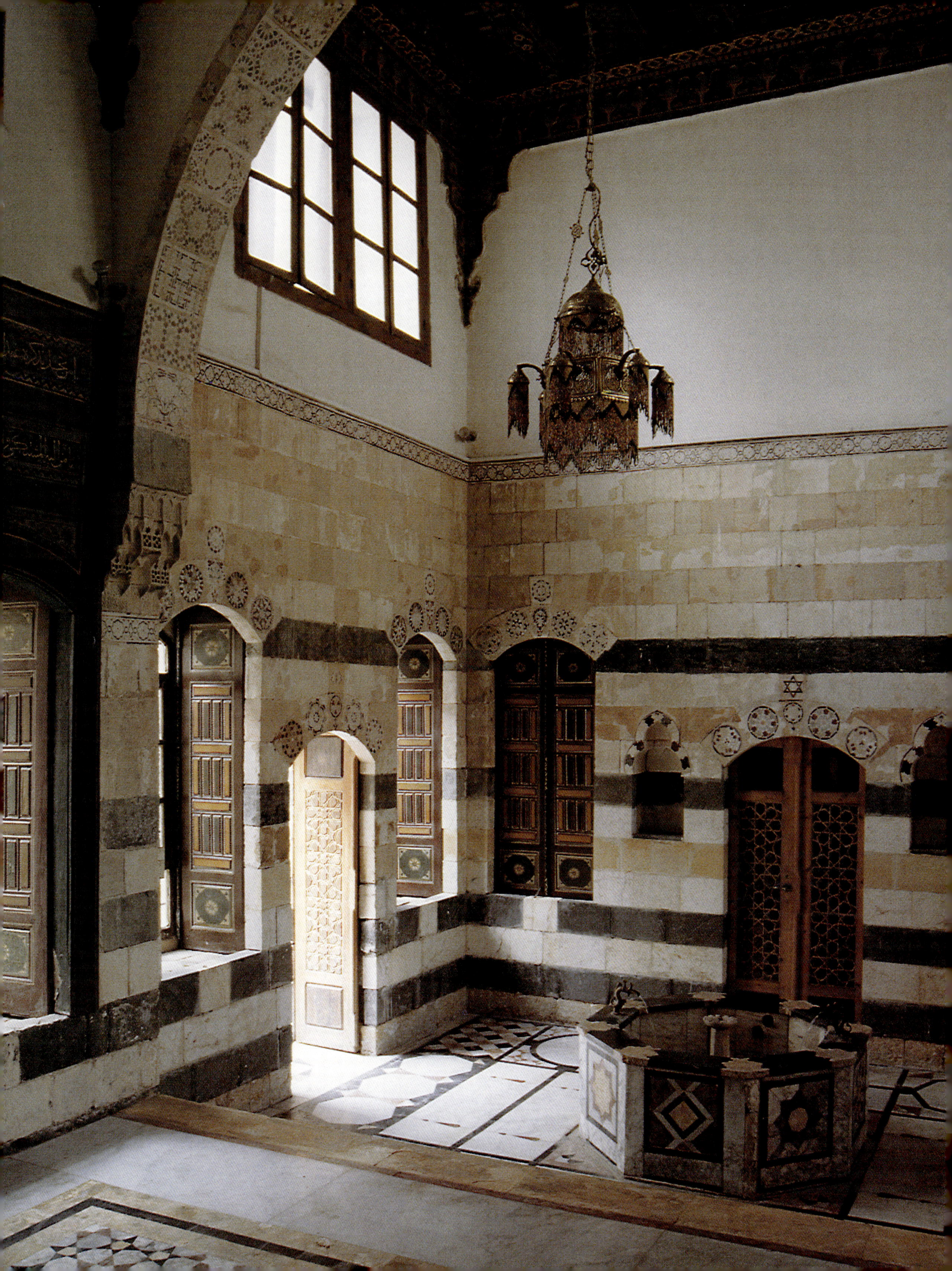

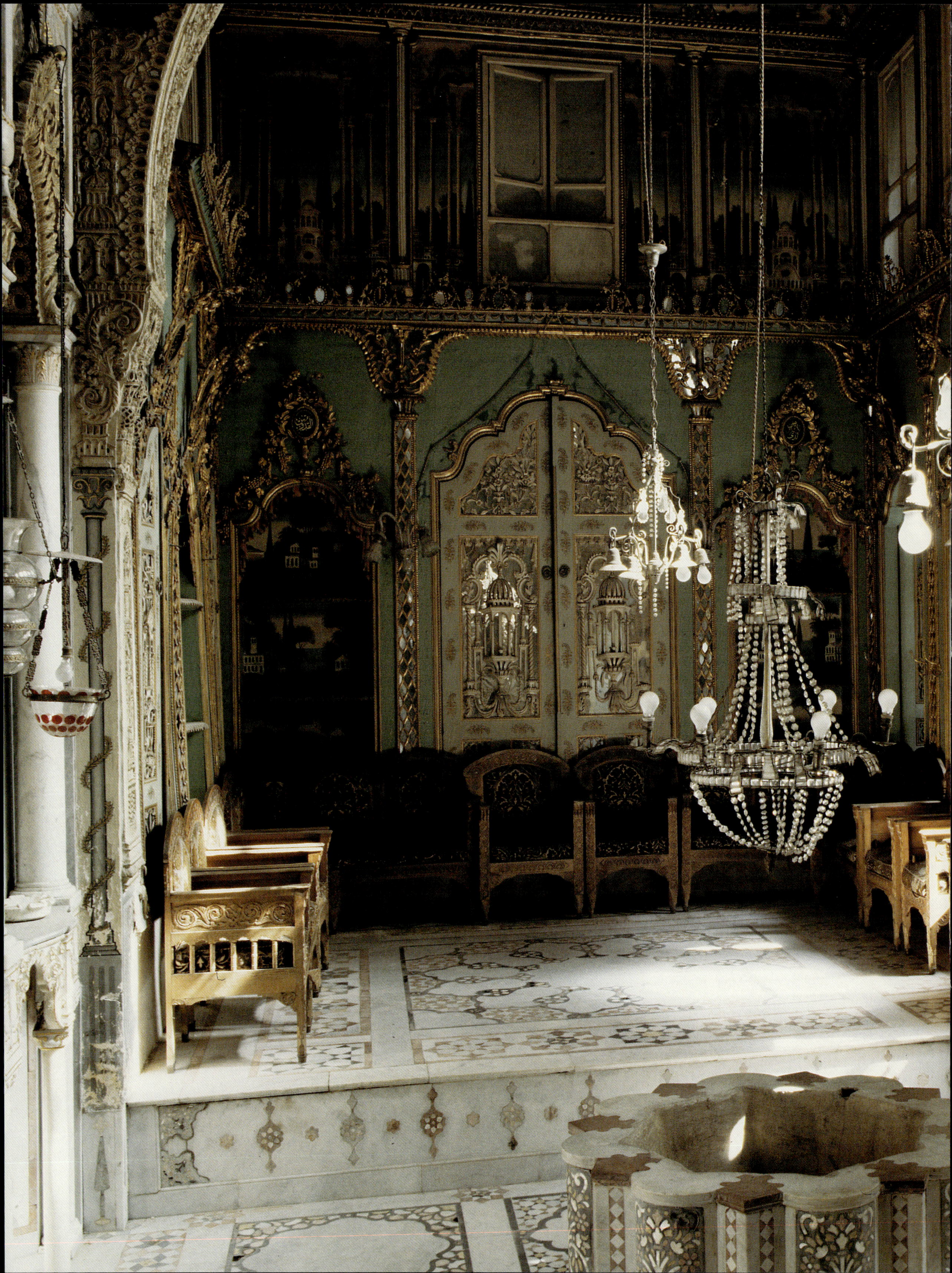

The main qa'a at Bait Mujallid (before restoration). The stone-decorated 'ataba in the foreground contrasts with the lavishly gilt and painted seating platform. This is the second seating area of the room shown on page 7.

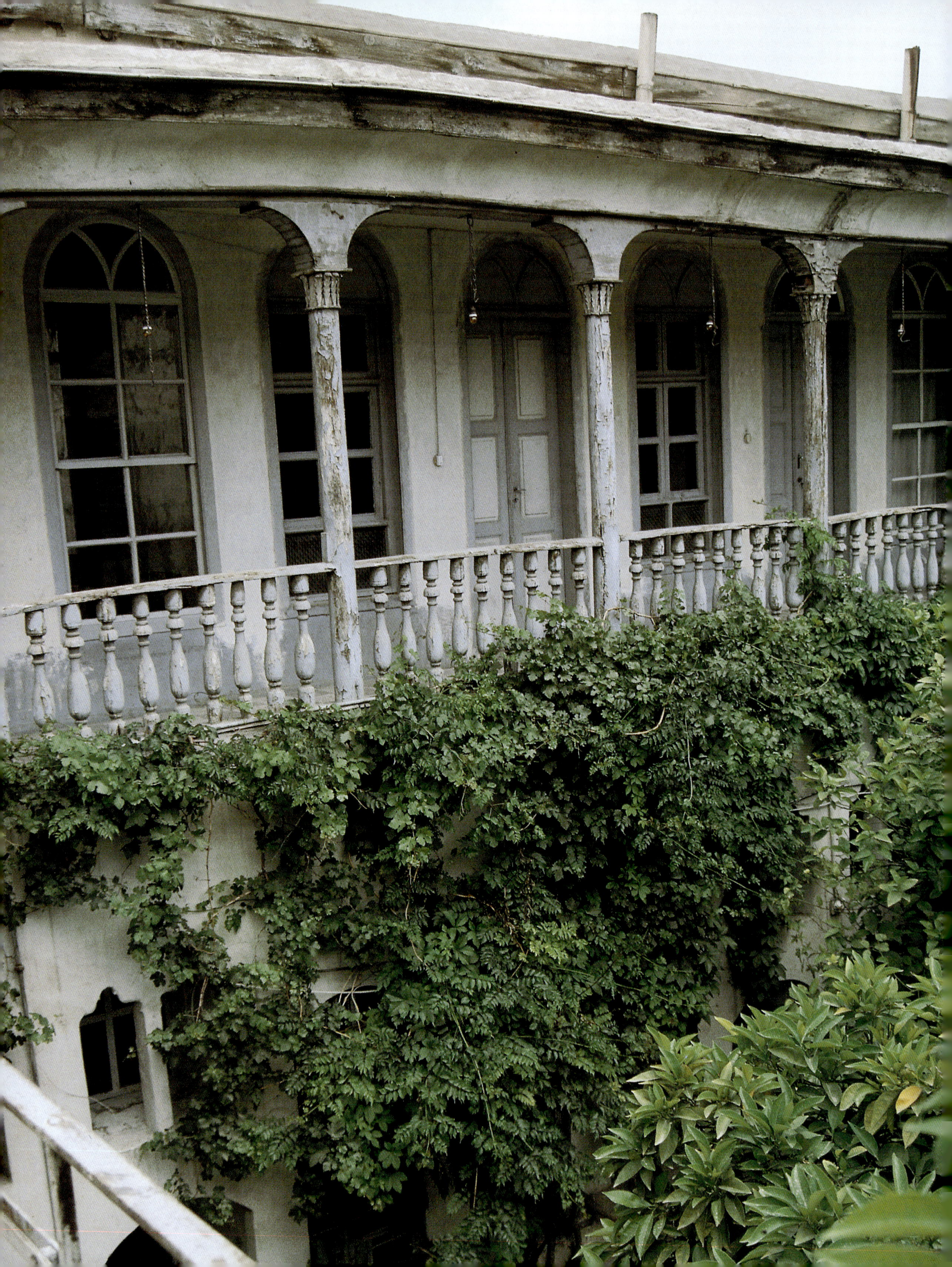

Opposite: A first-floor veranda runs round the courtyard and acts as a corridor to the bedrooms at Bait Shatta.

be instantly adapted to whatever function it was needed for – meals could be served on trays which would be removed afterwards and, at night, bedding could be taken out of the wall cupboards and the room would become a bedroom. A grand Damascene house might have two raised seating sections in the main qa'a, one on either side of a central 'ataba, and, in rare cases (such as Bait Siba'i and Bait Jabri), there could be three sections, one on either side of the 'ataba and one at the back. In some houses, the qa'a would be built above a cellar, in which case its entrance door would be at the top of a shallow set of steps.

Many big houses had more than one qa'a (Bait al-'Abd had six, but that was most unusual), and then there were other, smaller, multipurpose rooms (*murabba'*) around the courtyard, decorated almost as beautifully. Upstairs, on the first floor, there was usually some sort of veranda acting as a corridor round the courtyard from which the bedrooms opened, and on the top of the house there was sometimes a lone room, more like a kiosk, opening on to the roof. This was called the 'aeroplane' room (*tayyara*) because it was so near the sky.

During the First World War, soldiers of the German army were based in Syria (Germany being allied with the Turks) and among their number was a famous archaeologist and historian, Theodor Wiegand. Greatly impressed by the old city of Damascus, Wiegand persuaded the Governor of the time, Jamal Pasha, to allow two German engineers to come out and do a study of the city; and so, in 1917, Karl Wulzinger and Carl Watzinger (the similarity of their names is just a coincidence) arrived and took up residence in the House of the Spanish Crown, which had been the Spanish Consulate a few decades before. 'We were lucky to live for more than a year in one of the largest and most beautiful houses of the eastern city', they wrote in their wonderful study of Islamic Damascus, going on to describe the layout of the traditional Damascene house, its construction, water supply and so on. When they came to discuss the main reception room with its 'ataba and seating platform, they became quite fierce: 'It is considered very impolite to leave a guest standing in the 'ataba, like a servant or a beggar, but it is equally wrong for anyone to step on to the raised part of the floor wearing shoes.' Wulzinger and Watzinger went on to describe the seating arrangements: 'Cushions along the walls of the upper part provide for a place to relax; to put a chair or a settee on this higher area – as you see in many photographs of European consulates in Damascus – is quite inappropriate ...'. Traditionally, the Damascene house had little or no furniture; some small tables, perhaps, and the giant inlaid chest (*sunduq*) in which a bride kept her trousseau. As Alexander Kinglake wrote when he visited Damascus in 1834: 'There is no furniture that can interfere with the cool, palace-like emptiness of the apartments. A divan (that is, a low and doubly broad sofa) runs around the three walled sides of the room; a few Persian carpets are sometimes thrown about near the divan; they are placed without order, the one partly lapping over the other, and thus disposed, they give to the room an appearance of uncaring luxury; except these, there is nothing to obstruct the welcome air ...'.

The seating area and the 'ataba, though they were part of the same room, were decorated very differently. Both had elaborate painted wooden ceilings, but there the similarity ended. The decoration of the 'ataba was always in stone (marble mosaic, coloured pastework or carving), whereas the seating platform was decorated with painted wood panelling which ran all round its three walls to a height of 2.5 metres (about 8 feet 3 inches). In this panelling were set shelves for ornaments, and huge cupboards with ornate doors, in which the bedding and family treasures were kept. To create a harmonious 'whole', the windows of the room had shutters to match the cupboard doors.

Running like a frieze around the room above the cupboards there were painted panels of script, often with the date and the name of the builder, as well as lines from a poem or verses from the Qur'an, and a prayer asking God to bless the owner of the house and his family. The wooden panelling would end above this frieze with some sort of cornice – in 18th- and early 19th-century decoration this might be very elaborate and heavy, with 'stalactite' decoration, but the wall between the cornice and the painted ceiling would be left white and blank (as in Bait Shirazi). Later on, towards the mid-19th century, when it became the fashion to paint this blank wall with frescoes, the cornice became less elaborate – in Bait Mujallid it is like a thin strip of delicate lace in gilded wood.

Below: Painted panels, shutters and doors at Bait Qasim.

Bottom: Painted wooden panels for the seating area at Bait Dahdah.

Opposite: The raised seating platform at Bait Kuzbari.

There is a description of the houses of Damascus being 'richly decorated' with lacquered wood from as far back as 1401, the time of Tamerlane's sack of the city. (In fact, the chronicler, who was pro-Tamerlane, gives this as an excuse for why the houses burned so quickly then.) But the earliest panelled room from Syria that still exists is dated 1603. It is in the Berlin State Museums and comes from a house called Bait Wakil in Aleppo (the house is now a charming little hotel, no less attractive for being without its original wooden panelling). The room was bought from the Wakil family in 1912. It has a Persian type of design, with flowers and stylized foliage and, most unusually, animals and people. The family that commissioned the room was Christian, which meant that the Muslim taboo about representing real life in art didn't have to apply – although it should perhaps be pointed out that the Shi'a Muslims of Iran were, in any case, much less concerned with this rule than the Sunni Muslims of Syria. The painting on the Aleppo panels is flat – simply a design painted on wood – whereas a little later on it became the fashion to 'draw' the main part of the design on to the wooden panels with a mixture of gesso and gum arabic – rather like icing a cake – so that the pattern was slightly raised. The elaborate painting and gilding went on top and the panels were finished off with a coating of lacquer. This technique is called 'ajami work.

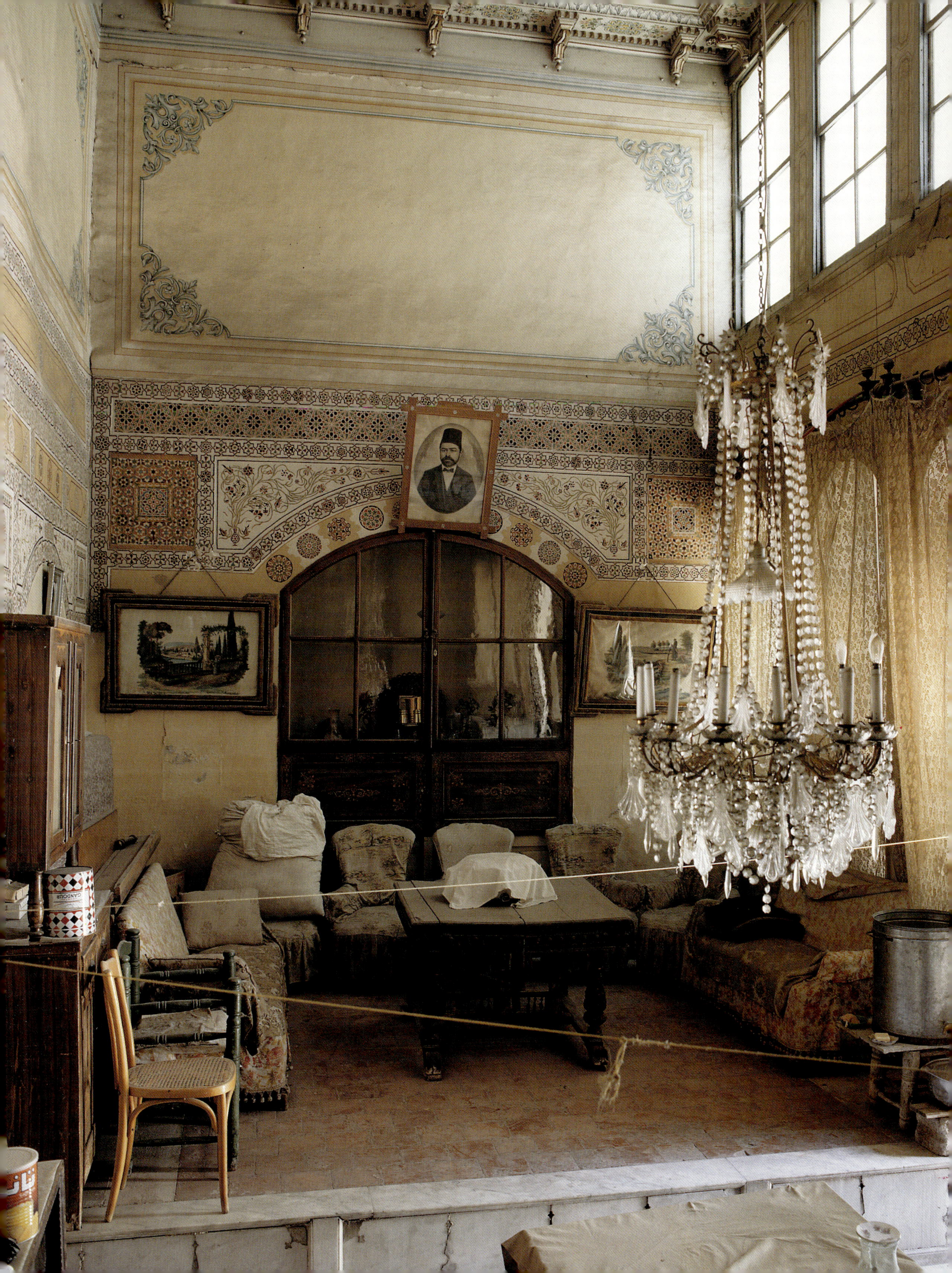

Ceilings

The traditional ceilings of Damascus houses are glorious – so finely painted that, from a distance, they look more like oriental carpets than painted wood. There are several phases of ceiling decoration: at first, the beams were exposed and painted; next, they were boxed in and more elaborately decorated, often with 'stalactite' (muqarnas) borders and corners; later, they were covered by wooden planks to make another, flat, ceiling which would then be decorated; in the last stage, under European influence, the traditional wooden ceilings were concealed under canvas which was painted with flowers and arabesques in Western fashion.

Above: These painted beams were found under a later canvas ceiling at Bait Mujallid.

Opposite: Bare beams at Bait Quwatli (a) painted so intricately that they look almost like embroidery.

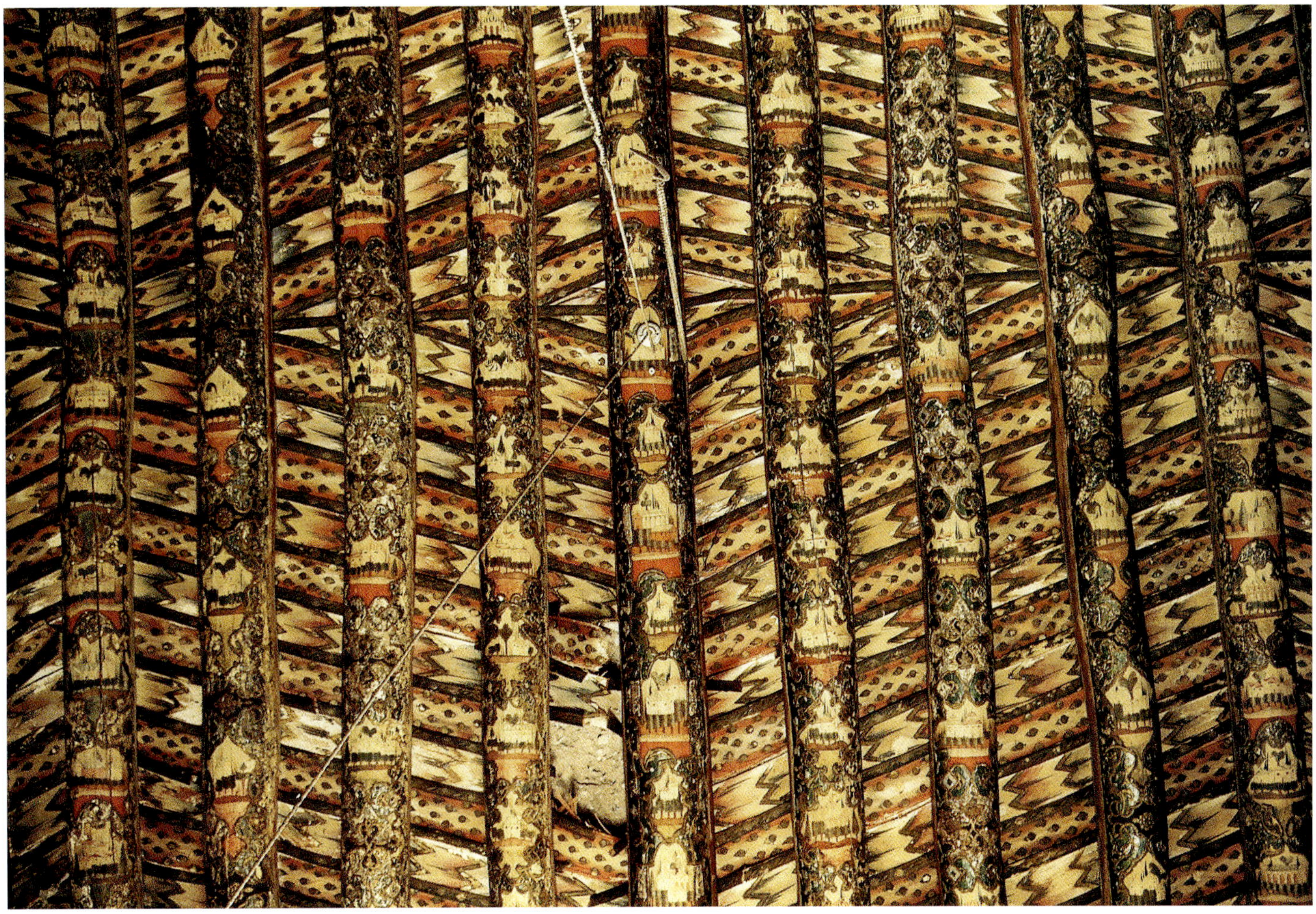

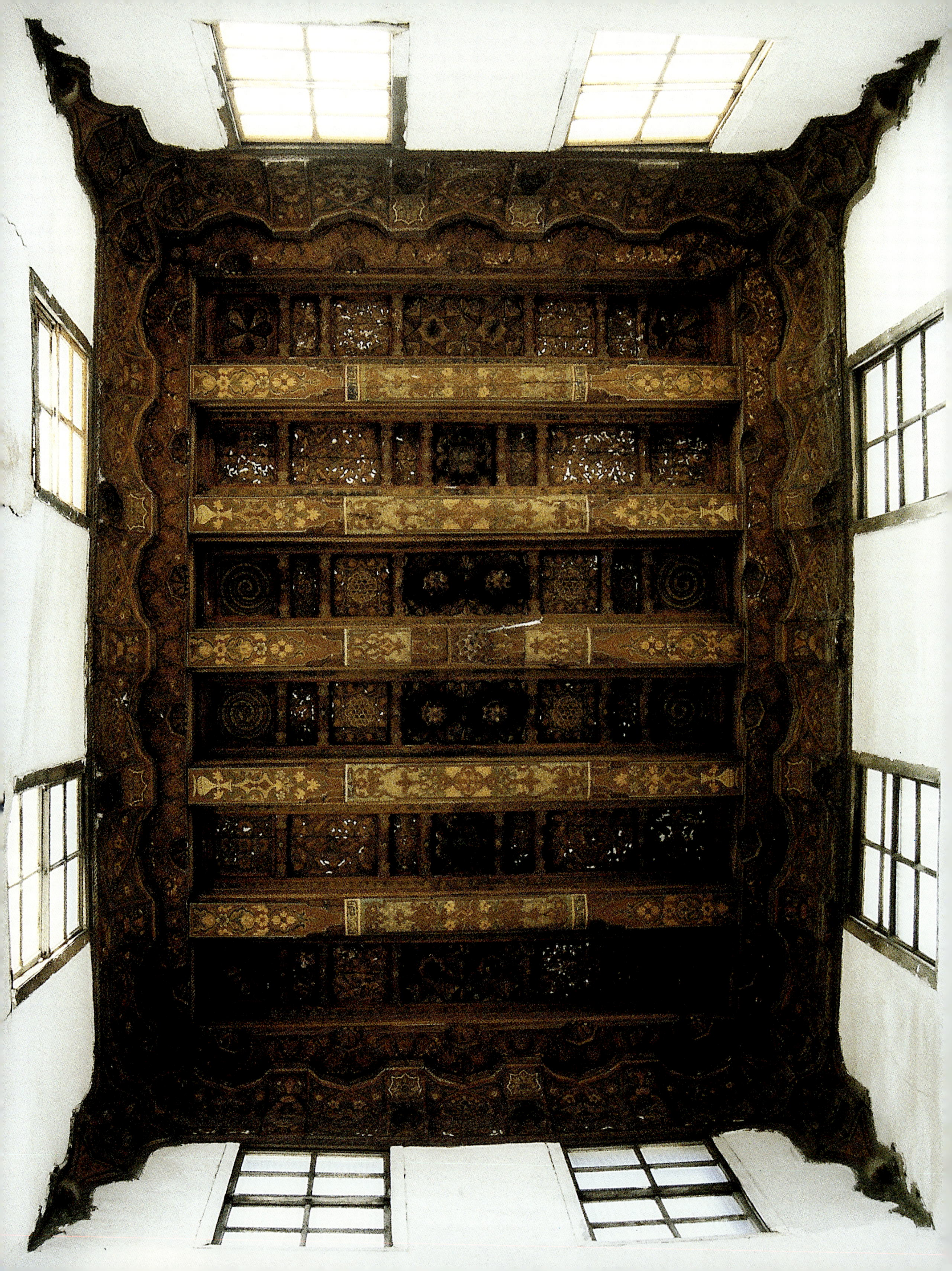

Ceilings

Opposite and above: Boxed-in beams with elaborate decoration – often including muqarnas work – were popular from Mamluk times up until the 19th century.

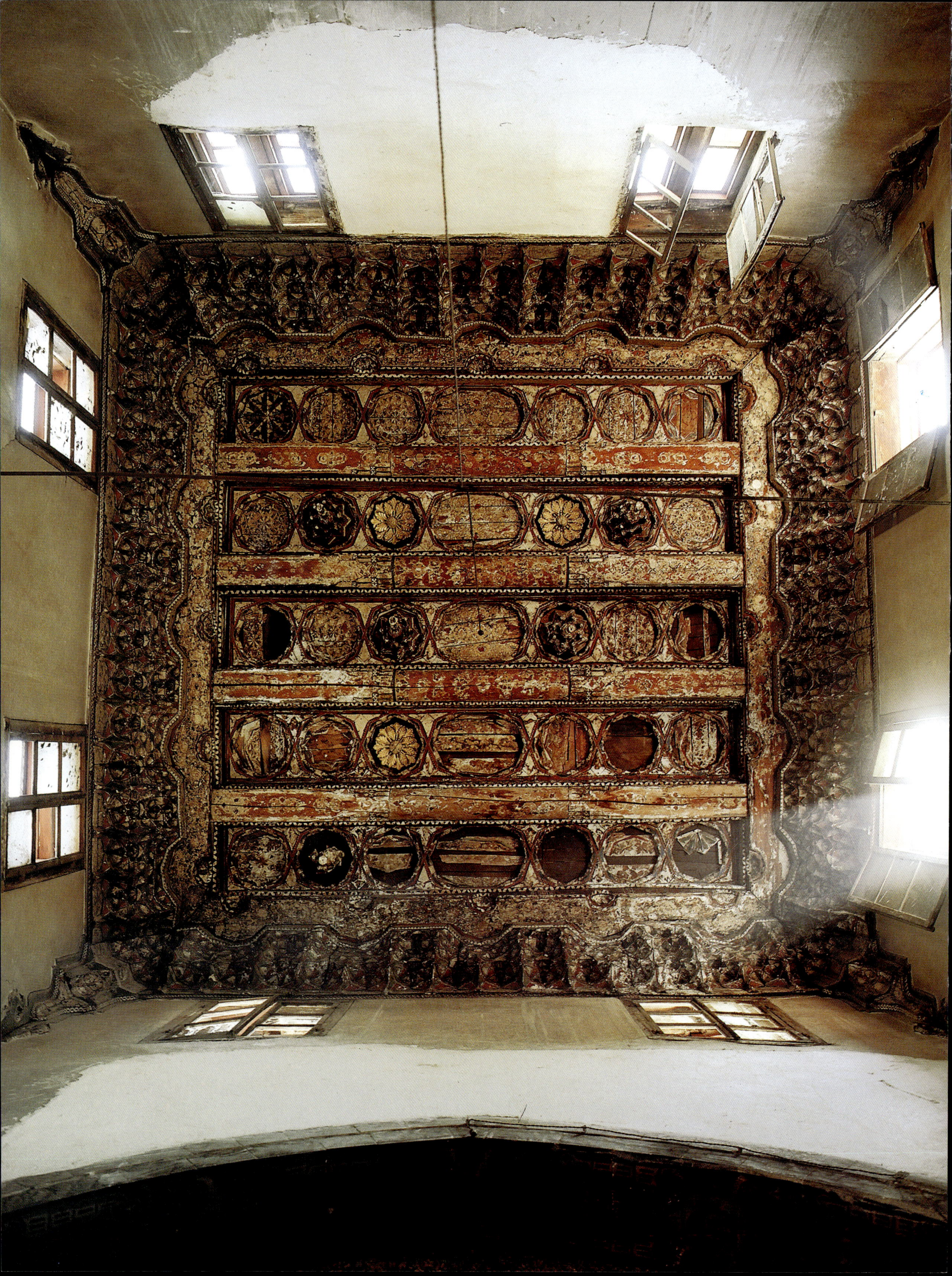

Ceilings

Opposite: Boxed-in beams with muqarnas work at Bait Shirazi.

Above: A new kind of ceiling at Bait Tibi; beams covered by flat planks, painted and patterned.

Overleaf: The flat wooden ceiling reached heights of magnificence with muqarnas work and central spiral at Bait Shirazi.

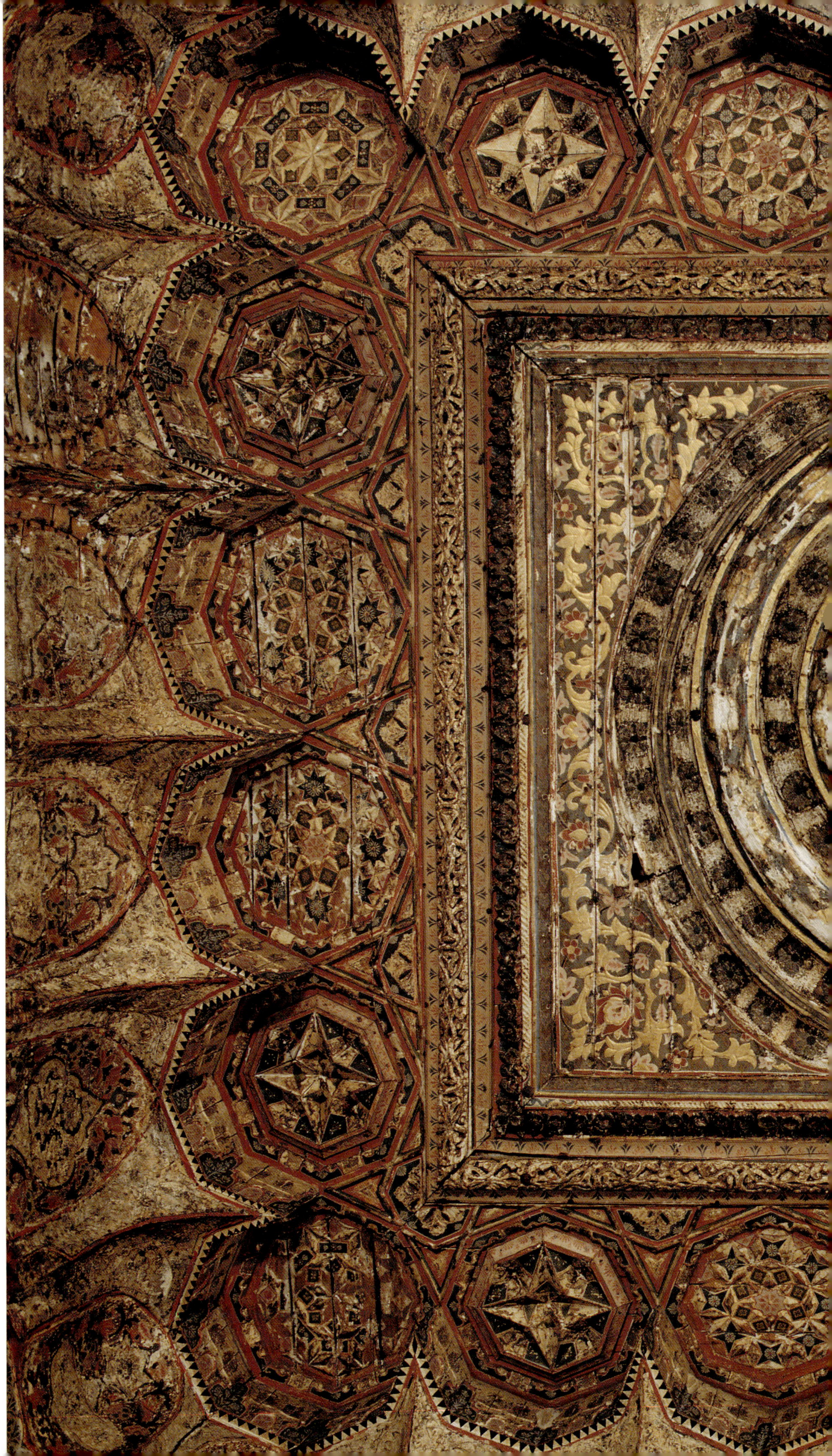

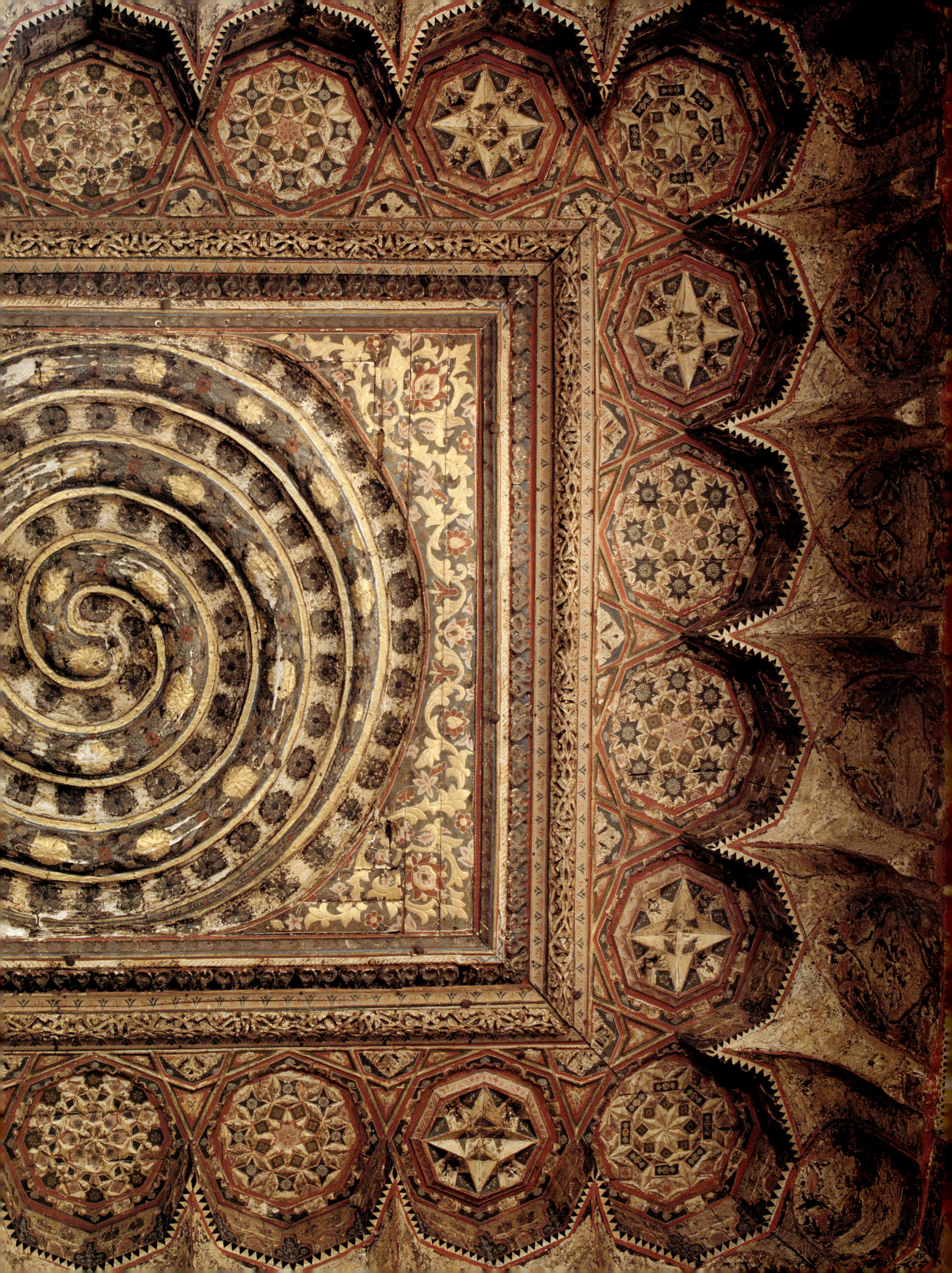

Ceilings

Examples of European influence on ceilings: canvas and wood decorated in a variety of Western patterns.

Left and below: At Bait Shirazi.

Opposite: At Bait Lisbona.

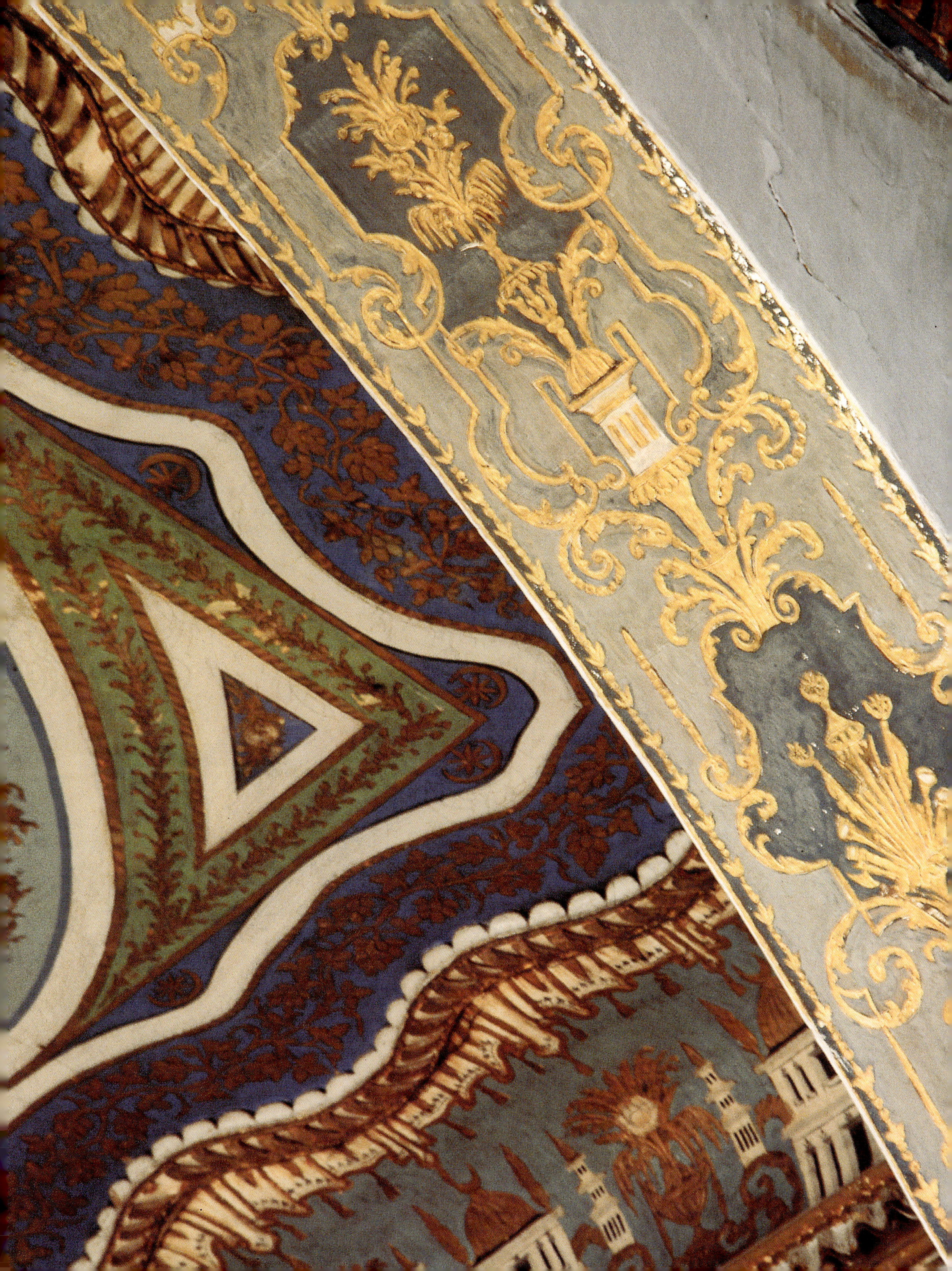

Painted and gilt doors in the rococo reception room at 'Ali Agha's house (Bait Nizam), described by both Charles Addison and Josias Porter.

The ceilings of all the reception rooms were even more elaborately decorated – if that were possible – than the panelled walls. Traditionally, Damascus ceilings were made of poplar beams backed with thin wooden slats, all painted so exquisitely that, from a distance, they look more like oriental embroideries than wood. Mamluk decoration of ceilings often included a border and deep corners done in the same heavy 'stalactite' work as the cornices described earlier, and this type of design continued to be used in the 18th century (as in Bait Shirazi). But there were other variations – the slats were sometimes concealed with planks and the beams boxed in, or planking went below the beams to cover them altogether with a flat ceiling. This flat ceiling would then have slivers of wooden beading tacked on in geometric patterns, which would then be painted.

In all Damascus, there is one house that does not conform to the traditional scheme of things, and that is Bait Tibi. The Tibis were a distinguished religious family, but it is not known which of them built this unusual house. Inscriptions inside give two dates for the decoration: 1786/7 and 1820. Modest, compared to the great palaces of other leading families, Bait Tibi has the usual courtyard and liwan, but the liwan is flanked by two small decorative kiosks. There is the traditional magnificently painted qa'a, or reception room, off the courtyard, but then, quite unexpectedly, on the first floor is another small room as exquisitely painted, gilded and mirrored as a Fabergé jewel box, which must have been the ladies' qa'a. The kiosks and the upstairs qa'a are the only ones of their kind in Damascus. There is a strong feeling in Bait Tibi that, behind all this extra prettiness, there must have been a remarkable woman with wonderful taste.

In the centuries of Mamluk rule, Damascus was naturally influenced by the styles of Mamluk architecture and design coming from Egypt, but from the 16th century, when Syria became part of the Ottoman Empire, Damascus followed the fashions in Istanbul, so that when, two hundred years later, a craze for everything European (especially French) swept that capital, Damascus followed suit. More and more, European-style flowers and fruit – in vases, in bouquets, in bowls – became a popular motif to use in the painting of the wall panels instead of the Arab and Persian geometric patterns and arabesques. (This period was named the Tulip Era, and perhaps the best illustration of what that meant to interior design is the ravishing dining room in the Topkapi Palace in Istanbul, commissioned by Sultan Ahmet III, which is decorated all over with nothing *but* bowls of fruit and flowers.)

Later, in 19th-century Istanbul, the delicate designs of the Tulip Era were put aside in a new craze for European-style baroque. As ever, Damascus followed suit and European baroque (as interpreted by Ottoman architects and craftsmen) erupted all over the old city, with unbelievably intricate mirror work and gilded wood decoration, painted plaster flowers and zinc fruits and vegetables, and swags and drapes and pineapples and pillars minutely carved in stone and marble. Wall paintings began to fill the traditionally blank white space on the walls between the wood panelling and the ceiling. Charles Addison was in Damascus in the mid-1830s and visited 'Ali Agha's house, where work was in progress on just such a room (the artists, he wrote, were from Istanbul). 'The walls, a short distance below the ceiling, were gaily painted in the form of buildings, fantastic porticoes, and columns through which in the distance were glimpses of the sea, and blue mountains, and here and there foregrounds of the weeping willow and the cypress … then cup-boards … around them were scroll patterns of clusters of arms and weapons, and portions of the wall either side were richly inlaid with tortoise-shell and mother-of-pearl.' Josias Porter visited this same house between fifteen and twenty years later and commented: 'The style of decoration in this mansion may be called the modern Damascene, the painting of the walls and ceiling being a recent innovation. In the more ancient houses, the ceilings and wainscoted walls are covered with the richest arabesques, encompassing little panels in deep blue and delicate azure, on which are inscribed in elegantly interlaced Arabic characters, whole verses and chapters of their law.'

The room they both describe can be seen by visitors today – it is the baroque reception room in what is now known as Bait Nizam. Now it is furnished with brown upholstered benches, but in Porter's day the divans round the walls were covered 'with the richest purple satin, embroidered with gold, in chaste designs of flowers and scrolls and having a deep gold fringe descending to the floor.… It resembles, in fact, some scene in fairyland …'.

The 19th century was the time of sweeping reform in the Ottoman Empire, when schools, courts, hospitals and town halls began to be built on European lines. It was also the time when Istanbul reinforced its grip on the administration of its Empire, recruiting local 'notables' into its service rather than allowing them to go their own independent way. All this was reflected in the interior decoration of the houses.

Above: Cornice decorated with fruit and architectural motifs at Bait 'Araqtanji.

Left: Flowers in a vase painted on a wooden panel at Bait Quwatli (a).

Above: New, bigger windows gave houses a European look, as here at Bait Tuta.

Opposite: Painted doors dated 1711 in the Damascus room at the Cincinnati Art Museum.

To demonstrate the new allegiance to the centre of the Empire, wall paintings of Istanbul and the Bosphorus (complete with little ships flying the Turkish flag) became hugely popular, while the European/Ottoman baroque style became more and more exaggerated. Now the handsome old wooden ceilings were concealed by canvases stretched below the beams and painted in completely European fashion; it became fashionable, too, to finish off the roofline round the courtyard with a wooden cornice (called *simis*), which occasionally had a wavy edge.

Wulzinger and Watzinger, who greatly admired the art of the painted Damascene wall panels, were slightly less enthusiastic about some of these late 19th-century developments. 'In a few cases', they wrote, 'the decorations become overpowering and perverse because of too much white marble … too large mirrors or too many landscape and figurative views which were inappropriate for local talents.' They went on to say, rather unkindly perhaps, 'Examples of this kind we mainly find in the Jewish and Armenian quarters.'

Towards the end of the 19th century, it became the fashion to alter not just the style of painting inside, but the houses themselves. At this time, the traditional raised part of the qa'a was sometimes lowered to make the floor all one level, European-style; dining rooms, like the splendid one at Bait Mujallid, were added; and more and more windows appeared in the traditionally blank outside walls – as at Bait Barudi, Bait Marie Qatash and Bait Tuta – until the façades of the houses became positively Western-looking. A *Yearbook of the Ottoman Province of Damascus* at this time mentions that from four hundred to five hundred houses were under renovation each year – which explains why there are so very many examples of the interior design and architecture of this period in Damascus today.

The changes in interior decoration continued into the 20th century. When the well-known Damascene Fakhri Barudi returned from a visit to Paris in 1911, he redecorated the qa'a of his famous house in Damascus with giant paintings (probably copied from postcards) of views of Europe. The Barudi house became *the* gathering place for Damascene intellectuals and, later, one of the centres for all who opposed French rule in Syria. (It is said that, if Fakhri Barudi walked through the souk and made a secret signal, the shopkeepers would immediately pull down their shutters and go on strike until he told them to open up again.) To show how modern and up-to-date they were, owners of houses at this time would commission artists to put new inventions, such as trains and tramways and aeroplanes, into the wall paintings, and during the French Mandate period in Syria, the painted steamships in the frescoes would occasionally be depicted flying French flags.

European furniture, chandeliers and ornaments had also become the fashion, changing the Arabian Nights atmosphere of the houses into something altogether more humdrum. Théophile Gautier, the great French 19th-century man of letters, praised a Damascene room: 'It was as elegant as it was lavish', he wrote, going on to describe the magnificent Turkish carpet, the painted and gilt ceiling and walls, the long divan in yellow and blue satin. 'Unfortunately,' he continued, 'this Oriental deluxe was mixed up with a chest of drawers with a marble top on which stood a clock covered with a glass dome and two vases of artificial flowers, also under glass; nothing more and nothing less than you might see on the mantelpiece of any suburban Parisian.'

Another French writer, Gustave Flaubert, who was in Syria in 1850, mourned the 'over-elaborate' chandeliers of Venetian glass that had suddenly appeared in Damascus rooms; Eugène-Melchior de Vogüé, in 1872, lamented 'the invasion of European furniture which has brought the deathblow to the old houses'; Pierre Loti, in 1894, deplored 'these atrocious imports'. By the 1920s, it was no longer a question of imports – Syrian craftsmen themselves were fashioning their traditional marquetry work into ugly, square Art Deco sofas and armchairs, and exquisitely inlaying, with mother-of-pearl, ungainly European-style wardrobes.

By the start of the 20th century, so many travellers were coming through Syria that it was only a matter of time before one of them had the idea of buying a whole painted-wood Damascene qa'a to take home, which is why you can find these exotic interiors in such unlikely places as Dresden, Cincinnati and Pittsburgh.

Each of the displaced rooms has its own story. The one in Dresden was bought by the German photographer Hermann Burchardt in 1898, when he accompanied Kaiser Wilhelm on his famous visit to Lebanon, Syria and the Holy Land that year. Burchardt got bored with photographing the Kaiser and ended up taking hundreds of pictures of the ordinary people he came across (frustratingly for architectural historians, he took no pictures of houses or monuments in Damascus). He bought the Damascene room for a collector friend in Germany and shipped it home, only to find that the collector had changed moods and was now going in for modern art. The room was sold, or given, to the Dresden Museum instead, where it was deposited in a cellar and forgotten about. In 1997, it was rediscovered and is now being restored. Its painting is dated 1810.

The Cincinnati Art Museum has a particularly attractive painted room dated 1711. This was bought by Andrew Jergens, of the millionaire Jergens soap family, in 1932, when he visited Damascus on a tour of the Holy Land. He bought the room from a Syrian dealer, who had, in turn, acquired it when the mansion it belonged to was demolished for the widening of a road. (That was during the period of the French Mandate in Syria, when roads were being widened all the time.) Mr Jergens bought the room to decorate his own Gothic mansion in Cincinnati, where it stayed until 1967, when the house was demolished and the Damascus room went to the local museum.

The University of Pittsburgh bought a Damascus room from an art dealer in New York in 1940. Their room dates from 1782.

Hagop Kevorkian, an Armenian collector, bought two rooms from Damascus in the 1930s. One, dated 1707, was donated to The Metropolitan Museum of Art, New York, in the 1960s and has become famous. It is known as the 'Nur al-Din' Room, since no-one knows which house it originally came from. The other room, dated 1797, which is said to have come from the Quwatli house which was the British Consulate in the 19th century (there were *four* Bait Quwatlis), he gave to New York University.

Gayer Anderson, the British explorer and eccentric, whose marvellous house in Cairo is now a museum, bought a Damascus room for it in the 1930s. He was told that it had come from one of the many houses belonging to the Azem family.

There is another Damascus room, at the Manial Palace in Cairo, which may have a romantic story behind it. When Egypt controlled Syria briefly between

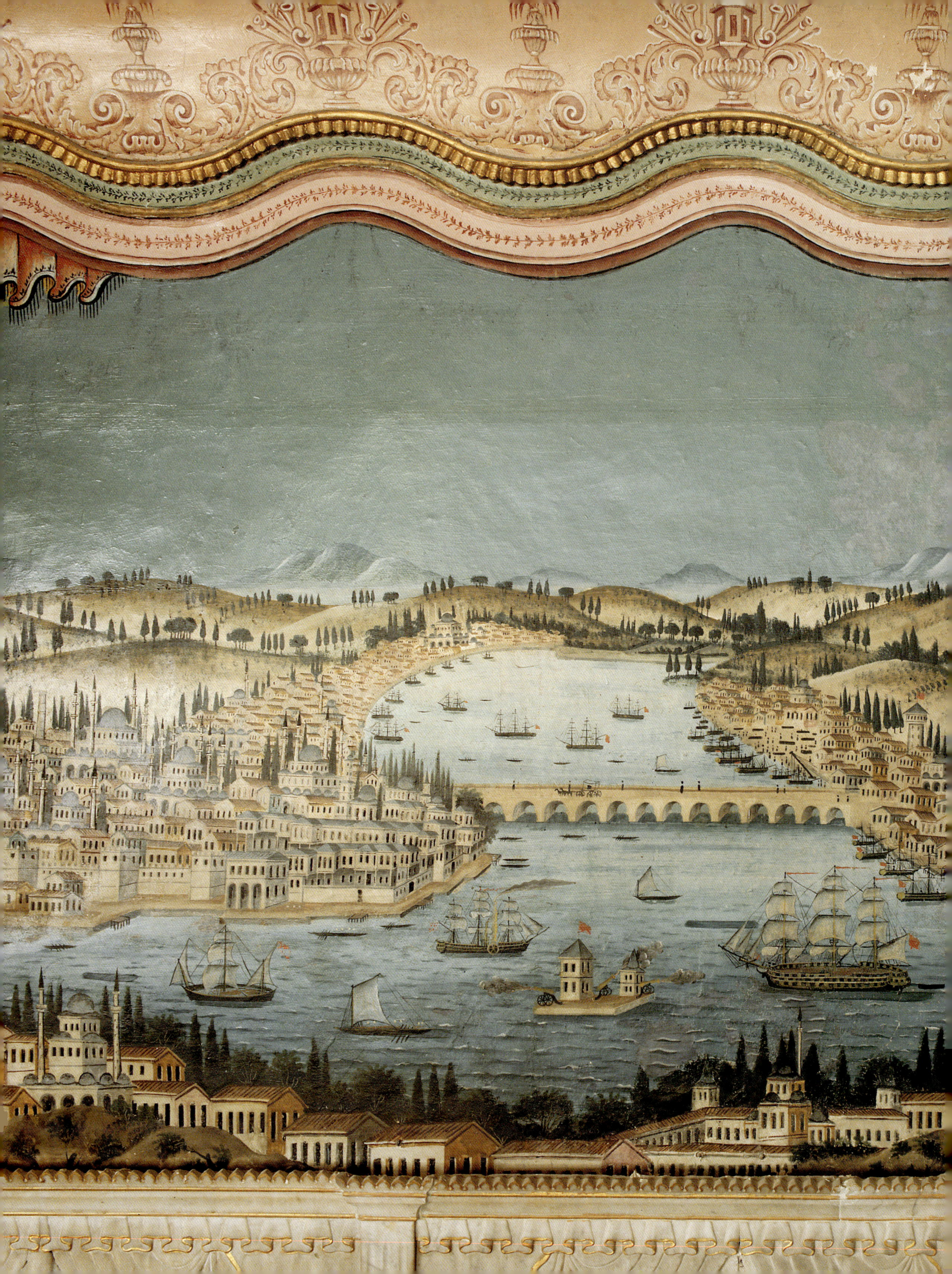

Wall Paintings

Wall paintings became fashionable in the early part of the 19th century, when pictures of anonymous buildings and landscapes began to appear. Later, as the Ottoman Empire reformed, and administrative power returned to the centre in Istanbul, views of Istanbul or the Bosphorus became hugely popular. Still later, at the turn of the 19th and 20th centuries, when modern inventions such as steamships and railways came to the Empire, they began to feature in the wall paintings too.

Left: A painting of the Bosphorus is the centrepiece at Bait Mujallid.

Above: Two delicate paintings from the liwan at Bait Shamiyya.

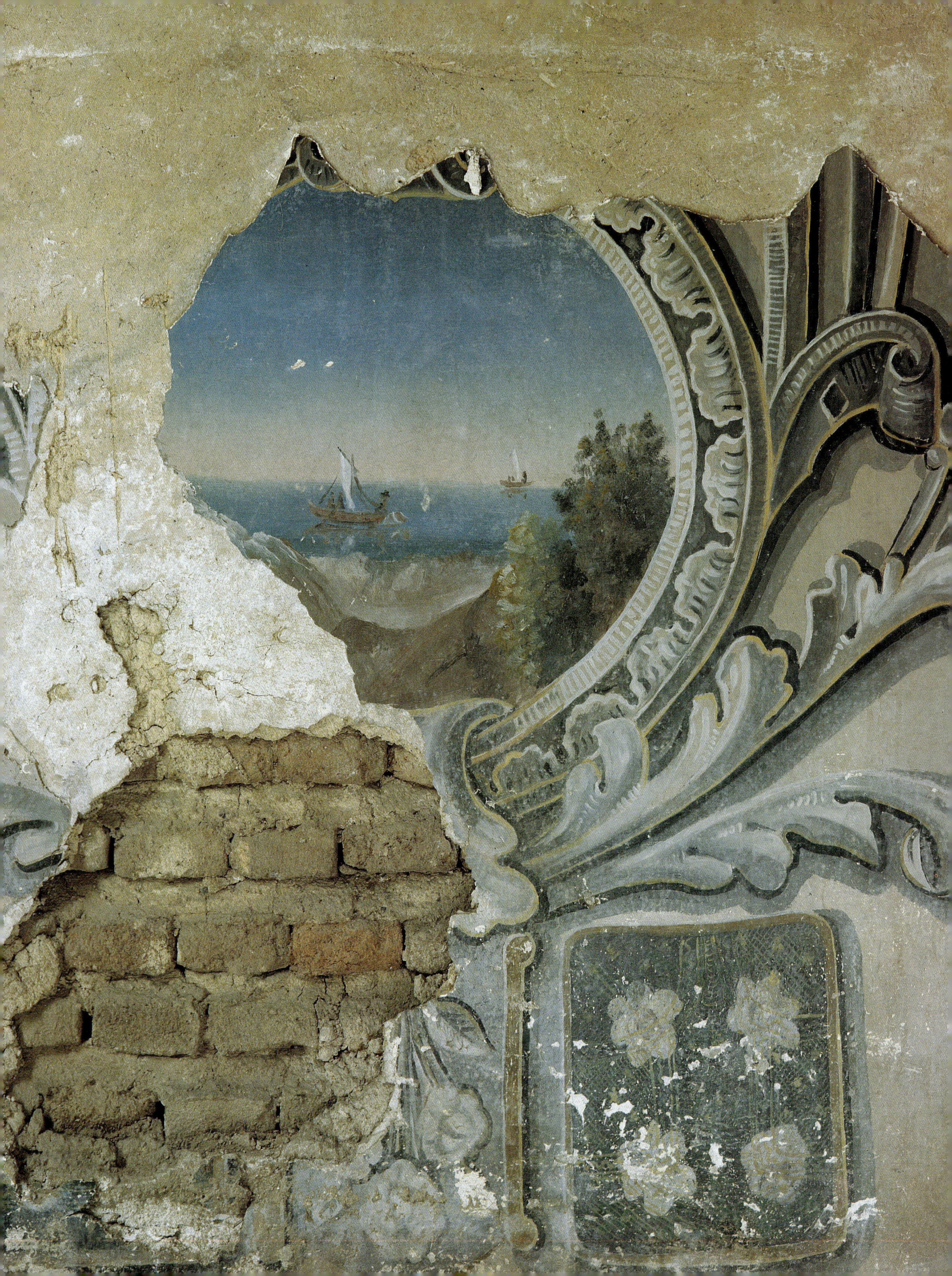

Wall Paintings

Opposite: Crumbling wall painting at Bait Barudi, now under restoration.

Above: A giant view of Florence decorates a wall at Bait Barudi.

Wall Paintings

Right: Detail of the painting on the wall above a shelf at Bait Mujallid.

Overleaf: Landscapes with trees are painted around the walls at Bait Mujallid.

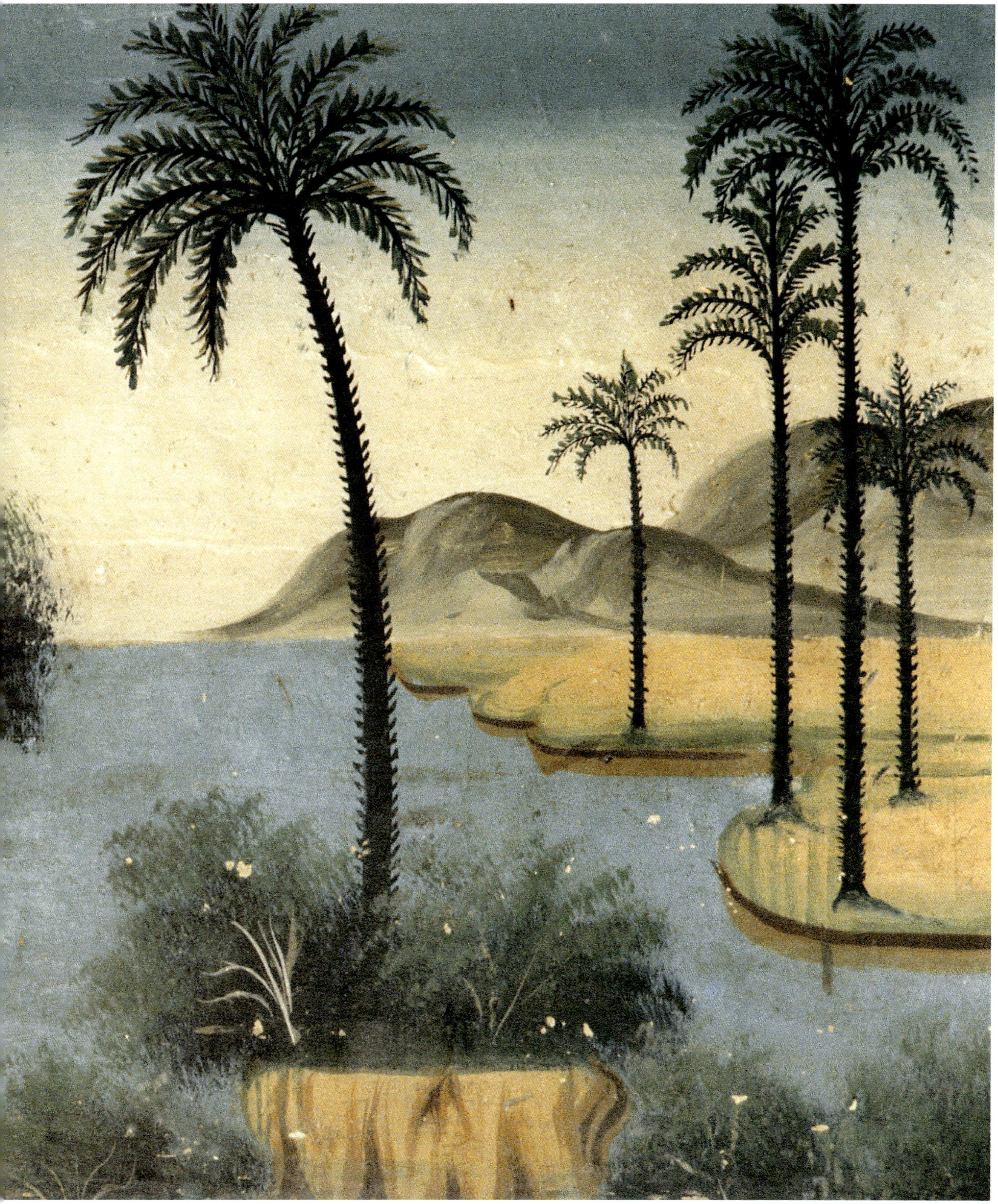

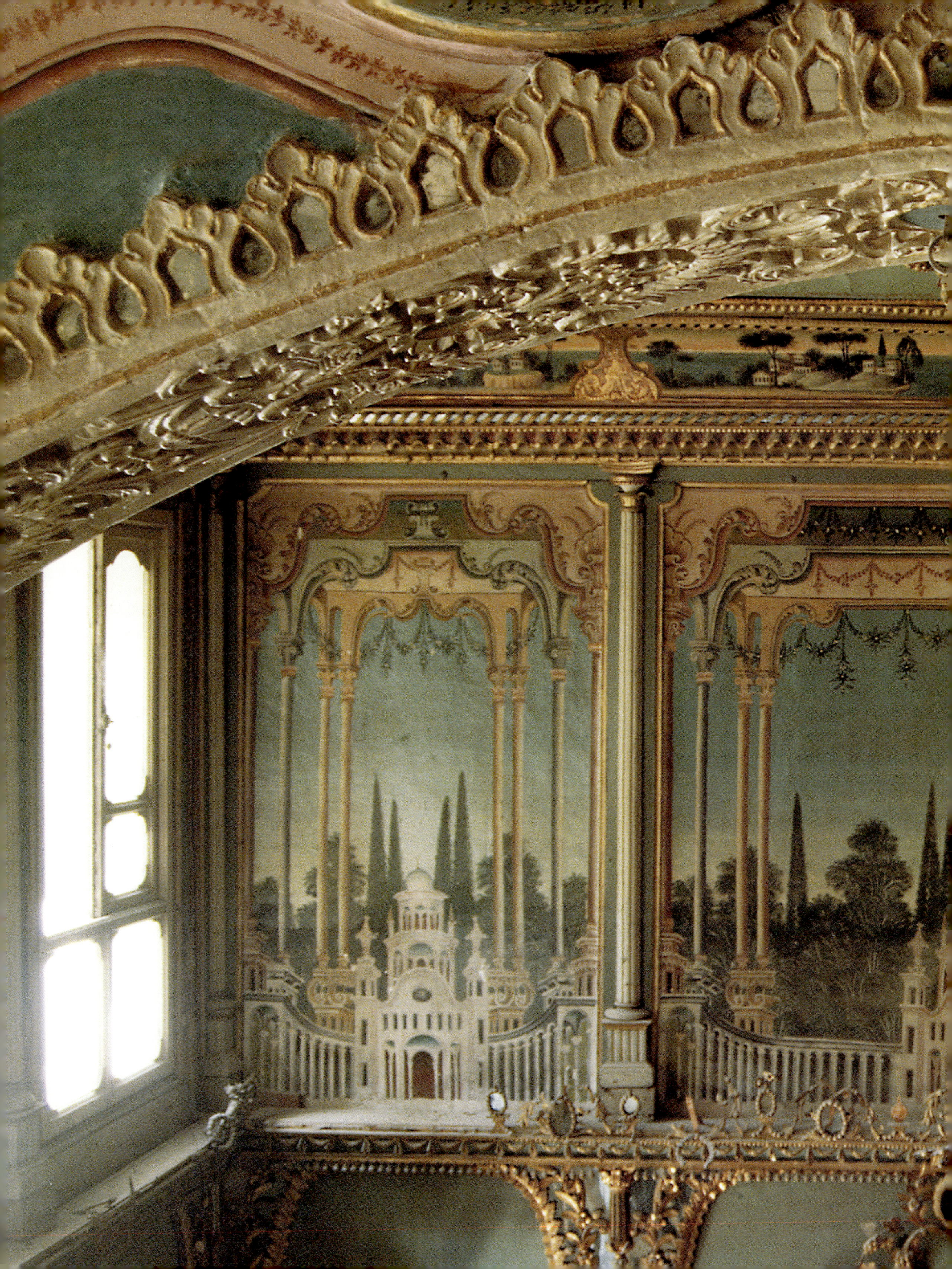

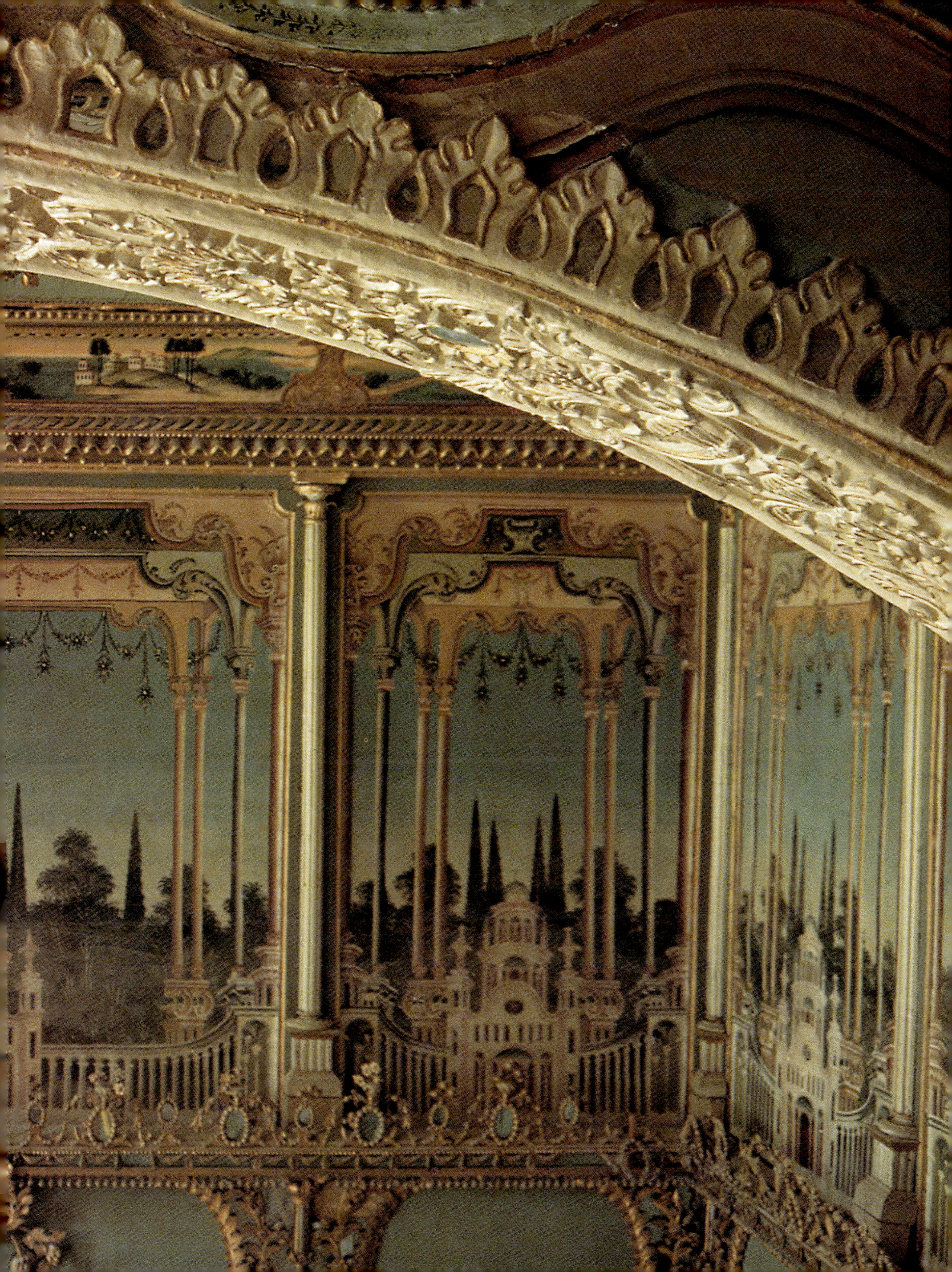

1832 and 1840, Sharif Pasha, a member of the Egyptian ruling family, was appointed Governor of Damascus. He is said to have arrived in the city and, hearing of the legendary beauty of Farlan, one of the daughters of the prominent Azem family, asked for her hand in marriage. She was already pledged to a cousin, but the family decided that Sharif Pasha was probably a better match and agreed to allow that marriage to go ahead instead. Farlan returned to Cairo with her husband, where she built a mosque called the Sitt al-Sham (meaning Lady of Damascus); perhaps she arranged for the Damascus room to go with her.

Henri Pharaon, a Lebanese banker, government minister and businessman, who owned the port of Beirut and was proud of the fact that his post office box number, in French-speaking Lebanon, was Boîte Postale 1, began collecting Damascus rooms of great quality for his museum-like house in Beirut in 1929. The earliest piece of the many he acquired dated from the 17th century. And there are Damascus rooms in the great palace of Beiteddine (Bait al-Din) in the Druze mountains of Lebanon.

The Victoria and Albert Museum in London had a Damascus room, acquired from European dealers in 1880 and 1881, but it was damaged by a flying bomb during the Second World War, and when, in 1957, it was found to have woodworm as well, a decision was made to destroy it. Four panels were saved, which are now in storage and only available for scholars to look at. 'Our Damascus room', says a curator, 'is only a memory', though photographs of it still exist.

To this day, panelled rooms are being dismantled from the old Damascus houses and sold abroad. It is a dilemma – is it better to leave them in the old city to collapse with their houses, or to remove them to safe-keeping – even if it is outside Syria?

As mentioned earlier, each new conqueror of Damascus tried to set his mark on the place by building his own grand palace, usually on the site of the previous ruler's. With one exception, all these palaces have long since disappeared (though many of the stone-built khans and schools and public baths can still be seen). The only one that remains is the Azem Palace, which is now the Museum of Popular Arts and Traditions of Syria. It was built by As'ad Pasha, the most famous member of the Azem family, which ruled Damascus for thirty-seven

Opposite: The entrance to the Azem Palace (now the Museum of Popular Arts and Traditions) is carefully designed so that no one can see the courtyard from the door.

years in the 18th century. As'ad Pasha had already built a mansion in Hama (where he had been Governor) – it is now a museum – but, undaunted, in 1749 he began the construction of his new palace on the site of the Palace of Gold that had been the seat of the Mamluk Governor, Tengiz. Eight hundred workers took two years to build the Azem Palace, while agents scoured the old city for works of art in stone and wood, antique pieces and other rarities that could be incorporated into the new building; Roman pillars were even brought from Bosra for the courtyard. According to al-Budairi (a barber in Damascus who kept a diary of what was going on in the city), it was impossible for anyone else to find a builder while the work was in progress, since all of them were employed by As'ad Pasha, and the water supply to ordinary houses was cut off while the city's plumbing was reorganized to suit his new palace. However, when it was finished, even al-Budairi was awed: 'Those who have travelled and seen many things say there is nothing like it in the whole Ottoman Empire, not even the palace of the Sultan himself.'

The house followed the traditional Damascene layout, but on a vast scale – the haramlik, or family courtyard, is so large that it is often now used as the venue for concerts. There were three kitchens and the house had its own hammam that was almost as big as a public bathhouse.

The current head of the Azem family, Ziyad al-Azem, was told by his grandfather, who lived in the palace, that it was his custom there to share a meal regularly with all the children of the house – on one occasion there were no less than eighty of them; perhaps not surprisingly, he didn't know all their names. (This grandfather had ten sons and six daughters, so the story is not as unbelievable as it might sound.)

Everything was done within the palace: sheep were brought in flocks to be butchered, bread was baked throughout the day, the furnaces of the hammam never went cold and there was even a resident midwife. There were servants in the house, but it was the women of the family who took charge of the gigantic feat of logistics that went into just keeping the place going from day to day. Ziyad al-Azem says proudly: 'Our women were not

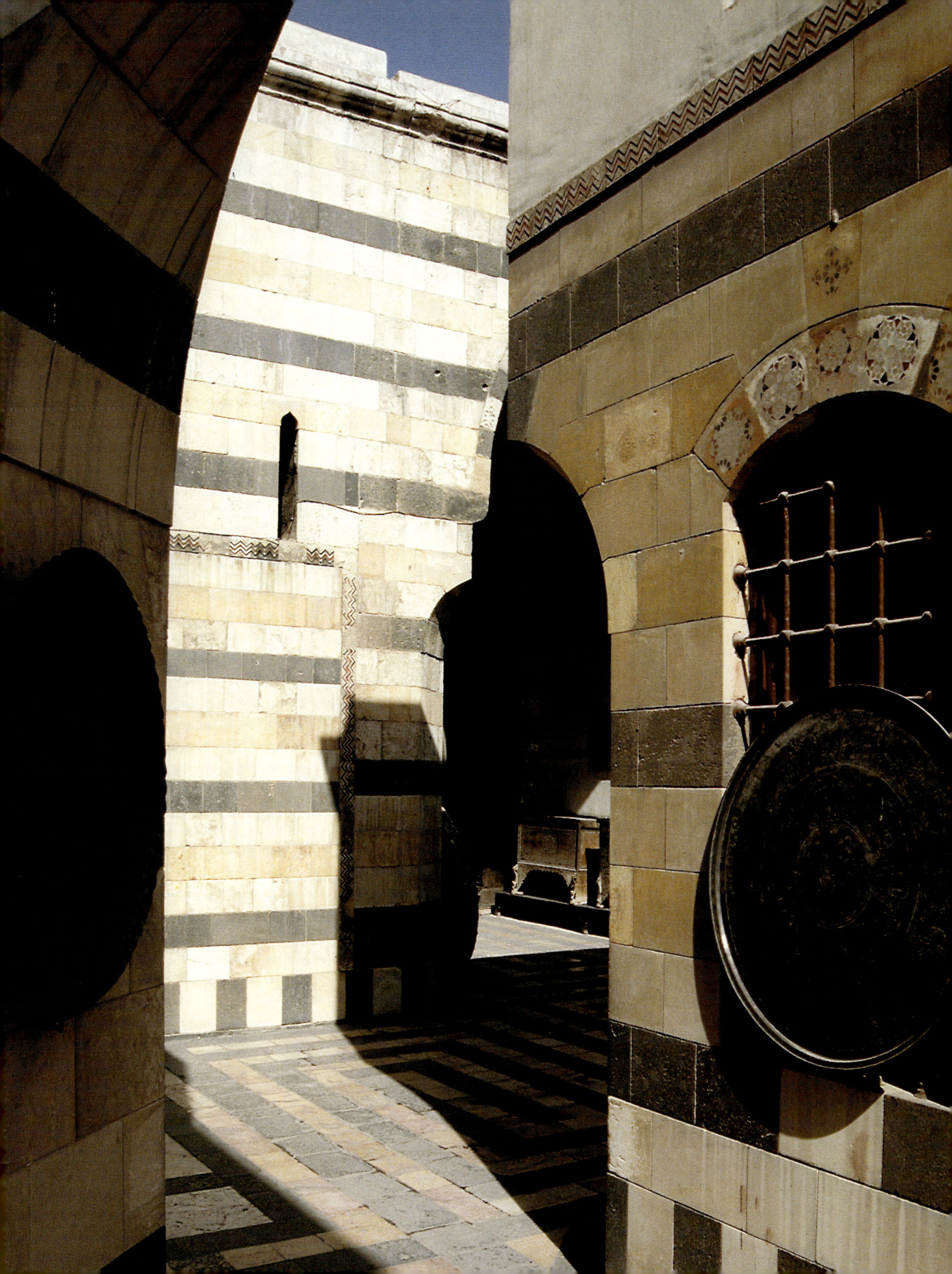

idle French duchesses, they worked hard … indeed, for a daughter to be known as a competent organizer was almost as valuable an asset as beauty when it came to finding a good husband.'

Damascene women, in those days, rarely left their houses, except on family visiting days and to go to the bathhouse (though not at the Azem Palace, which had its own). But this didn't necessarily mean they were uneducated. In the grand families such as the Azems, they were expected to be literate and to speak languages. Only those men and women not permitted to marry each other by religion – father/daughter, brother/sister – were allowed to see each other; in every other circumstance, the women had to be veiled (the same rule applies to women wearing the *hijab*, or scarf, today). Josias Porter, describing the scene in the souk in the 1850s, wrote: 'The strange figures that are seen mingling with the throng, enveloped from head to foot in white sheets, are women.'

At the Azem Palace, two main meals a day were served – one between 10 and 11 a.m., before the men of the family rode off to their estates and villages, and another in the evening at sunset. The *beys*, or lords of the house, and boys over eight, ate first; the women, girls and small children afterwards; and then the servants. No food was ever thrown away – it would be given to people in need. After the last prayer at night, the house would be locked and – in theory at least – no-one was allowed in or out; but men were known to slip away down to the 'free' Jewish quarter. 'There can hardly have been a man in Damascus', says Ziyad al-Azem, 'who did not have a Jewish *petite amie*.'

The Azem family sold the palace to the French Government in 1922 for 22,000 gold livres, but the sale was fraught with frustrations – for a start, there were sixty-eight heirs involved and some of them refused to part with their share. Eventually though, the Institut Français d'Archéologie et d'Art Musulman moved into the haramlik and the French High Commissioner, General Sarrail, made his headquarters in the salamlik. This proved to be disastrous for the palace, for in the uprising against the French in 1925, General Sarrail was an obvious focus of hatred and the revolutionaries attacked the house. Finding him absent, they ransacked the rooms and set fire to the building. The palace burned for two days and many priceless treasures in the library and little museum there were destroyed or lost or stolen, including an archive of two thousand photographic plates. But 'The Azem Palace is far from being entirely ruined', said the indomitable Director of the Institute, M. de Lorey, and restoration work began. In 1946, when the French left Syria, the building became the property of the Syrian State and was later opened as a museum. It seems only fair, given that As'ad Pasha made his fortune out of the people of Damascus through taxes and monopolies and confiscations and speculations, that the Government of Syria should now own his two magnificent buildings – the Azem Palace and the Khan As'ad Pasha nearby.

Among the aristocrats of Damascus in the 19th century and beginning of the 20th, there were seven super-élite families whose sons and daughters traditionally married each other: the Azems, the Mardam Beys, the Ghazzis, the Hamzas, the 'Abds, the 'Ajlanis and the Yusufs. Four of these were religious families, but the Mardam Beys,

Opposite: European-style Art Nouveau mirror at the Historical Museum.

Right: A corner of the haramlik at the Azem Palace.

Below: Traditional mother-of-pearl inlaid sunduq, or chest, at the Historical Museum.

147

Coloured Pastework

Coloured pastework is a technique by which a pattern is incised in a block of stone and then filled in with pastes made of different coloured stones, ground up, giving the effect of a complex stone inlay. It was invented by the Mamluks in the 14th century, but it was Damascus craftsmen who took the art to heights of beauty and perfection over the succeeding centuries. It was a favourite decoration until the 19th century.

Above: Traditional designs in pastework above a door at Bait Siba'i. Geometric star designs are often used in Islamic decorative arts.

Opposite: Coloured pastework and carved stone decoration at Bait Dahdah.

Overleaf: Elaborate coloured pastework decorates all the walls of this reception room at the Historical Museum.

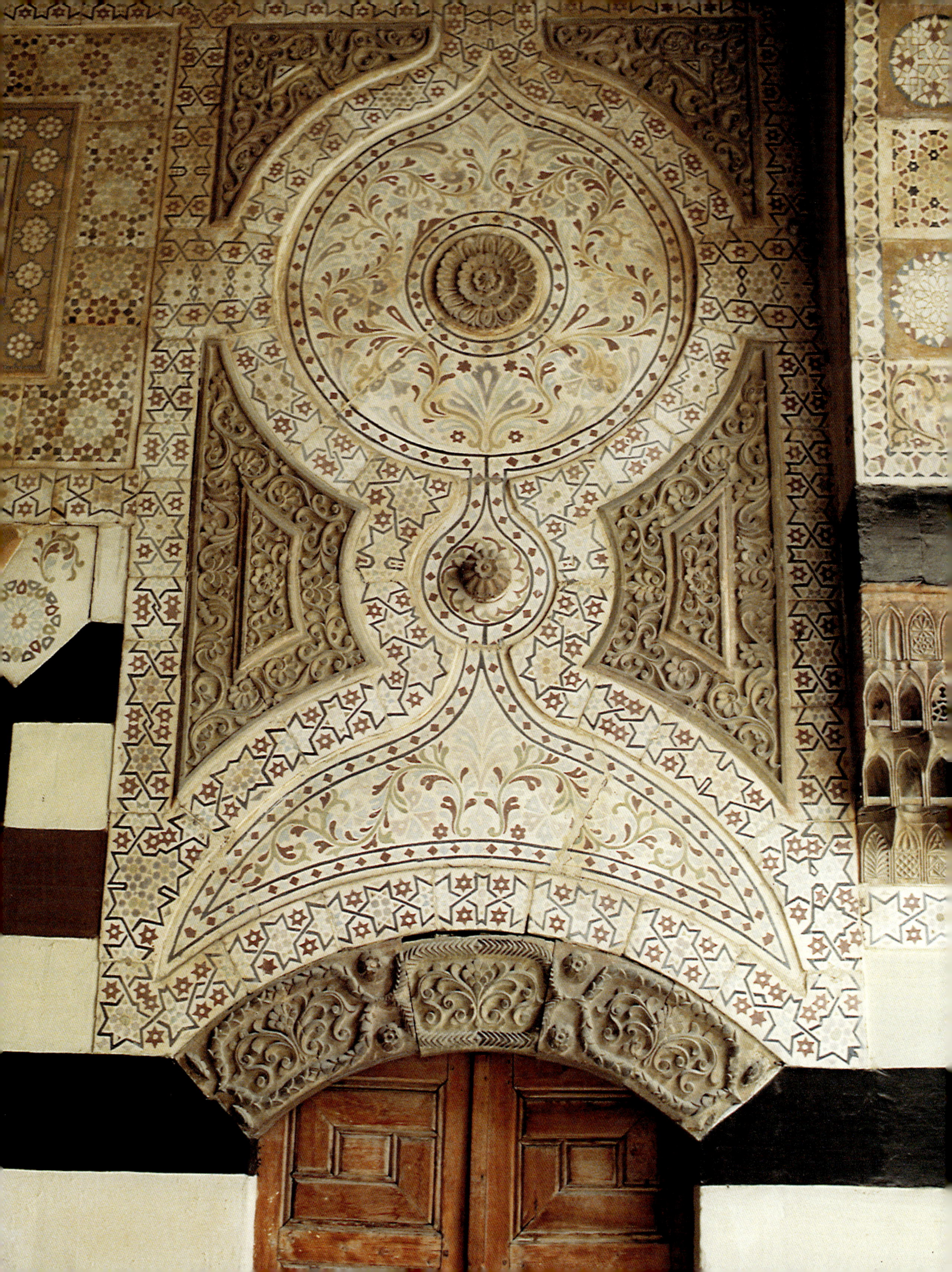

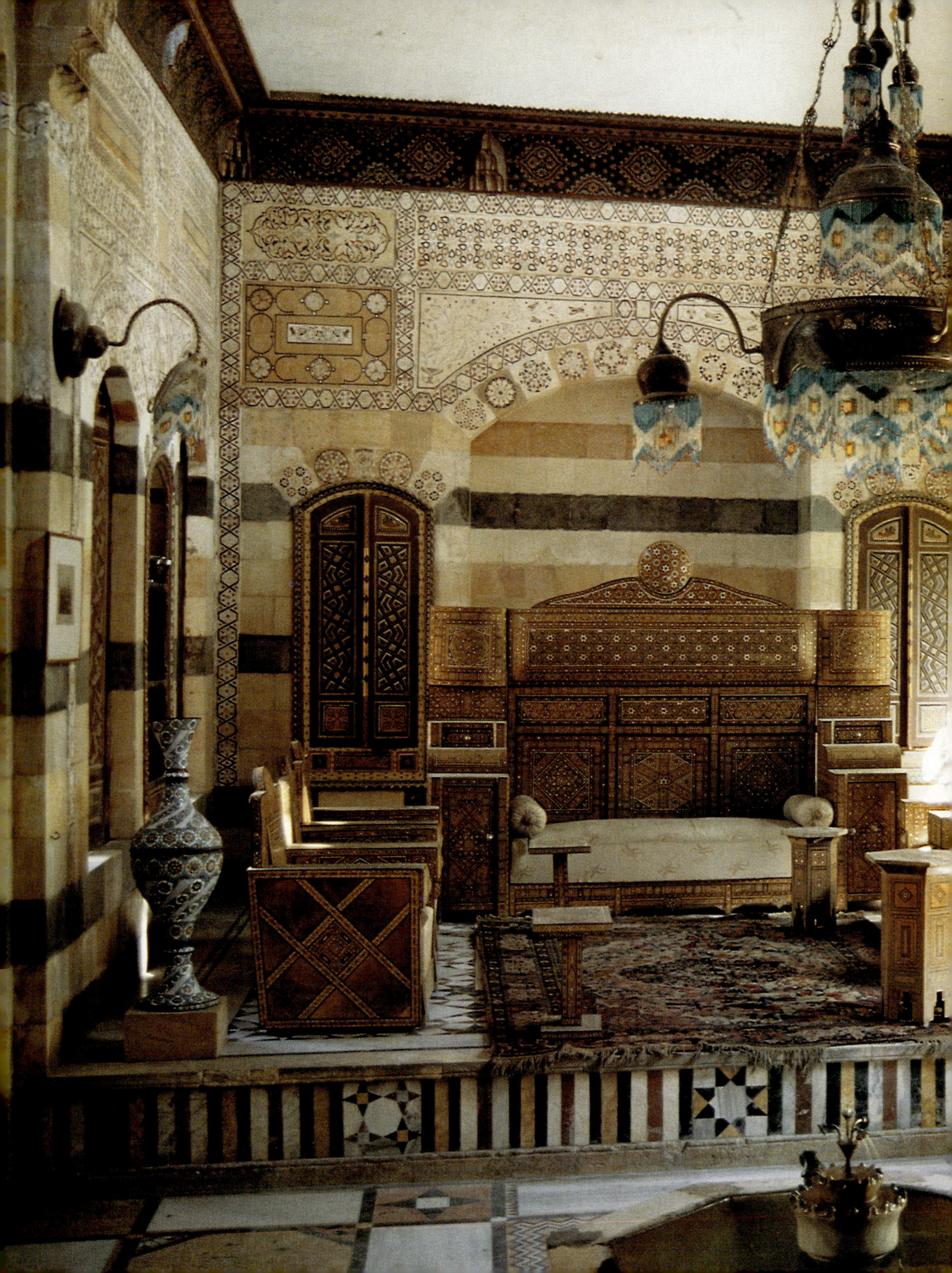

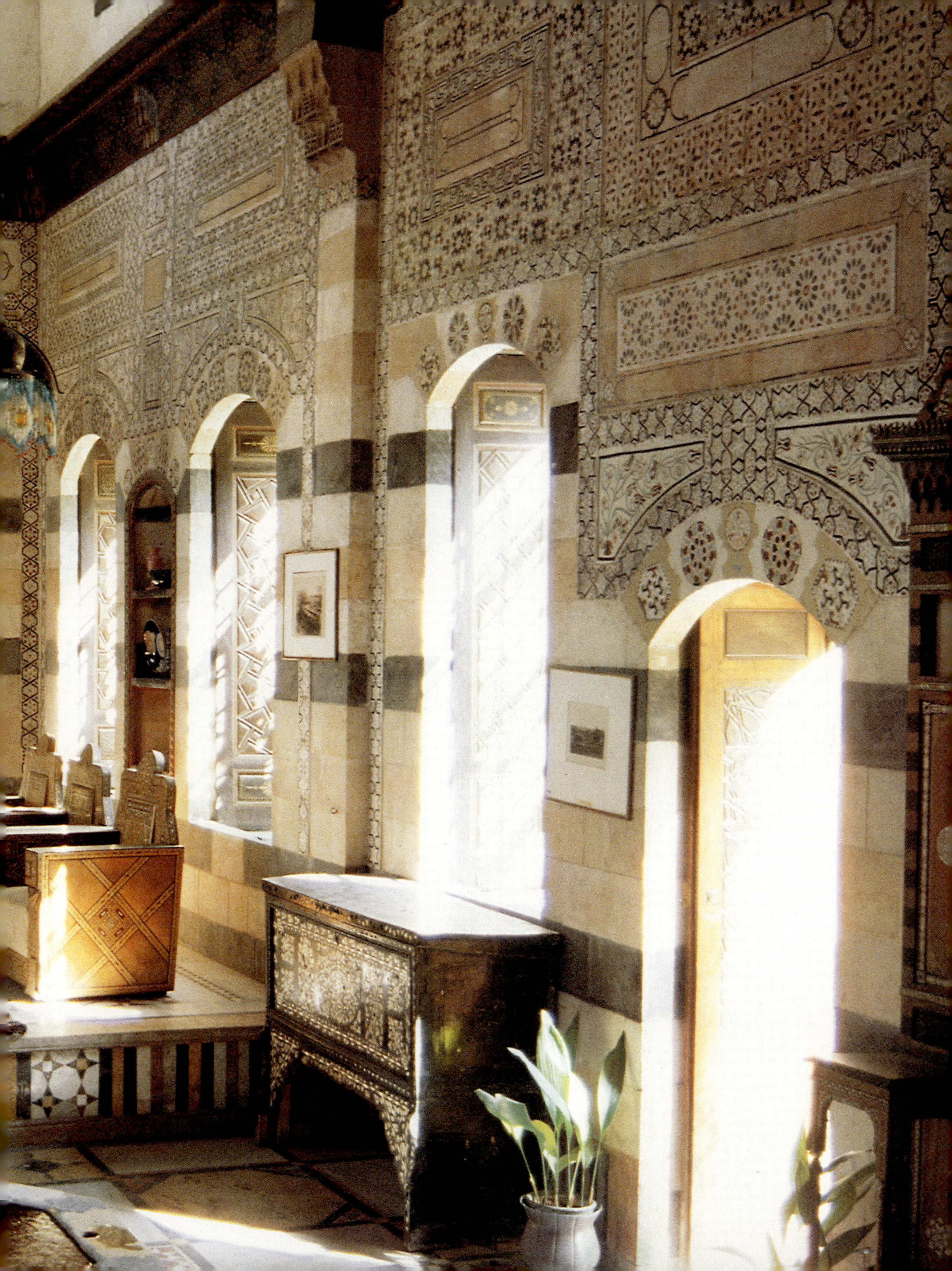

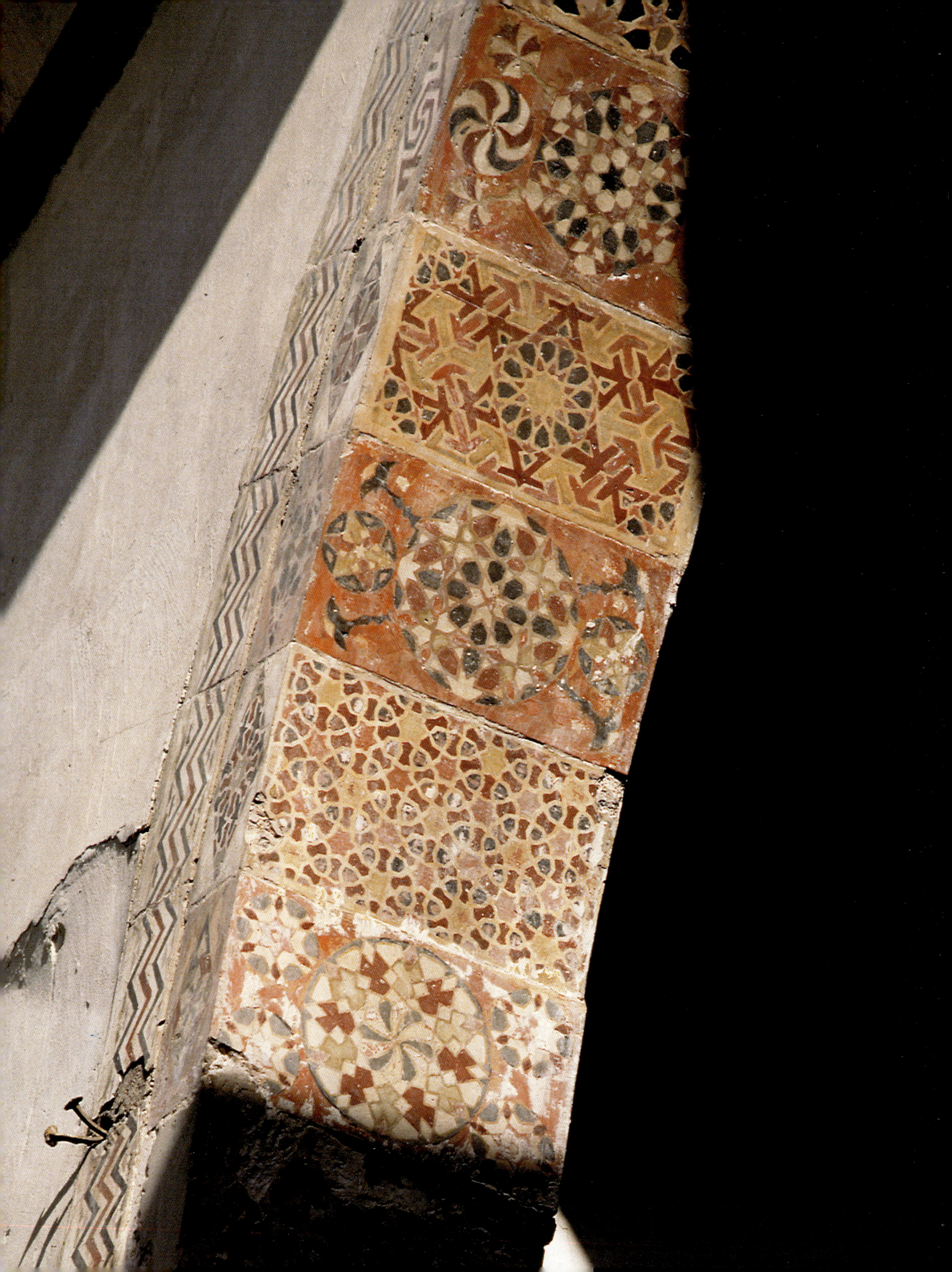

Coloured Pastework

Opposite: An arch of pastework-patterned stones at Bait Sayrawan.

Above: Fine coloured pastework walls set with geometric wooden doors at Bait Siba'i.

Left: The interior façades of Bait al-Istwani are finely pasteworked.

Above: The reception room of the German Consulate near the Suq al-Hamidiyya in the late 19th century.

Opposite: The enormous reception room at Bait al-Yusuf is flamboyantly decorated in Ottoman baroque style.

the 'Abds and the Azems had won their status through gaining political power – the Azems in the 18th century and the other two in the 19th.

It is reliably recorded that, from the time of their first famous ancestor, Isma'il, the Azem family grew, in only three generations, to number more than four hundred people. (It should be remembered that it was not uncommon for a rich man to have four wives in those days and, consequently, huge numbers of children.) By the 19th century, there must therefore have been hundreds and hundreds of Azems and it seems likely that many of the big houses in Damascus, now known by other names, started off as homes for them. There was certainly a big Azem house next to the Madrasa 'Abdullah Azem, where today there is nothing but a large gate with ruins behind it, for tragically this house was destroyed years ago for a development project which was never eventually realized.

Just outside the wall of the old city, among the drab new cement buildings of Suq Saruja, hides another palace that once belonged to the Azems. Like the more famous Azem Palace, it is now a museum – the Historical Museum of Damascus – where the city's records and archives are stored. But it is better known as the house of Khalid al-Azem, who was Prime Minister of Syria in 1962. No-one is sure of the history of this house before the beginning of the 20th century, when it was lived in by Khalid al-Azem's father, Mohammed Fawzi Pasha, a minister and one of the grandest of the 'notables', who every morning received his many visitors in traditional style in the salamlik of the great house. When he wished to bring these receptions to a close and retire to eat with his family in the haramlik, he would throw the tube of his narghila to the ground as a signal that the time had come for the guests to leave.

The house is thought to have been the Prussian Consulate between 1849 and 1862 – this is deduced from sketches that the Consul, Johann Gottfried Wetzstein (a scholar and orientalist), made of the place and sent home in letters. A friend of the Consul, who stayed in this house during a journey round the Middle East, wrote that the first courtyard had colossal fig trees the size of oaks, as well as the traditional orange and lemon trees and vines. 'The liwan and the three other reception rooms', he went on, 'are each one more beautiful than the other.' The Consul himself described the main qa'a of his house as being like the interior of a church, with coloured glass windows.

The main courtyards housed the offices of the Consulate, the servants' quarters and stables, as well as a large kitchen and a hammam. The Consul and his wife lived on the first floor 'which they could not fill', and from the roof there was a magnificent view of the mountains. In a letter that Consul Wetzstein sent to the Prussian envoy in Istanbul after the massacre of the Christians in 1860, he described how the house had provided temporary shelter for no fewer than 604 people. No wonder that the next Consul moved out into something smaller. The Consul at the end of the 19th century, Ernst Lütticke, lived near the Suq al-Hamidiyya and seems to have been extremely popular. The indomitable English traveller Gertrude Bell, revisiting Damascus in 1905, wrote: 'When I had come to Damascus five years before, my chief counsellor and friend – a friend whose death will be deplored by many a traveller in Syria – was Lütticke, head of the banking house of that name and honorary German consul.' (Prussia had become part of unified Germany by then.)

Next door to the house of Khalid al-Azem, in Suq Saruja, is another enormous palace called Bait al-Yusuf. The two houses have a connecting door – in fact, it is thought that they might at some time have been one house. Nadia Khost, a writer and journalist in Damascus, says that when the French shelled the Syrian Parliament in 1945, the members fled along the back streets of Suq Saruja to take shelter in Bait al-Yusuf, and when that, too, came under attack, they dashed through the communicating door into the Khalid al-Azem house and from there escaped into the city.

Bait al-Yusuf was famous at the beginning of the 20th century as the home of another of the grandest Damascene notables of the time: 'Abd al-Rahman Pasha al-Yusuf. The Yusuf family were Kurdish; they had come to Damascus in about 1800 as sheep traders, but the next generation did extremely well in the service of the Ottomans and an advantageous marriage to the only child – a daughter – of the rich and prestigious (and fellow Kurdish) Shamdin family sealed their destiny. 'Abd al-Rahman Pasha was the son of that marriage. He inherited, in 1892, not only wealth and prestige but, from his father-in-law, the post of Commander of the Pilgrimage to Mecca, or Amir al-Hajj. He was, in fact, to be the *last* amir of the hajj, for the post ceased when the Ottoman Empire collapsed. He was assassinated in 1920 at the time the French took over Syria. 'Abd al-Rahman enlarged and redecorated the family house, Bait al-Yusuf, in fabulous, flamboyant style and it became a centre of hospitality, not only for the rich and powerful, but for the poor from Akrad, the Kurdish area of Damascus, who would be fed from a kitchen outside the house. Today, Bait al-Yusuf is divided up between thirty-five families and small businesses and has fallen, over a long period, into a bad state of repair.

The Ibish family, also Kurdish, came to Damascus as traders in livestock – this time horses, not sheep – and did well for themselves. Their family home was also in Suq Saruja; it is now the restaurant of the Syrian Workers' Union – a pleasant place to eat. At the end of the 19th century, the grandfather of the present

156

Left: Another view of the astonishing reception room at Bait al-Yusuf, a gathering place for society in the early part of the 20th century.

Right: 'Abd al-Rahman Pasha al-Yusuf, one of the most distinguished of the Damascus notables, and Amir al-Hajj, photographed in 1910.

generation traded thoroughbred horses all over the Middle East and in this way became friendly with Prince Yusuf Kamal, a member of the Egyptian royal family, to whom he introduced his son, Husain. The Prince was a passionate big-game hunter and in no time he had persuaded young Husain to join him on a major hunting expedition to Africa. Three times the two men went off to Africa and India together – in 1910, 1915 and 1926 – each time for a couple of years or more. The animals they 'bagged' were divided between them and sent to be stuffed in London. Prince Yusuf Kamal's share was integrated into the Hunting Museum at the Manial Palace in Cairo ('not a place for animal lovers', says the *Lonely Planet Guide*), but Husain's was exhibited in the qa'a of the family home, where it remained, locked, even after the house became the property of the Workers' Union. You could peer through the windows of the qa'a and see a surreal sight: set against the traditional painted walls and on the marble floor were elephants' feet, lion skins, a giraffe's head and myriads of horned skulls. In 1998, the collection was taken over by the Syrian Government and transferred to the qaʻa of Bait Sibaʻi, where it is now, as inappropriate and surreal as ever it was in its original home.

One of the problems of researching the histories of Damascene houses is that each one is known by the name of its proprietor of the time, so that, when ownership changes, so does the name of the house. And it's astonishing how quickly things are forgotten – or maybe it isn't: how many of us know anything about the previous owners of our own homes?

Another difficulty is that numbers of the well-known houses have disappeared. Some were cleared away for modern redevelopment (particularly those in Suq Saruja); some were destroyed by the French in the rebellion of 1925 described on page 211; and some just collapsed through neglect. For instance, the house of the Basha family was apparently pulled down when the road from Straight Street to Bab al-Saghir was widened – happily, the spectacular stonework from its main reception room was carefully dismantled and stored, and then, in the 1980s, re-erected in one of the State guest houses, where it is known today as the Damascene Hall.

A mystery was the whereabouts of the house of ʻAli Agha. This was described as one of the finest houses in Damascus by several European travellers in the 19th century, including Charles Addison and Josias Porter, whose descriptions of it are quoted earlier – but it seemed to have vanished. ʻAli Agha's story is a sad one. He was a Turk, but he married an Azem daughter, which gave him an entrée into that grand family, and he worked for the Egyptians in the short period that they ruled Syria, 1832–40. Indeed, it was his daughter Farlan, whose marriage to the Egyptian Governor of Damascus, Sharif Pasha, has already been mentioned. Despite this close family connection with the rulers, ʻAli Agha was accused of treachery and condemned to death in 1839. By all accounts, he had been extremely rich and a man of great taste and refinement, and he was obviously very open to foreigners, for his is one of the few Muslim houses that was written about by Westerners. Twenty years after ʻAli Agha's death, Murray's *Handbook* described his house as having been turned into a hotel;

Left: The stonework from Bait al-Basha now decorates a Presidential guest house.

Above: An unusual decorative design for the corners of the liwan at Bait Nizam.

Opposite: The large reception hall at Bait Nizam, formerly the house of ʻAli Agha, which was visited by several Western travellers in the mid-19th century.

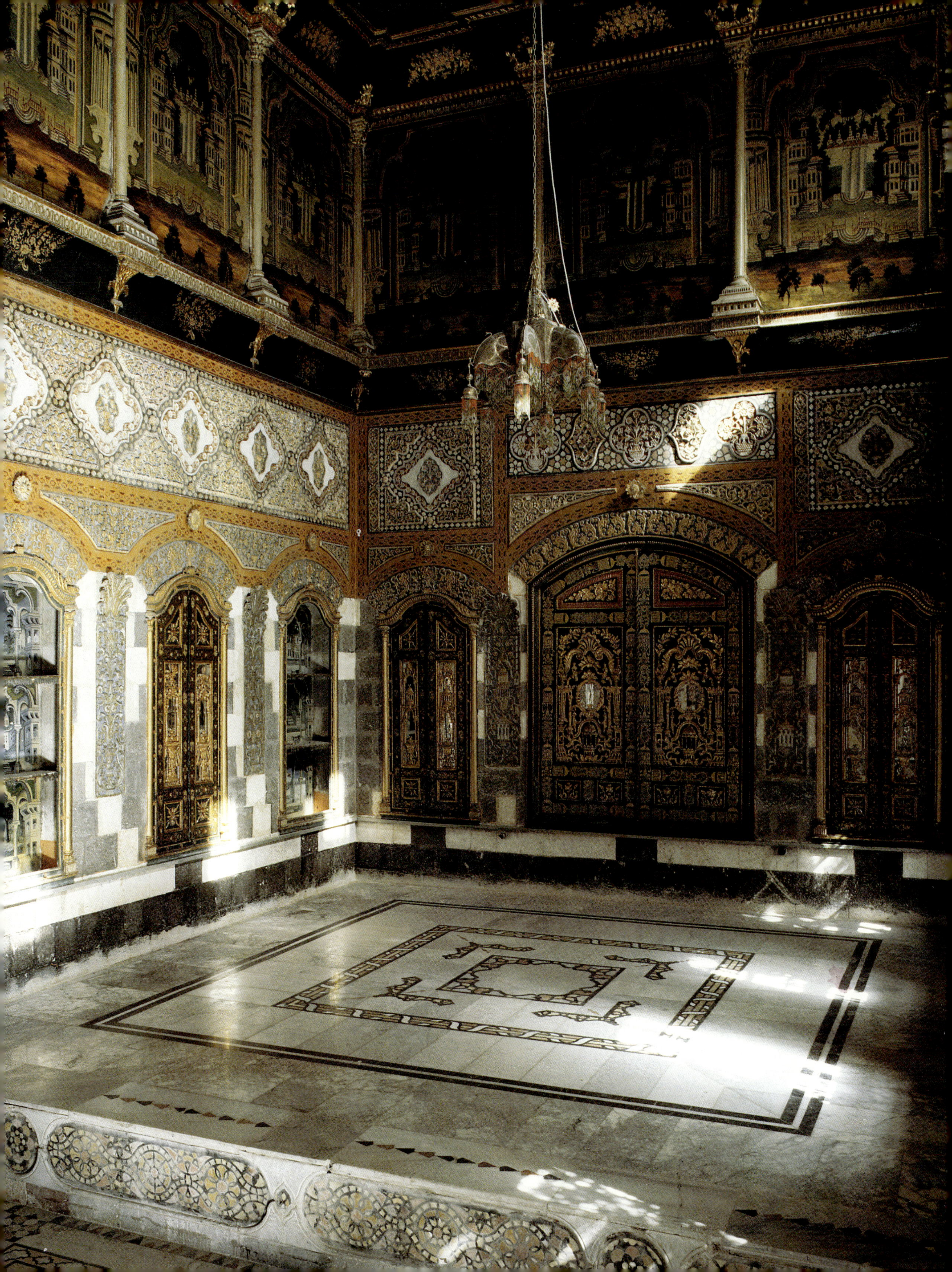

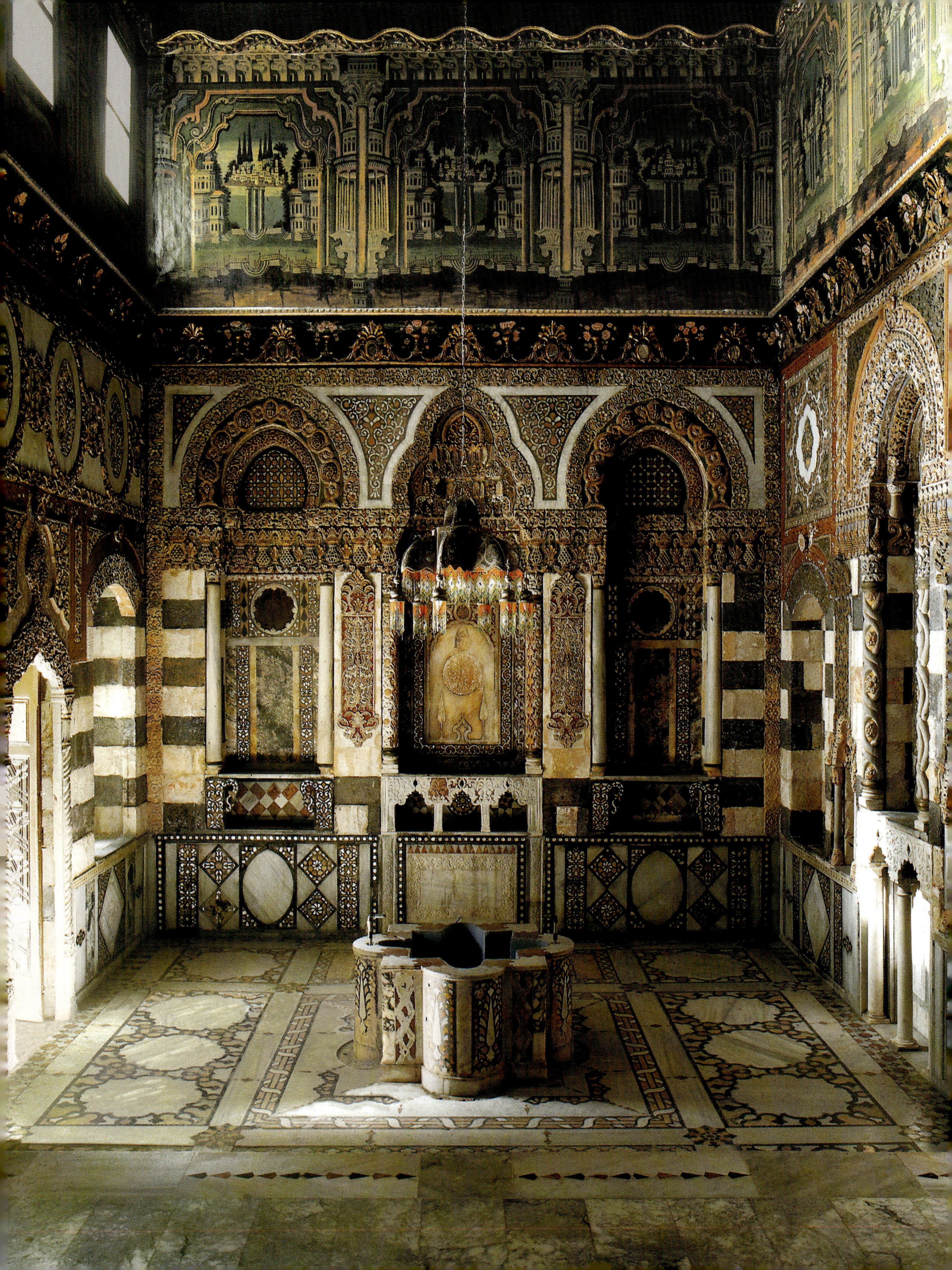

then it seemed to disappear. But recently, Stefan Weber of the German Institute of Archaeology in Damascus learned from court records that 'Ali Agha's house is the one known today as Bait Nizam, now owned by the Syrian Government and can be visited in the mornings, or hired for parties.

Just around the corner from Bait Nizam lies another beautiful palace, Bait Siba'i, which is also owned by the Government and can be visited – since 1998 it has housed the Ibish collection of stuffed hunting trophies. Bait Siba'i's origins are not clear – some say that it once belonged to the great religious family, Hamza; others that it was an Azem house. For a couple of years in the 1990s, the German Ambassador to Damascus and his wife rented it as their official residence, in an effort to make people more aware of the glories of the old city. It was not the first time that the house had had a European connection – in the 1950s, it was the home of the Belgian Consul, the Marquis Louis de Sau, who became a notorious figure in the diplomatic world. It's an interesting story: the Marquis was Consul in Lebanon with responsibility for Syria as well, which meant that he was constantly travelling between Beirut and Damascus. To this day, no-one knows exactly what he was doing, but he was caught at the Syrian/Lebanese border with guns in his car and, since he was known to be pro-Palestinian, he was accused of smuggling arms to them. It was a big scandal and the Belgian Government demanded his return to Brussels. The Marquis was obliged to leave the foreign service and he went to live quietly in Arna, a beautiful village in the mountains of Syria, where eventually he married his housekeeper, a local girl who was thirty years younger, and had a daughter. In his new life he took a passionate interest in gardening and fruit-growing – importing new varieties of plants from Belgium to improve local production of apples and strawberries. The Marquis never again returned to Europe, but the two sons of his first, Belgian, marriage often came to see him in Syria. He later moved from the mountains to a village near the sea at Tartus, where he died in 1994.

In the 19th century, three other most unusual foreigners came to live in Damascus, two of whom ended their days there, while the third spent less than two years in Syria before being recalled to London. They were 'Abd al-Qadir al-Jaza'iri, an Algerian amir, or prince, exiled

Opposite: The 'ataba of the reception hall at Bait Nizam shown on the previous page.

Below: Detail of carving at Bait Nizam.

from his own country by the French, who had taken it over; the second was Jane Digby, who had exiled herself from England; and the third was the extraordinary explorer and linguist Richard Burton, who was in Damascus as British Consul. The three became extremely good friends: 'If you ever find Abd al-Kadir, Mrs — and Captain Burton together, you will have a rare treat of conversation and different experiences', wrote Burton's wife, Isabel. (She always referred to Jane Digby as 'Mrs —', to avoid giving the appearance of gossip or scandal.)

'Abd al-Qadir arrived in Damascus in 1852 with an enormous entourage of family and bodyguards. He purchased several houses along the Barada river near Bab al-Faradis, where they settled. According to one historian, his arrival sent shock waves through

Damascus society. He had everything: he was clever, knowledgeable, spoke many languages and was rich (with a pension from the French). He was also a descendant of the Prophet and a Sufi sheikh, but most of all he was a hero. For in Algeria 'Abd al-Qadir had fought the French bravely for fifteen years, trying to oust them from his country, though in the end he was forced to surrender. The deal had been that he and his lieutenants would be allowed to go into exile, but once on the ship supposedly taking them to Beirut, they were told that they were, in fact, going to France, where they would be imprisoned. 'Abd al-Qadir and his colleagues were kept prisoner in various châteaux of the Loire for four years until Napoleon III came to power. The Emperor had sympathy for exiles, since he had been one himself, and, so the story goes, he came himself to the château where 'Abd al-Qadir was being held and announced to him, '*Émir, vous êtes libre*' ('Amir, you are free'). In his book *Mirror to Damascus*, Colin Thubron paints a poignant picture of this time: 'I could not think of his wars, only of his incongruous imprisonment on the Loire, and of his release by Louis Napoleon; of the emperor and the emir squatting down to eat cous-cous on the floor of the Château d'Amboise, of Abd El-Kadir kneeling to afternoon prayer in the vestibule of St Cloud and of his accidentally seeing the standards of his warriors among the captive banners hanging in the Hôtel des Invalides …'.

He was liberated, but not free to return to Algeria, and so he decided to live out his exile in Damascus, where he very quickly became the most eminent citizen. His charm was legendary – when Isabel Burton told him that his herb tea cured headaches so well that she would have to come to drink it every time she had one, he laughingly said that, if that were so, he hoped she would have a headache every day. 'His mind is as beautiful as his face', she wrote. 'He is every inch a Sultan.' 'No visit to Damascus was complete without a call on this noble emir', wrote Henry Jessup, the American missionary, who knew him. 'He was seen by European notables, French nobility, English lords, American tourists, Protestant and Catholic missionaries and Mohammedan pilgrims from Asia and Africa. He declared all men to be his brothers.'

This proved to be no idle boast: eight years after his arrival in Syria, 'Abd al-Qadir became a hero all over again. In 1860, when Muslims attacked Christians in Damascus, he was not in the city but, on hearing that there was trouble, he rushed back and played a vital role in saving lives. ''Abd El-Kadir and his men stood between the living and dead', wrote Dr Mishaqa, a Syrian Christian whose account of the massacre is the only one written by a survivor. They formed the terrified Christians into groups and took them, under guard, to the Citadel, where they were safe. But meanwhile 'Abd al-Qadir's own houses by Bab al-Faradis were filling with hundreds of fugitives – 'European consuls and native Christians' – and soon the mob turned on him. 'The hero coolly ordered his horse to be saddled, put on his *cuirass* and helmet and, mounting, drew his sword. Singly, he charged into their midst. "Wretches," he exclaimed, "Is this the way you honour your prophet? Shame upon you.… Not a Christian will I give up. They are my brothers."'

'Abd al-Qadir rescued hundreds of Christians and he was rewarded with medals and gifts from heads of state all over the world – a pair of gold-mounted revolvers from the President of the United States, a sword from the Queen of England, a medal from the Pope – but perhaps the most gratifying to him, certainly the most ironic, was the *Légion d'Honneur* he received from the French government, his old enemy.

The amir married five wives in all (his first, an Algerian cousin, had grown fat and ugly, but was still the only person allowed to remain seated when he entered the qa'a of his house) and he had sixteen children.

When 'Abd al-Qadir died in 1883, he was buried in the Muhi al-Din mosque, next to the tomb of the Sufi sheikh Ibn 'Arabi, whose teachings he had followed. But after Algeria gained its independence from France in 1962, the new government asked for the body of their resistance hero to be returned to its native land. His great-granddaughter, Amira Amal al-Jaza'iri, accompanied the coffin back to Algeria, where it was greeted with a 101-gun salute and a minute of silence. All members of the family were invited to resettle in Algeria with homes and pensions. Most of them took up the offer, but Amira Amal chose to stay in Damascus where she has played a pioneering role in women's education and is greatly respected. She is the proud inheritor of her grandfather's *Légion d'Honneur* on its pretty pink-and-green ribbon, so, at least for now, the medal remains in Damascus, the city in which it was bravely won.

'Abd al-Qadir al-Jaza'iri wearing his medals, including the sash of the *Légion d'Honneur*.

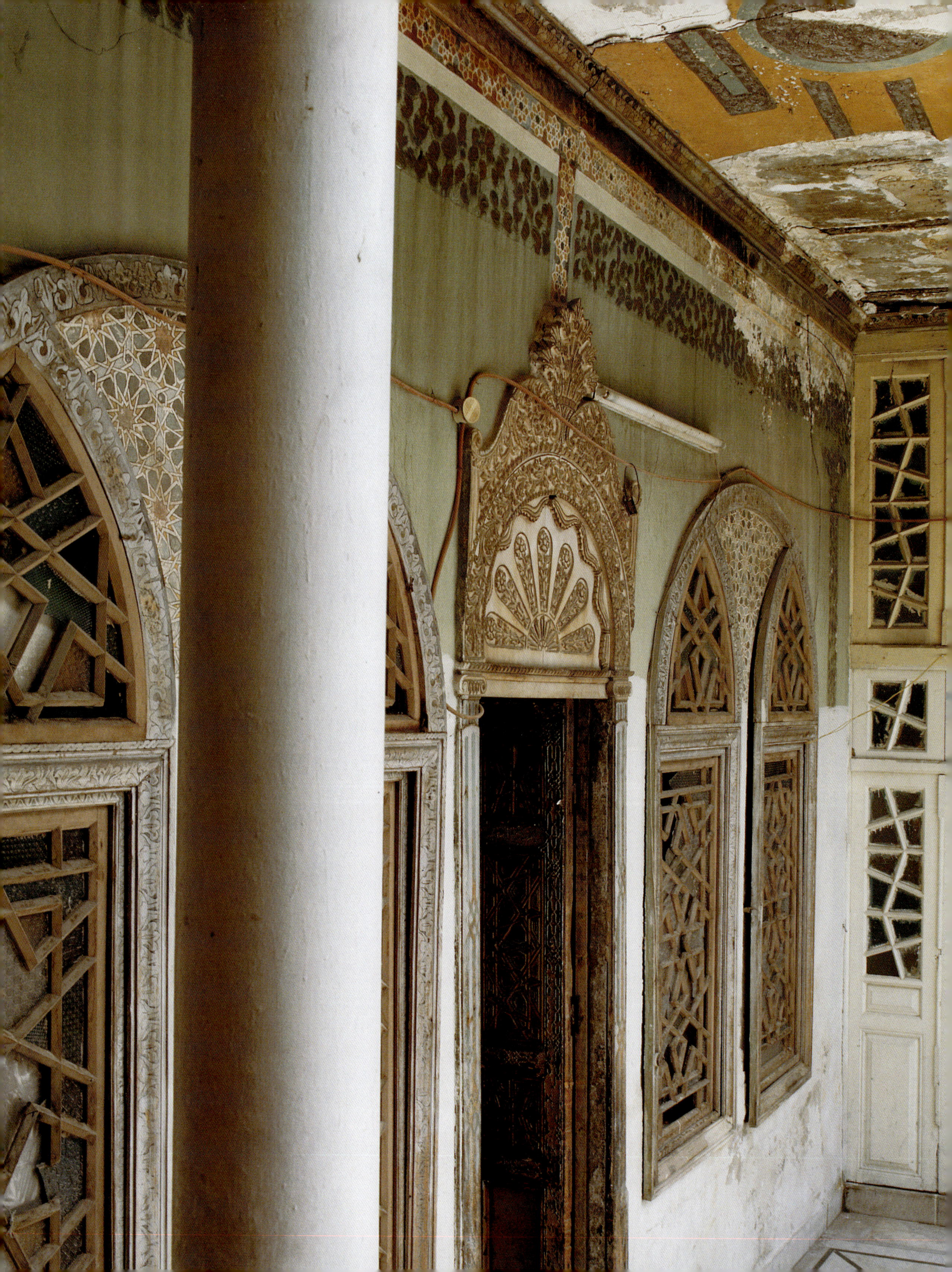

Left: One of 'Abd al-Qadir's houses has distinctive North African decoration. It was lived in by one of his sons.

Below: The liwan of 'Abd al-Qadir's own house on the river.

Bottom: Architect's drawing of the liwan and façade of 'Abd al-Qadir's house.

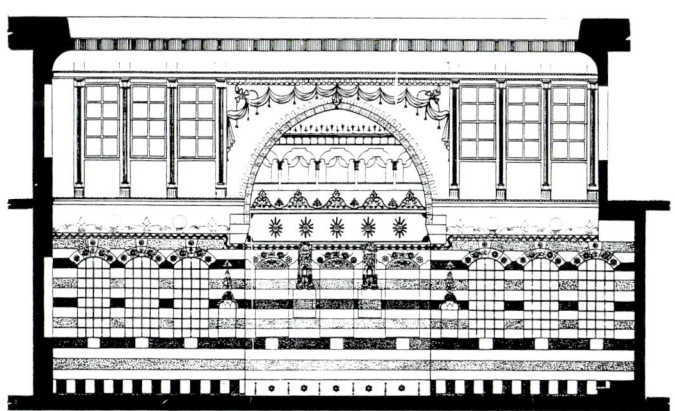

'Abd al-Qadir's houses along the river have new occupants now. His own, a classic Damascene palace with striped black-and-white walls, is now an old people's home; it has long been deteriorating and there is no clue either that he once lived there or that the great and the good of his time passed through its doors. Nearby, however, is another house that belonged to one of his sons, which has distinctive North African Arab decoration. There is a motto on the wall: 'Be as humble

165

Above: The ceiling of the octagonal room in Jane Digby's first house as it is today.

Left: View of the river taken from the bridge behind 'Abd al-Qadir's house.

Opposite: Detail of a window in 'Abd al-Qadir's North African-style house.

as the crescent moon reflected in water, not arrogant like smoke which, though it is nothing, tries to reach the sky.' Not long ago, the house was used as a school for Palestinian refugees and on the facing wall are sad graffiti. But there is one joy – 'Abd al-Qadir had his own bridge over the river, and it is still there. Gertrude Bell, visiting his sons after his death, was taken across it. 'At last I was led over a little bridge … into a garden full of violets, through which we passed to stables as airy, as light and as dry as the best European stables could have been.' Today, there are no stables and no violets, only ugly concrete buildings, but it is possible to stand on the bridge and imagine how it must have been when there were orchards and gardens beyond, amongst which, not so very far away, stood Jane Digby's house.

The year after 'Abd al-Qadir settled in Damascus, Jane Digby, a handsome English aristocrat, arrived in the city as a tourist. She was forty-five years old and had led an extraordinary life in which she had been married to an English lord, a German baron and a Greek count and had had numerous lovers, including King Ludwig of Bavaria. In Syria, she became attracted to the sheikh of the Bedouin tribe that controlled the routes to Palmyra, whom she had met when looking for a guide. He was twenty years younger than her, but, to the deep disapproval of the British Consul of the time, she married the sheikh and they lived happily ever afterwards until her death in 1881.

The agreement with her husband was that she would spend some of the year in the black tents of the tribe in the desert, and some of it in Damascus. Even before her marriage, she had bought a plot of land outside the city walls amongst the gardens and orchards and streams that could be seen from 'Abd al-Qadir's bridge, and there she began what was her favourite occupation – designing, building and furnishing a house. In its basic layout, Jane Digby's house conformed to the classical Damascene form, but she added certain English touches – on the ground floor was a room with a high octagonal ceiling, decorated with European wallpaper but with the traditional ornate wooden cupboards set into the walls. For the rest, the house was built around the usual central court. On the upper floor, Jane and her sheikh had separate apartments: hers, she furnished in English style – her drawing room had straw-coloured curtains and English furniture, which she ordered from Europe. Her family sent out things she requested, including seeds for her vegetable and flower gardens and clothes, so that she could keep up with the fashions back home. On one occasion, Isabel Burton, Jane Digby and Signora Castelli, the wife of the Italian Consul, were invited to the wedding of the Governor of Damascus's daughter. The ladies of his household, who knew the three Western women well, begged them to come in their European ball dresses – and so they did. It must have been a wonderful sight – the three foreign women with their nipped-in waists, billowing hooped skirts and off-the-shoulder bodices, and the ladies of the harem in their oriental finery.

Jane Digby's house became an essential port of call for travellers to Damascus – all of whom had heard the gossip about her scandalous life, knew of her marriage to the sheikh and were agog to see how she lived. Unfailingly, they were surprised and impressed by the refinement and elegance of her surroundings. Jane herself would not receive anyone without a letter of introduction. She was even surprised as to why the young Prince of Wales, on a visit to Syria in 1862, would want to meet her – 'mere curiosity, I suppose', she wrote in her diary. He wrote, in his, that Jane was still very good-looking for a woman of over fifty and that her house was 'charmingly arranged … as is her garden which is full of roses'.

Not everyone was so open. An American traveller, Charles Dudley Warner, was embarrassed to come across her in church. He wrote, horribly piously: 'We found a little handful of worshippers at the mission church and among them – heaven forgive us for looking at her on Sunday! – an eccentric and somewhat notorious English lady of title, who shares the bed and board of an Arab sheikh in his harem outside the walls. It makes me blush … when I see a lady sated with the tame civilisation of England throw herself into the arms of one of these coarse bigamists of the desert.'

Jane's garden was her pride and joy – her courtyard had the traditional trees and plants and a fountain in the middle, but in the huge garden around the house she created herbaceous borders and paths, built herself a little summer house covered with jasmine and roses and planted all sorts of unusual trees and shrubs. It is Jane Digby who is supposed to have introduced the magnolia to Syria. 'I have no gardener but myself and books, nothing but a native man who – when I attempt a rockery and have toiled all day scratching my hands to pieces – goes and throws it all down, calling it rubbish!' she wrote.

In 1862 Jane decided to sell the house she had spent eight years creating. 'My love of change and occupation will easily induce me to sell if I could get my price …', she had written some time earlier. That year she obviously did receive a good offer, for she bought a plot of land nearby and began work on a new 'pleasant and more compact house'.

Mary Lovell's 1995 biography of Jane Digby kindled such an interest in her life that visitors to Damascus today are as keen as ever they were a hundred years ago to see where she lived. Since her time, however, the whole area in which Jane constructed her houses has become a heavily built-up quarter of Damascus with a busy main road, King Faisal Street, separating it from the old city. Nonetheless, Mary Lovell and her Syrian guide, Hussein Hinnawi, tracked down Jane's first house, which, though now divided up among thirty poor families and in a terrible state of repair, can still be identified by the octagonal roof and the European wallpaper. Her second home has not been found.

Isabel Burton was in Damascus at the time Jane Digby lived in her second house. This seems to have been similar in design to the first, except that it is described as having a hammam, as well as spacious quarters off the courtyard for members of her husband's tribe visiting Damascus, and a conservatory. As in the first house, Jane and her sheikh had their rooms upstairs: 'A suit of apartments which is elegance itself. Family and home treasures and little reminiscences of European life, old china and paintings, are mingled with Oriental luxury whose very atmosphere bespeaks refinement', wrote Mrs Burton.

Jane Digby and Isabel Burton became very good friends in the time that the Burtons were in Damascus. They had much in common: both were deeply in love

Opposite: Jane Digby in her Arab dress, painted in 1859 by Carl Haag. She stands in front of the ruins of Palmyra, where her husband's tribe ruled.

with strong, independent men who were often absent, and they were self-reliant and practical women. They both had hen-houses stocked with all sorts of chickens, geese, ducks and guinea fowl for the table, they were keen gardeners, and both were capable horsewomen who knew perfectly how to look after their livestock and stables. They exercised their horses side by side; Jane acted as interpreter for Isabel when they visited Arab ladies; and she helped with the official reception days that Isabel held at the Burtons' residence.

Jane Digby and the Burtons shared the friendship of 'Abd al-Qadir, who had a summer villa near the Burtons in Salihiyya, and Isabel wrote that she would never forget the evenings they spent together on the roof of their house talking about all manner of subjects, with the view of Damascus and the mountains all around: 'It was all wild, romantic and solemn; and sometimes we would pause in our conversation to listen to the sounds around us: the last call to prayer on the minaret-top, the soughing of wind through the mountain gorges and the noise of the water-wheel in the neighbouring orchards.' But all this came to an end after less than two years – when the Burtons were recalled to London.

One of Jane Digby's last European visitors was a Dr Lortet from Lyons, who was taken to see her on a visit to Damascus in 1880. His party was received in a 'ravishing pavillion' in her garden, 'furnished in oriental style, decorated with mirrors and a thousand precious ornaments …'. Dr Lortet was struck by her beautiful white hands, her well-preserved looks, and by the fact that 'in spite of her great age, this noble woman was preparing to leave for the desert with her husband'. As Dr Lortet wrote later in the account of his travels, this was to be her last journey; she died the following year, and was buried in the Protestant cemetery in Damascus. Her grave, under a tree, is English and ordinary except for a piece of stone added at the foot, on which her husband carved her name in Arabic. Until the mid-1990s, this unkempt cemetery was a peaceful, rather wild place, but various well-intentioned folk have since then 'improved' the grave with a chain fence and paved the cemetery. Fatie Darwish, a wonderfully eccentric (and knowledgeable) elderly English lady who has lived

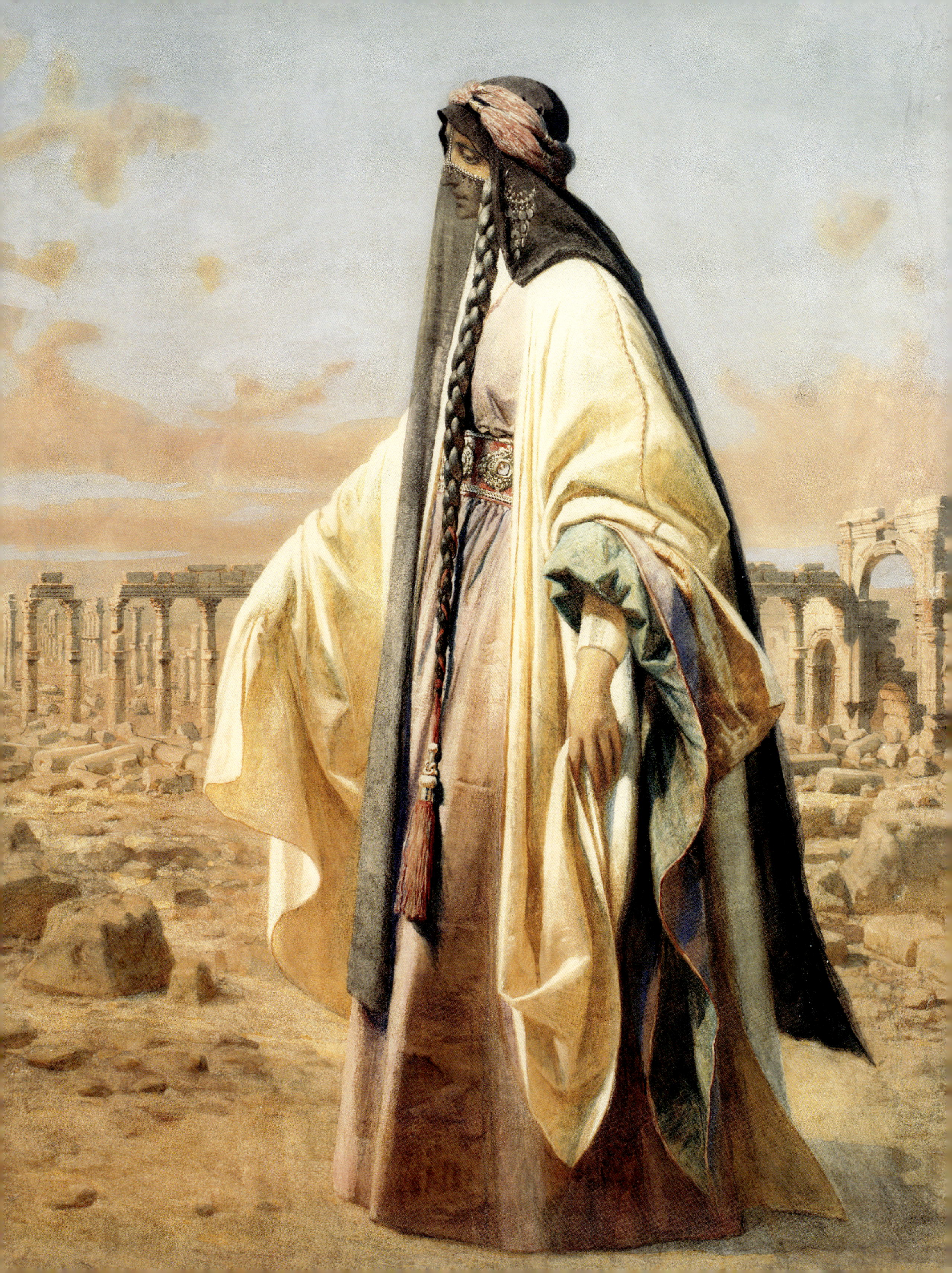

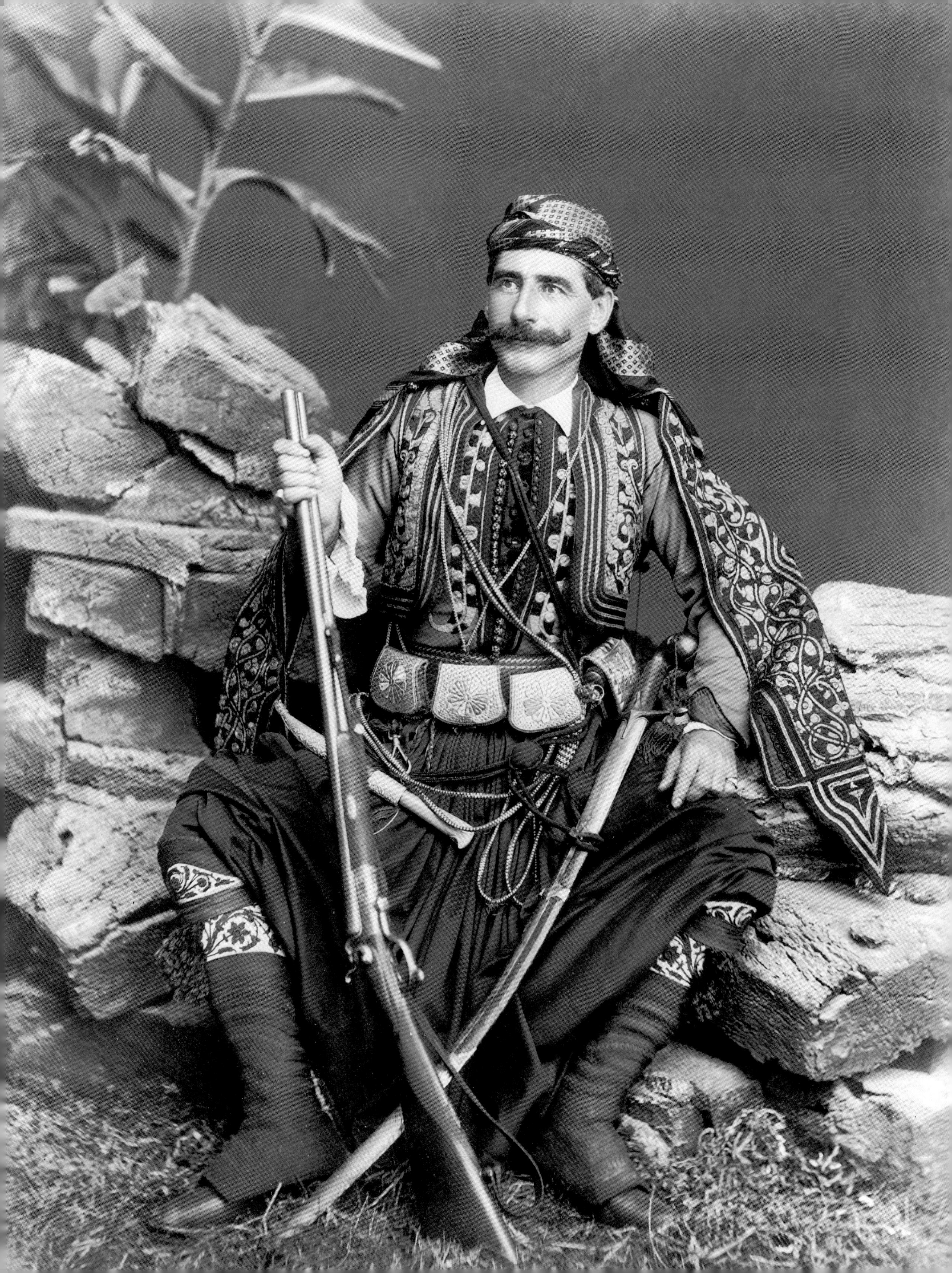

Opposite: A dragoman in his uniform, photographed by Bonfils in the 1870s.

in Damascus since 1948 (she is married to a Syrian doctor) swears that Jane Digby appears in her dreams, demanding that her grave be put back as it was.

Richard Burton, the new British Consul in Damascus in 1869, arrived ahead of his wife, Isabel, and put up at Dimitri's Hotel, which was where all Westerners stayed. Though Dimitri's was an old courtyard house, it was the first European-style hotel in Damascus. It stood on a corner near Marja Square, which in those days was the site of the horse market. (Later, another hotel, the Victoria, was built nearby, where Lawrence of Arabia lodged after he entered Damascus with the victorious Arab army in 1918.)

Great Britain had been the first European country to open a consulate in the Syrian capital, in 1834, but it had not been easy. Damascus was a holy city, hostile to Westerners. Those who visited took care to dress *à la turque*, as they called it, so that they blended with the crowds and would not be noticed. Lamartine, journeying to Damascus in 1833, wrote: 'The arrival of a European in Western dress causes terrible upset and we are rather afraid that the news of our journey will have reached Damascus ahead of us and expose us to serious dangers. We have taken every possible precaution. We are all strictly dressed in Turkish costume ...'.

The first British Consul, John Farren, was appointed in 1830, but the Ottoman Sultan refused to give him the necessary permission to go to Damascus, so he kicked his heels in Beirut for more than two years, writing that 'Damascus gloried in an implacable resistance to the admission of European intercourse.' In 1832, the Egyptians invaded Syria and, when they had established themselves firmly as the new rulers, they made it clear that Farren would be welcome in Damascus. He rode into the city in February 1834 with a cortège of five hundred (Egyptian soldiers, janissaries, his own staff, English residents, etc.) and, to his own astonishment, met with no hostility from the enormous crowd that had turned out to see him.

By the time the Burtons arrived in Damascus thirty-five years later, there were still very few Westerners in the city – only thirty Europeans, according to Isabel Burton, including three British (who were, of course, Jane Digby and the Burtons themselves). 'Whoever lives in Damascus must have good health and nerves, must be charmed with Oriental life and must not care for society, comforts or luxuries ...', she wrote.

But on the other hand, life was full of fascination and adventure to Isabel; even a walk in the souk was utterly absorbing: 'I cannot say enough on the subject of the bazaars, and the picturesque figures to be met with in Damascus', she wrote. 'The Circassians and Anatolians, the wild Bedawin Shaykhs, the fat, oily, cunning, money-making Jew, the warlike-looking Druze, the rough Kurd, the sleek, fawning, frightened Christian, the grave, sinister Moslem, the wiry Persian, the soft Hindi, the waddling Turk, the quiet, deep-looking Afghan, the dark and trusty Algerine – every race, every costume of Asia, every sect of religion, all talking different tongues, all bringing their wares to sell or coming to buy; jostling one another and struggling through strings of mules, camels, donkeys and thoroughbred mares, with gaudy trappings.... The *Kawwases* [Consulate guards] swaggering before and behind their Consul calling out "Make way".' Mrs Burton described how the souks were (as they still are) divided up into different trades and merchandise. Her favourite was the marquetry bazaar. 'There you buy clogs, or tables and chests, all inlaid with mother of pearl. A bride is obliged to have her *trousseau* packed in one of these monster lockers and a pair of clogs at least a foot high, all similarly inlaid. She walks about the courtyard on these Oriental stilts very gracefully and drops them before ascending the Ka'ah [qa'a].'

Ten years earlier, Josias Porter, writing in Murray's *Handbook*, had been struck by the fact that, though the souks were full of brilliant colour and 'costumes of every fantastic form that tailors could invent', to the exotic characters in the souk it was the ordinary Englishman's hat that was an object of awe. The first European who entered the city wearing a hat, earlier in the 19th century, had it knocked off his head by angry Damascenes, but now they couldn't take their eyes off one. 'It attracts universal attention. The flower-potted Derwish stares at it; the Persian, with his furred sugar-loaf, a yard in length, exclaims '*Mashallah*'; the little Turk, with his red nightcap stuck on the back of his bullet head, looks up at it in amazement; village sheikhs, who seem to have got their whole bed-clothes wrapped round their heads, stop to gaze at the phenomenon ...'.

Captain Richard Burton, British Consul in Damascus from 1869 to 1871.

The Burtons believed they would be in Damascus for years and years and, as soon as she arrived at Dimitri's Hotel (which she found damp) on 1 January 1870, Isabel began planning for the long term. At first, she was tempted by the idea of having a marble palace in the old city ('the decorations of some of the salons are gorgeous', she wrote yearningly), but eventually she decided, mostly for the sake of her husband's health, to live in Salihiyya, a suburb of Damascus on the foothills of the Qasyun mountain. Though the area, at 750 metres (2,500 feet), had beautiful views, fresh water, clean air and lovely light, the selection of houses on offer was second-rate. In the end, they rented half a house – the haramlik courtyard of a big mansion. (Had they been able to have the salamlik courtyard as well, she wrote, 'it would have made a first-class residence', but that had been sold to a different landlord.) However, the situation of the house was perfect, set among apricot orchards and gardens with streams running through them. Their new home overlooked a small road, across which Mrs Burton hired a stable for twelve horses.

The village of Salihiyya has long since been absorbed into the modern city of Damascus – where it is still considered a most desirable area to live, even though there are no apricot orchards any more. Not a trace of the Burtons' house remains, but it is thought to have been near where the Italian hospital is today.

Isabel Burton's description of it shows that their house had the traditional layout: 'I want to take you through my home,' she told her readers, 'which is quite of the second class. Firstly you enter a square courtyard, vulgarly painted in broad stripes of red, white and blue, planted all around with orange, lemon and jessamine trees and in the middle plays the inevitable fountain. The most conspicuous object is the Liwan, a raised room with one side taken out of it; that is, the front opens onto the court: it is spread with carpets and divans.... It is the custom to receive here on hot days and to offer coffee, lemonade or sherbet, Narghilehs, cigarettes. On one side is our dining room and on the other a cool sitting-room when it is too hot to live upstairs. Upstairs the rooms are six and run round two sides of the courtyard. A long terrace occupies the other two sides …'.

Helped by Jane Digby (who usually stayed on to dinner afterwards), Mrs Burton held her official receptions every Wednesday, when church dignitaries, Turkish officials, notables, the Consular Corps, missionaries and friends would come to call. Men and women were entertained in separate areas and Mrs Burton, dressed 'as for visiting in London', would divide her time between the two.

For the rest, Isabel Burton did good works in her neighbourhood, tried to learn Arabic, made calls on Arab ladies in their harems and visited the hammam. Indeed, when she returned to England, she missed the hammam so much that she decided to try the Turkish baths in Jermyn Street in London. She took her Syrian maid with her, who said it was the first time she had been warm since arriving in England, but their general verdict was 'Jermyn Street is a parody of the real eastern bath. It has all its disagreeables without its delights, extreme heat without graduation, stuffy rooms without any comforts or luxuries …'. In the real hammams of Damascus a bath took about four hours, during which, Mrs Burton reported, you moved gradually from warm rooms to hot rooms; were scrubbed with a pad of blond fibre (made from palm fronds), sluiced down with water, shampooed again all over, and ended up in the cool room, with your head wrapped in a cold towel, being fed with iced sherbets, before starting the whole process again.

'We now return to the hall where we first undressed, enveloped in silk and woollen cloths, and we recline on divans. It is all strewed with flowers, incense is burned about us, cups of very hot and bitter coffee are handed to us and Narghilehs are placed in our mouths. A woman advances and kneads you like bread; you fall asleep during the process.… When you awake you will find music and dancing, the girls chasing one another, eating sweetmeats, cracking nuts, and enjoying all sorts of fun.' Mrs Burton was glad not to be a Muslim woman, having to be hennaed and waxed (Muslim women traditionally removed all body hair) and perhaps tattooed – the tattoo artist waited in an ante-room for his clients. At the end, she wrote, 'it appears to me that one's first skin is wholly peeled off … one feels very light after these baths, and the skin is wonderfully white'. (A visit to a hammam in Damascus today provides a similar, though rather less luxurious, experience, taking several hours.)

Most of Mrs Burton's time, however, was taken up with looking after the household and the menagerie of animals she had accumulated. She bought a camel, and a

Isabel Burton enjoyed visiting the hammam. This is the vault of a once-popular bathhouse in the Tailors' Souk (Suq al-Khayyatin), now filled with shops.

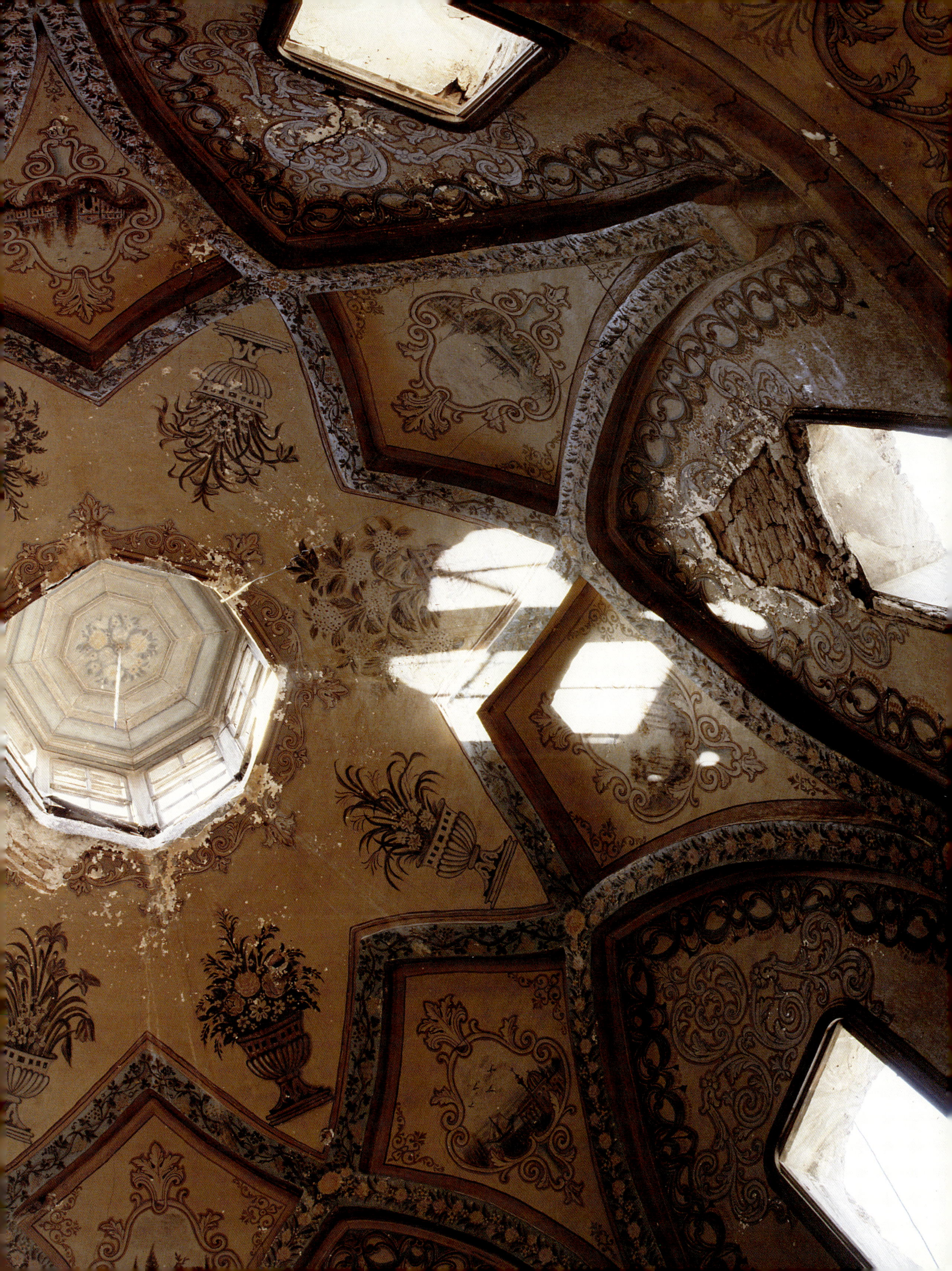

Dr Mishaqa, a greatly respected man of letters, who was the US Honorary Consul in Damascus in the mid-19th century. Like most of those selected by foreign countries to represent them in Damascus, he was a Christian.

white donkey to ride on. (There were places where foreigners were not permitted to ride horses – something which had thoroughly irritated another traveller, Henry Maundrell, in 1697. After visiting some gardens near Damascus, Maundrell wrote: 'Franks [Europeans] are obliged either to walk on foot or ride upon asses: the insolence of the Turks not allowing them to mount on horseback.' He advised that it was best not to complain, but 'to turn the affront into a motive of recreation'.) From England, Isabel Burton had brought with her five dogs, one of them a St Bernard, and to these she added a Kurdish puppy, a white Persian cat (bought in the souk), three milk goats, a hen-house full of various fowl, and some pigeons. The Burtons were presented, as gifts, with a baby lamb and a leopard cub, 'the idol of the house' (it was later poisoned and died), and she planted her vegetable and flower gardens with English seeds. Then the trouble began: the pigeons and chickens ate the seed, the cat ate the pigeons and chickens, the dogs worried the cat, the leopard killed the lamb and harried the goats and frightened the horses, camel and donkey. 'Captain Burton', she wrote, 'declares that it was like the House that Jack Built …'.

In spite of such domestic hazards, the Burtons loved life in Damascus, perhaps not surprisingly, for, as well as their home in Salihiyya, they had one of the grandest consulates in the city and a summer house in the mountains at Bludan (this was demolished only in 1994). Isabel was staying there, in fact, when a messenger arrived from Damascus with a note from her husband saying, 'Do not be afraid. I am recalled. Pay, pack and follow at convenience.' Burton had upset some of the Jewish community, because he would not condone their money-lending to poor peasants at extortionate rates; he fell foul of a couple of 'amateurish' missionaries, Mr and Mrs Mott, whom he criticized for handing out Christian tracts to Muslims; and the Turkish Governor had always distrusted and feared him. Between them, the three groups of enemies managed to make so much mischief against him that he was ordered to leave and return to London. Isabel was heartbroken. She described an afternoon spent on the mountain picnicking above Damascus, just before the political storm broke around their heads, as 'my last happy day'.

In the Burtons' time in Syria, the Consular Corps, besides the British, consisted of the French, Russian, Prussian, Austrian, Italian, Greek, Spanish, Persian and United States representatives. In spite of Isabel's belief that 'in a fanatical place like Damascus we are neither English, French, nor Prussians, but simply Europeans, and we are bound to hang together', it didn't, in fact, work out quite like that. As she wrote later, 'The difficulty of this European society is that it will split and separate into cliques….' The cliques were the missionaries, the religious orders, the Consular Corps, 'and the French who, as is natural, see little of anyone but themselves'. She herself seems to have liked the Italian consul, Signor Castelli, and his wife best; they gave 'charming little dinners'.

Isabel Burton did not count the missionaries in her tally of foreigners in Damascus, but there were, in fact, two British families and one American (all Presbyterian) as well as Mr and Mrs Mott, who were in charge of the British Syrian School (and fell out with Richard Burton). This school had been started by Mrs Mott's sister, Mrs Bowen Thompson, a widow who had been inspired by the gruesome stories of the Christian massacre to come to Syria and offer her services. She does not seem to have been an easy woman: Henry Jessup recalled how he had welcomed her warmly when she arrived in Beirut 'when not an English resident would recognise her'. The British Syrian School, also known as St Paul's, still stands in Bab Tuma, but is now a school for refugees from Qunaitra. It is a classic Damascene house, but the marble fountain in the first courtyard has written on it, in wonderfully Gothic Victorian letters: 'Presented by Augusta Mentor Mott'.

The Persian Consul was the most important member of the Consular Corps. He was, according to Isabel, '90, but looked 40' and was held in awe by the Governor and all the officials. His Consulate was in a magnificent house called Bait Shirazi, where descendants of the family still live today. Bait Shirazi has a beautiful stone-paved courtyard, a 'maze' fountain, a magnificent qaʻa with three seating areas, beautiful painted ceilings, and walls with 'stalactite' (muqarnas) decoration. The stonework is dated 1765.

When the Burtons arrived in Damascus, the American Vice-Consul was a greatly respected Syrian, Dr Mishaqa. To the gratification of the missionaries, Dr Mishaqa had converted from Greek Orthodox to Presbyterian. He had narrowly escaped being killed in the

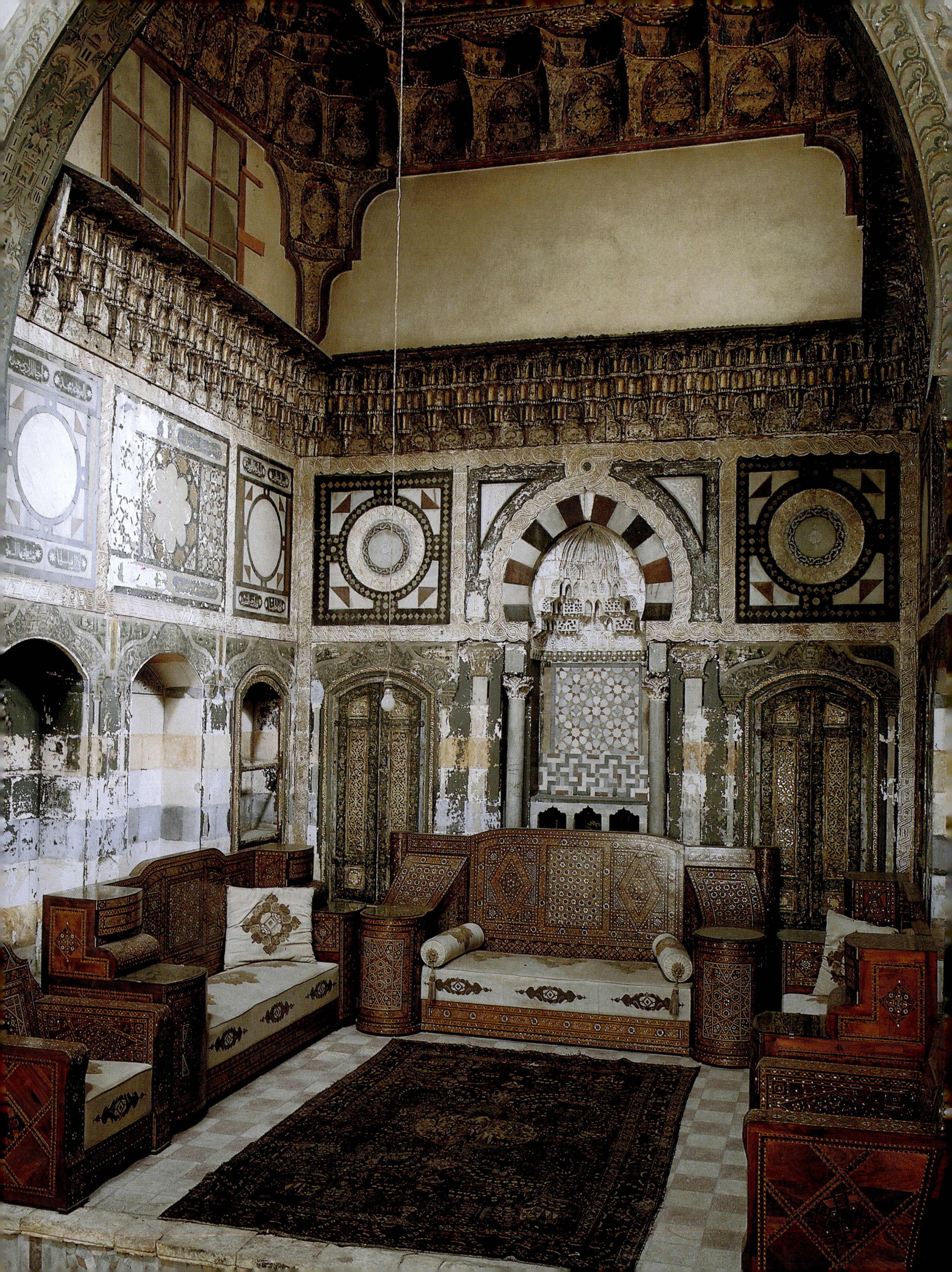

massacre of the Christians – it is his account of the affair and of 'Abd al-Qadir's heroism that has been quoted from earlier. The house that was the American Consulate is still in the Bab Tuma quarter, but in a rather poor state. (It has an interesting old kitchen.) When, in 1870, Dr Mishaqa retired from his duty representing the United States, his son Nasif, who was at the time a dragoman at the British Consulate, took over. All the consulates employed dragomans and kavasses – exotic-looking creatures in fantastic uniforms. Dragomans were an indispensable mixture of translator, secretary, guide and general fix-it man, who knew their way around in every sense. They were often unpaid, doing the job for its status and for the protection it offered. In 1872, the British Consul, Mr Kirby Green, complained to London that his allowance did not permit him to have a paid dragoman, 'the allowance of £200 failing even to cover my house rent'. He pointed out that the French had two paid, and one unpaid, dragomans. Occasionally a dragoman might be a foreigner – in the 1870s there was an American, Rolla Floyd, working as a dragoman for the United States Consulate; he specialized in guiding tourists. Kavasses were bodyguards, and the more that were employed, the greater the prestige of the consulate. Mr Kirby Green had three – the French five.

The Italian Consulate was, at around this time, in Bait Shamiyya in the Christian area, which is now a convent. The Austrian Consulate was in Bait Shawi, which is the house on the left as you drive down Straight Street, with a beautiful but dilapidated bay window jutting over the street. The Spanish Consulate was in the House of the Spanish Crown, where Wulzinger and Watzinger stayed in 1917 and where the grand Spanish coat of arms, carved in stone, now presides over a carpenter's workshop. According to the map in the Librairie Hachette guide *Orient, Syrie, Palestine* for 1890, the French Consulate at that time was in Bait Nizam ('Ali Agha's house).

Josias Porter, who knew Damascus in the 1850s, drew a map of the old city and marked the British Consulate as being in a house now known as Bait Quwatli. This is an enormous palace with a vast main courtyard and several smaller ones, some beautiful panelled rooms, a qa'a with wall paintings, and coloured pastework dated 1837. Sadly, today it is parcelled up between many families and a paper store – one of the dividing breeze-block walls actually goes across the huge stone fountain in the main courtyard. Later, the British must have moved, because in 1870 Isabel Burton locates her husband's Consulate outside the city wall, near the horse market, which was then in Marja Square. After that, its whereabouts become a bit of a mystery, compounded by the fact that a photograph taken by Bonfils in the 1870s of Bait Nizam is identified as the house of the '*Consul anglais*' (i.e., British Consul), when that house was supposed to have been the *French* Consulate. Bonfils is known to have made some mistakes in his captions; perhaps this is one of them. (After the First World War, the British Consulate was in a house in the Halbuni district, near the railway station. There, at a Christmas party one year, remembers Sir Richard Beaumont, who was Vice-Consul in Damascus from 1938 to 1945, the Prime Minister of Syria and his Foreign Minister danced the Lambeth Walk, the step that was all the rage at the time in England.)

The story of the Bonfils family and their photographs is a fascinating one. The original Bonfils, it is said, was a French military photographer who arrived in Beirut

Opposite: Magnificent Bait Shirazi was the home of Persian consuls until the 20th century.

Above: Veranda on the first floor of the British Syrian School (Madrasa Qunaitra).

Overleaf: Bait Quwatli (a) was the British Consulate in the mid-19th century. It is an enormous house with several courtyards and much decoration.

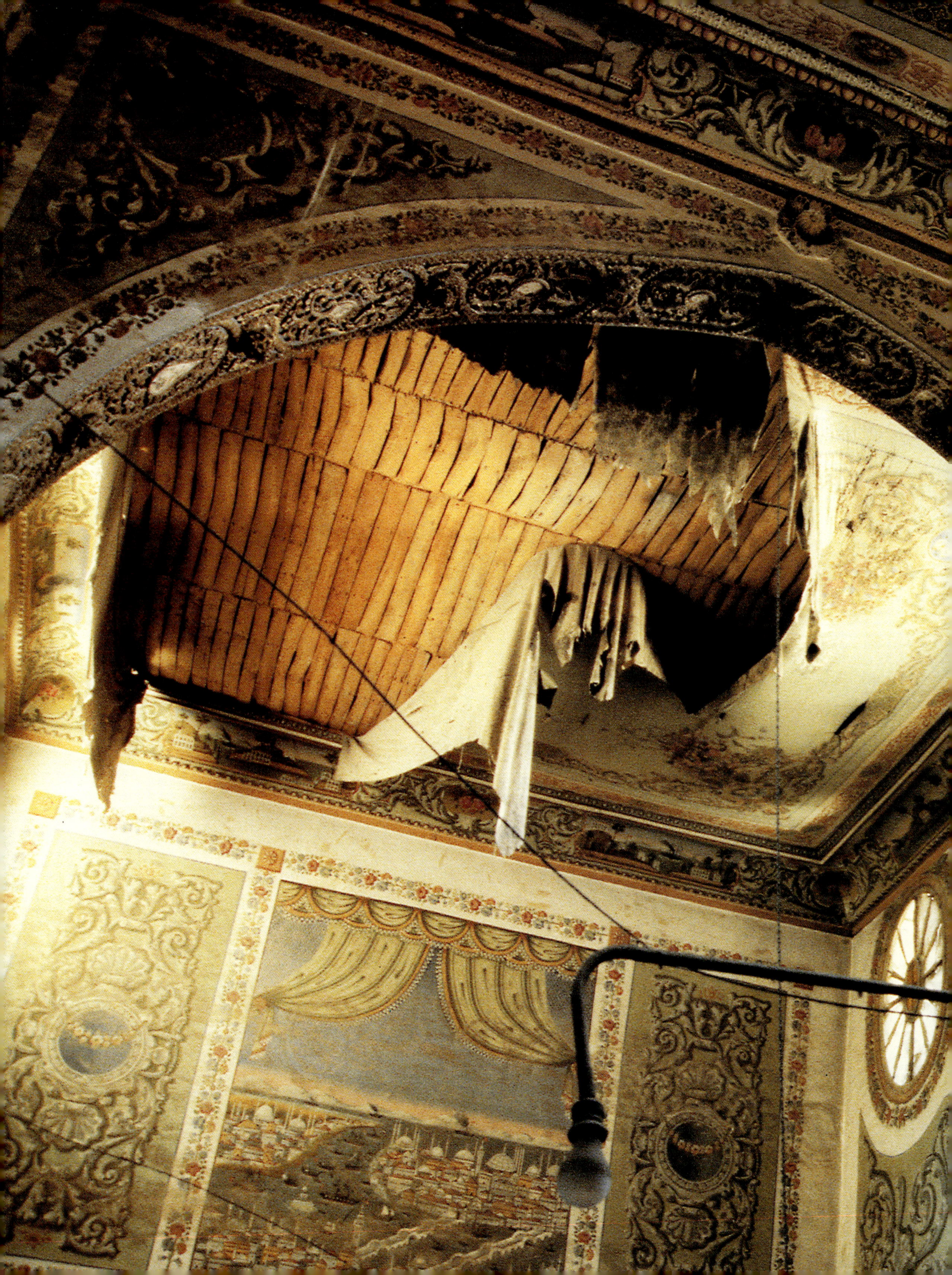

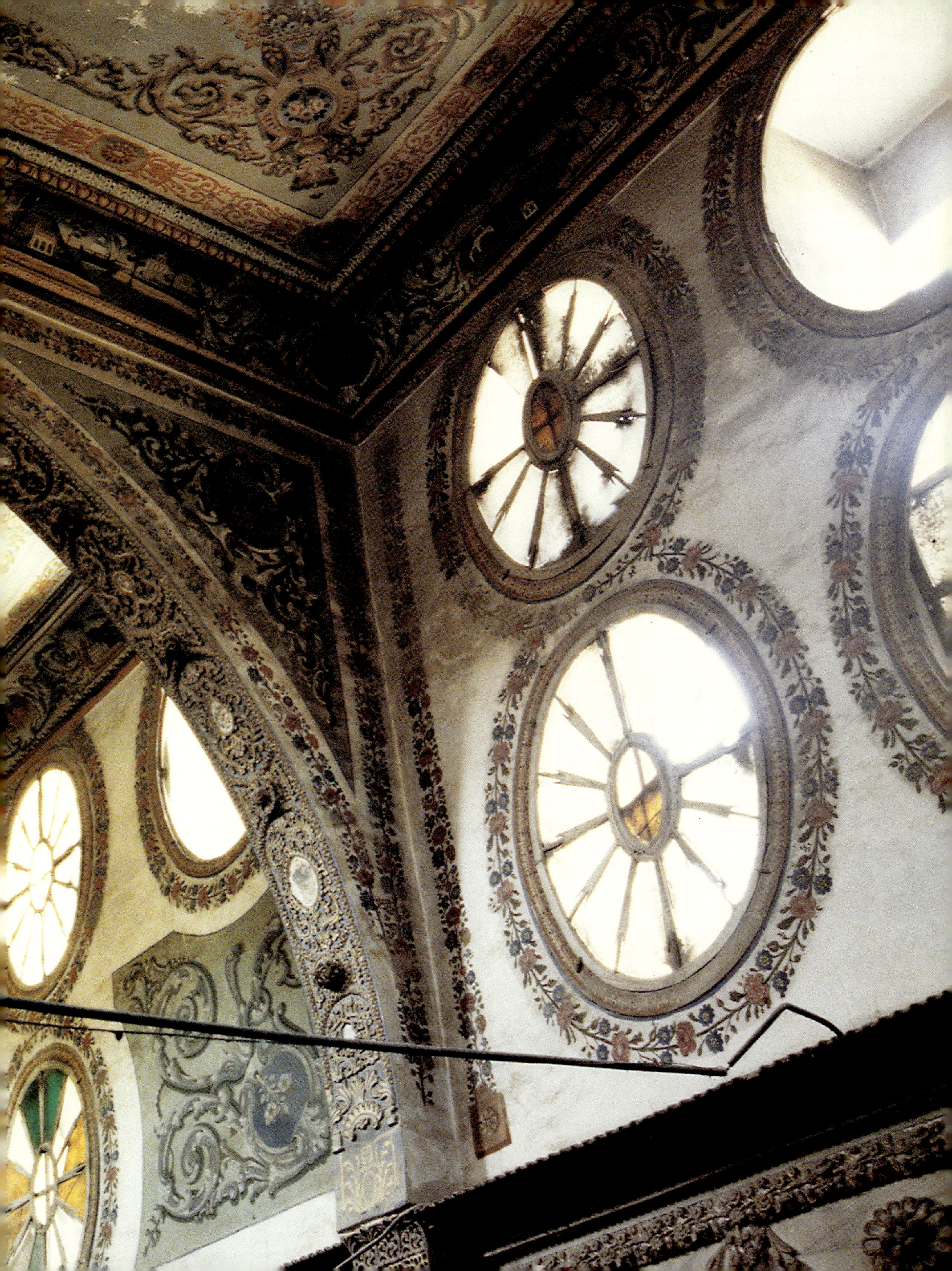

with the French troops sent out after the 1860 massacre of the Christians in Damascus, in case there was any more trouble. When the mission ended, he decided not to return to France, but to set up a photographic studio in Beirut. It became one of the most successful enterprises of its type – between father, mother and son Bonfils (they were all photographers) they produced some three thousand images of the Middle East.

In 1907, the family returned to France. The story does not end there, but shifts to America, where, in 1889, the Semitic Museum had been founded at Harvard. Its first Curator, Professor David Lyon, started collecting photographs of the Middle East – in particular, the Holy Land – buying them from agents of the big commercial studios, including the Bonfils *atelier*. By the 1930s, the museum had rather run out of steam and, when the Second World War broke out, the photographic collections were packed up and put in the attics; the top floor of the museum was rented to the Center for International Affairs, and soon everyone forgot that the pictures had ever existed. Years went by and, in the course of time, Henry Kissinger became a Fellow of the Center and kept an office there. In 1970, at the time of the Vietnam War (when Kissinger was National Security adviser to the US President), two young radical women tried to blow him up by planting a bomb in front of the building. No-one was hurt, but the blast

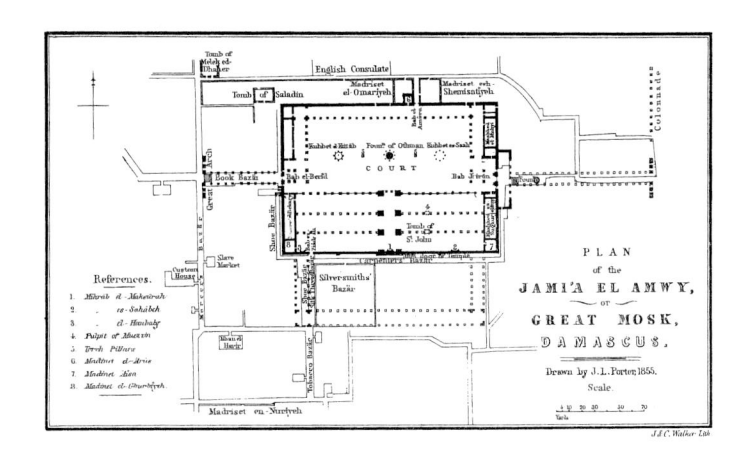

Above: Josias Porter's map of the Umayyad Mosque and surroundings, including the British Consulate.

Left and opposite: Two Bonfils photographs of the main reception hall at Bait Nizam, taken in the 1870s and wrongly captioned (in French) as the British Consulate.

33. Damas. Intérieur de maison. — Consulat anglais (Dujeni)

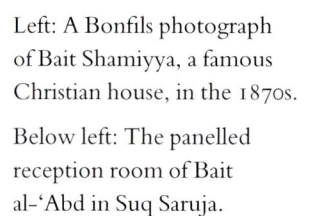

Left: A Bonfils photograph of Bait Shamiyya, a famous Christian house, in the 1870s.

Below left: The panelled reception room of Bait al-'Abd in Suq Saruja.

Below: Street elevation in the Qanawat district, just outside the old city wall.

Bottom: The striking European-style façade of Bait Yaghmur in Qanawat.

blew a hole in the ceiling of the Center and, when the damage was being inspected, the hidden pictures were discovered. They are a priceless record of the houses, streets and monuments of late 19th-century Damascus, but it is interesting to see that no grand Muslim house was photographed – only consulates and Christian and Jewish houses, these being accessible to foreigners.

The old city of Damascus had begun to spill over its encircling wall very early on in its history. The nearby village of Salihiyya was first settled in the 12th century by Muslim refugees from the bloodbath of the Crusader conquest of Jerusalem. In 1675, there was enough traffic on the road connecting Salihiyya with Damascus for the authorities of the time to have it paved, and a couple of years later the French Consul in Aleppo reported that 'most of the people of Damascus' had pleasant summer houses there. By the time Richard and Isabel Burton went to live in Salihiyya, it had 15,000 inhabitants.

Qanawat, a district only a few steps west of the old town, grew up around the Roman aqueduct which took water into the old city. Being so close, but not actually inside the wall, made it a favourite place for both Mamluk and Ottoman officials, as was Suq Saruja, also west of the walls. Suq Saruja had once been only fields of roses (cultivated for their oil) dotted with tombs and shrines, but by the 19th century it was so bustling with Ottoman civil servants and military men that it became known as Little Istanbul.

The village of Midan, a ribbon development trailing along the road south from the old city like the tail of a kite, was where the grain and the livestock that fed Damascus were traded, and it was also the route that, annually, thousands of pilgrims took on their way to Mecca. For this reason, it was a popular place (especially in the Mamluk period) for the rich and the powerful to do visible good works: the road was lined with mosques, schools, baths, tombs, orphanages and other public buildings for the benefit of the pilgrims – and to pave their donors' way to paradise.

Over the centuries, Midan gained a reputation for being rather a fanatical and backward area – which is probably why, in the middle of the 19th century, the 'Abd family established another large house in the newly fashionable Suq Saruja district. The 'Abds were already a powerful clan, but in 1850 a new member of the family was born who was to rise to dizzy heights in the Ottoman Empire. Ahmad 'Izzat al-'Abd became secretary of the Sultan and the second most powerful man in the Empire: 'The Mighty Shadow behind the Throne of Constantinople' is how the English traveller Gertrude Bell described him. According to a British intelligence report at the beginning of the First World War, 'Izzat Pasha was the most likely candidate to become King of Syria, should the Arab Revolt succeed – something the British were clearly not keen on, since the report describes him as an 'old intriguer, not religious, un-safe'. Instead, 'Izzat Pasha became Grand Vizier of Turkey at the end of the war, and responsible for armistice negotiations. An Austro-Hungarian general who knew him took a completely different view from the British, describing him as a 'knightly character' who was greatly respected.

Both the 'Abd houses are still standing – but in very poor repair. The palace in Midan had three courtyards and no less than six painted reception rooms. They are divided up between many families now, and much of the panelling and decoration has been removed, but a beautiful lintel in coloured pastework gives the date: 1745. The house in Suq Saruja also has three courtyards: one of them has been damaged by fire, but it is still, overall, a fine building.

By the late 19th century, these built-up areas outside old Damascus exceeded the size of the town within the walls, but they were all constructed in traditional style. Then came a dramatic new phase of development. With the great reorganization and reform of the Ottoman Empire (known as the tanzimat) there was a need, for the first time in the history of Damascus, for non-religious public buildings: a town hall, a court-house, a police station, a jail, a parliament building, schools, hospitals. Since it would have been impossible – and inappropriate – to crowd these into the dense alleyways of the old city, a new quarter had to be created, and Marja Square came into being. As Western as anything to be seen in a provincial town in England or France, Marja Square was built on the site of the old horse-market. Nearby, the new Suq al-Hamidiyya (named after the Sultan Abdul Hamid) was constructed, mod-

An early 20th-century portrait of Ahmad 'Izzat al-Pasha al-'Abd, 'The Mighty Shadow behind the Throne of Constantinople'.

elled on the new shopping arcades or *galleries* of Europe and using iron girders, supplied by Krupp of Germany, for the roof.

A series of modern-minded Governors were appointed to Damascus at this time – Midhat Pasha, the Turk who had written the constitution of the 'new' Turkey, arrived in 1878 and, in the two short years of his reign, rebuilt the Suq al-Buzuriyya, or Spice Souk, and a large part of Straight Street as they are today. These new men were not nostalgic for the old days, nor for the old city. 'Uthman Nuri Pasha, Governor from 1889 to 1890 and again from 1892 to 1893, built himself a European-style palace in Salihiyya with a large garden all around: today it is the French Embassy and residence.

The design of this house owed nothing to old Damascus (though a hundred years later, in the 1990s, a French Ambassador decorated three of the rooms with

Stonework

Craftsmen in Damascus seem always to have been able to carve stone as though it were wood, and an extraordinary feast of their work – from Roman to Ottoman baroque – exists in the old city, sometimes still in situ, *sometimes re-used in later buildings. Stone cutters and carvers excelled at the meticulous geometry and precision required in Mamluk decoration and architecture, and centuries later produced breathtaking feats of skill for the 19th-century rococo decoration (or redecoration) of some Damascus houses.*

Above: Carved marble rose on a marble door at Bait Barudi.

Opposite above: Mamluk carved stonework on the façade of the Tayruzi hammam.

Opposite below: Carved stone disc on a door surround at Maktab 'Anbar.

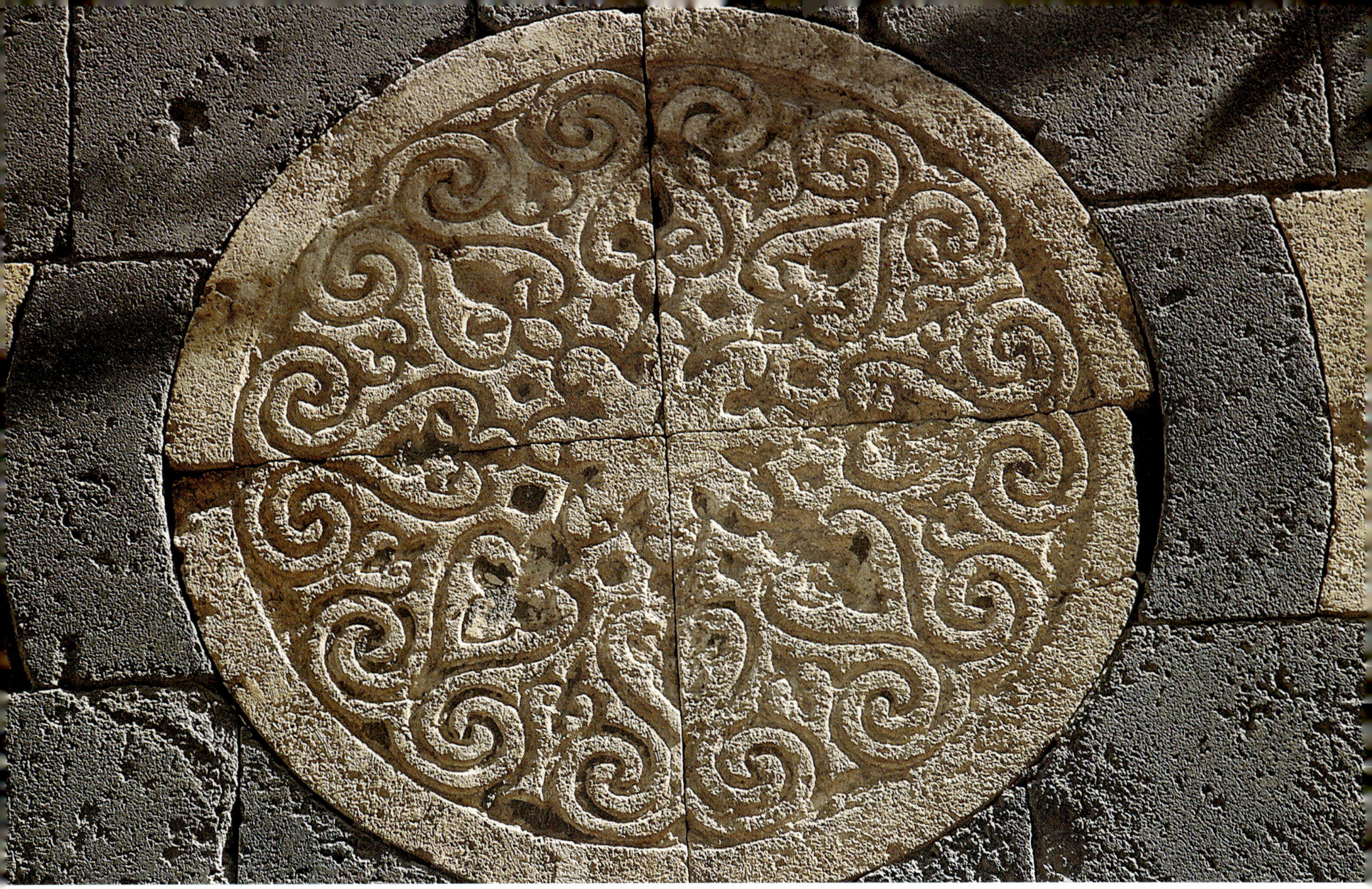

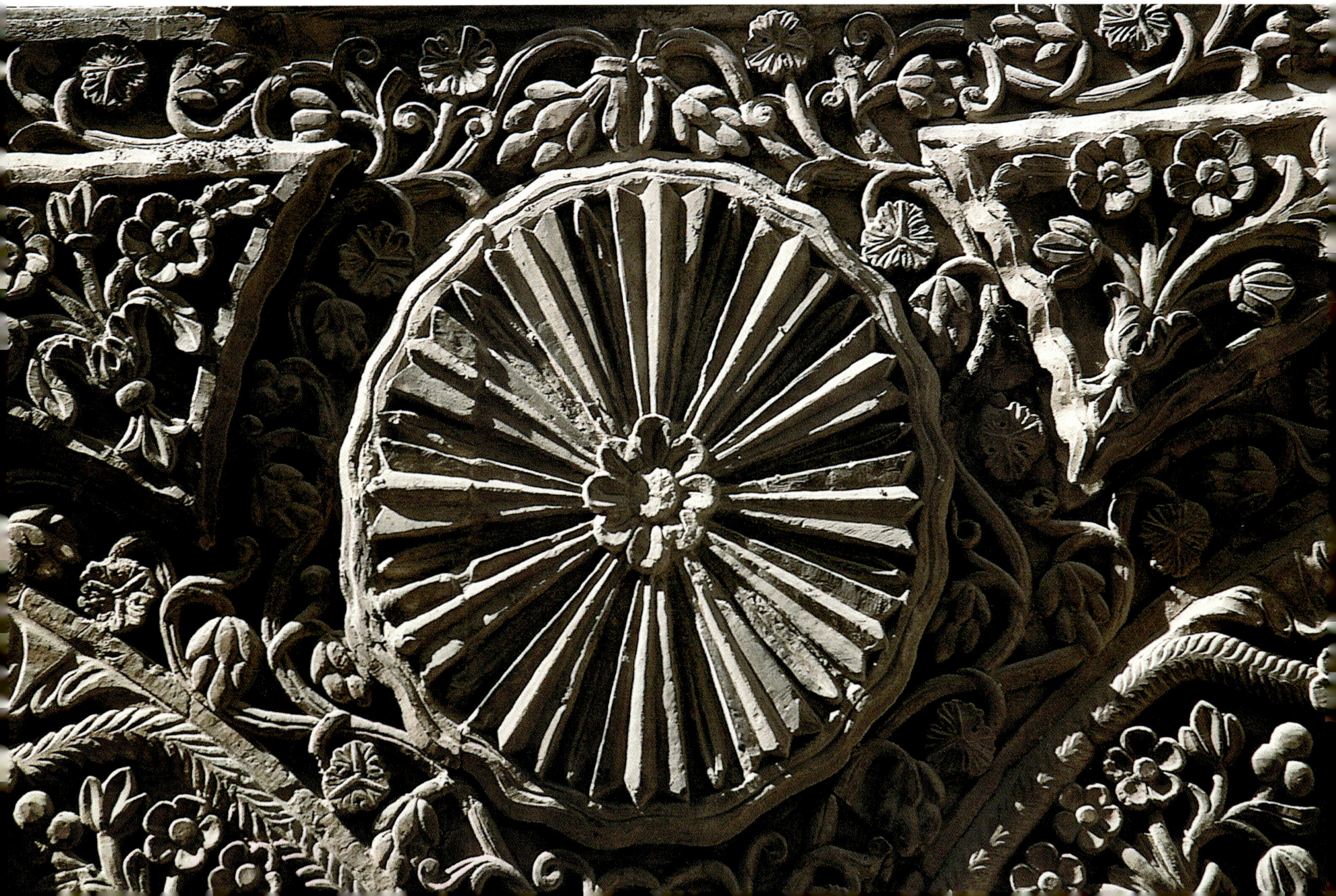

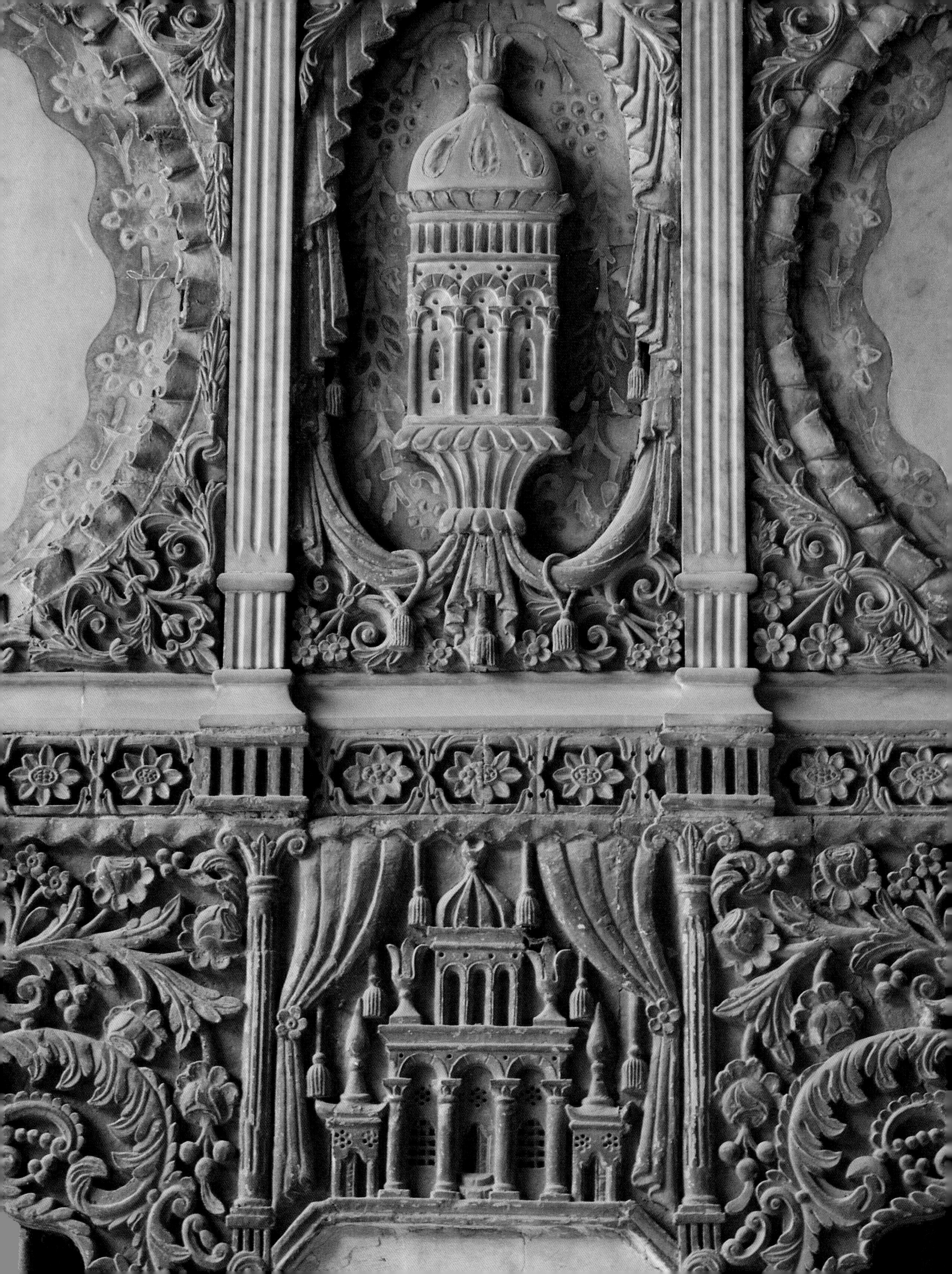

Stonework

Opposite: Intricately carved stone for the back wall of the liwan at Bait Lisbona.

Left: Detail of mother-of-pearl inlay into stone in the liwan at Bait Lisbona.

Below: Architect's drawing of the highly decorated liwan façade at Bait Lisbona.

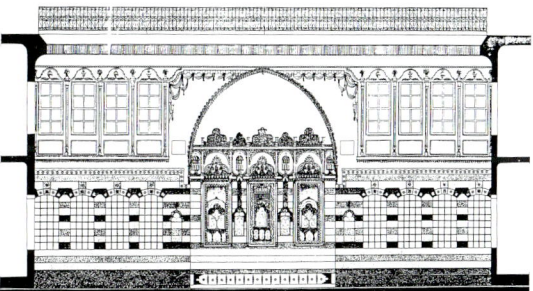

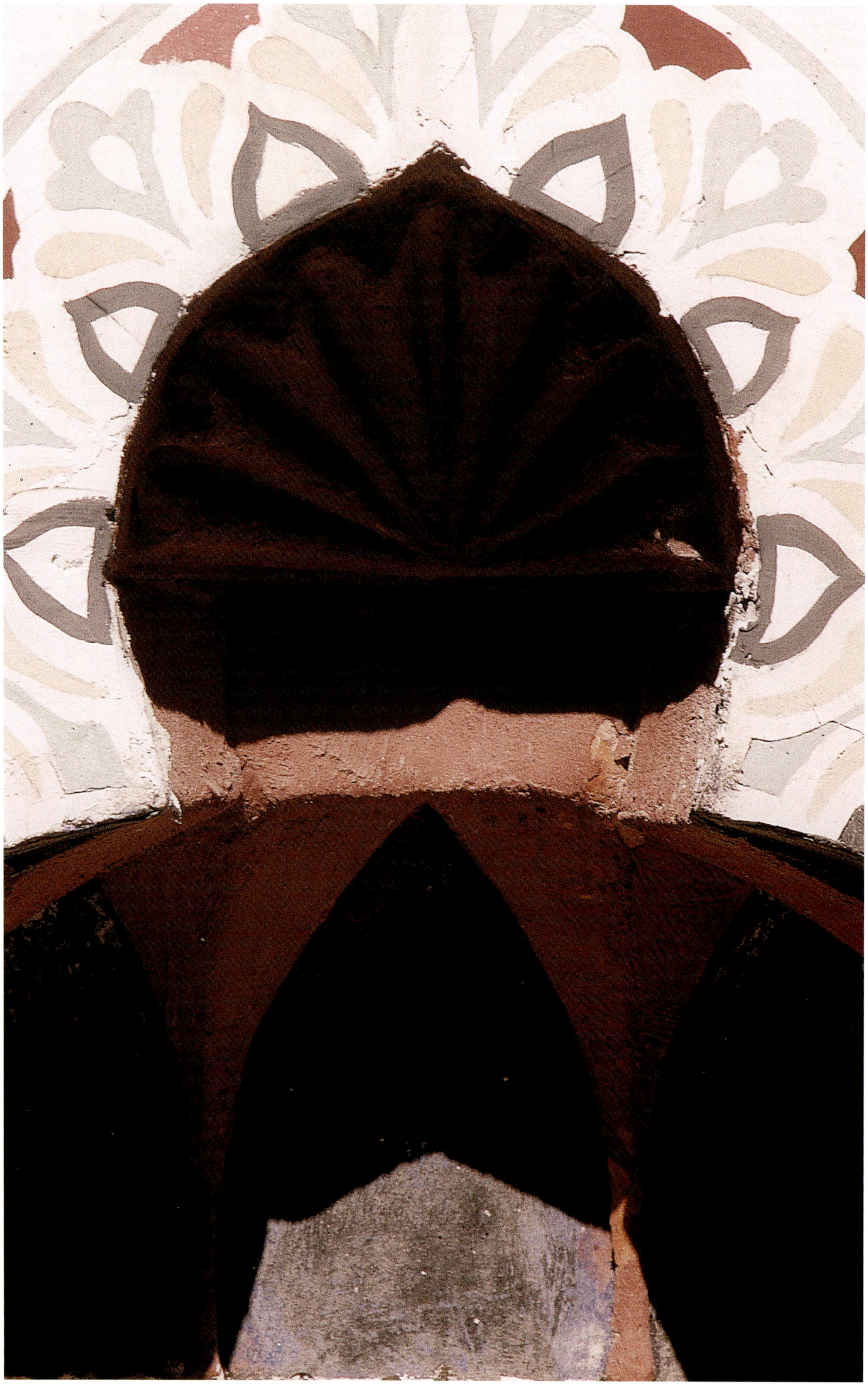

Stonework

Opposite: An 18th-century carved stone niche decorated with coloured pastework.

Top: Elaborately carved stone pineapple and arabesques at Bait Nizam.

Above: Detail of the stone carving at Bait Lisbona – drawn curtains were a favourite motif.

panelling from old houses). King Faisal, who was in power in Syria for only a couple of years before the French took over, lived in this house from 1918 until 1920, when he moved to the charming palace built by another modern-style ruler, Nazim Pasha, who was Governor of Damascus from 1895 to 1907 and then again briefly in 1909 and 1912. In his time, all sorts of innovations came to Damascus: the railway to Mecca was built, a new water supply to the old city from 'Ain al-Fija was organized, tramways and the telegraph arrived (the telegraph link between Istanbul, Damascus and Mecca is commemorated by the carved pillar in the middle of Marja Square).

When he first came to Damascus, Nazim Pasha had rented the house of Fakhri Barudi, but soon he started work on the new palace for himself in Muhajirin, on the slopes of Qasyun mountain, a previously unexploited area. Like the house of 'Uthman Nuri Pasha, Nazim Pasha's house, with its pretty neoclassical façade, stood four-square in a large garden. It is now one of the Presidential palaces. Gertrude Bell was invited to call on the Governor there. 'The *Vali* [Governor] has been eight years in Damascus', she wrote, 'and he has evidently made up his mind that in Damascus he will remain, if no ill luck befall him, for he has built himself a large house and planned a fine garden, the layout of which distracts his mind, let us hope, from preoccupations that can seldom be pleasant ...'. Miss Bell was taken to meet the Pasha's wife and children: 'I followed him upstairs into a sunny room with windows opening onto a balcony from which you could see all Damascus and its gardens and the hills behind...' The children recited French poems and played the piano for their English visitor, while 'the Pasha stood in the window and beamed upon them, the Circassian wife smoked cigarettes and bowed whenever she caught my eye; a black slave boy at the door grinned from ear to ear.' While Miss Bell was there, one of 'Abd al-Qadir's sons came to call on the Governor. His mother had been one of 'Abd al-Qadir's slaves, commented Miss Bell, and he was 'by complexion almost a Negro'.

Shortly after Gertrude Bell's visit to Damascus, John Kelman, another English traveller, remarked, 'It would be difficult to name an article that could not be bought in Damascus. The slave-market is supposed to be now suppressed, but it may be found if you know where to go for it.' He added, as a footnote, 'It is said that the

Left: Nazim Pasha's new palace was built in European style. Gertrude Bell visited him there in 1905.

Opposite: Marja Square at the beginning of the 20th century. The column, erected in 1905, marked the opening of the telegraph link between Istanbul, Damascus and Mecca.

price of a child lately offered for sale near Damascus was five sheep and a goat.' In Josias Porter's map of Damascus, the slave-market is marked not far from the entrance to the mosque, near the 'Customs House' (Khan al-Jumruk). John Bowring's 1840 *Report on the Commercial Statistics of Syria* lists 'slave trade' alongside glass, paper and woollen cloths. It was not, he wrote, carried out to a large extent in Syria; nevertheless, 'in the houses of the opulent a few negroes are to be seen and, among the wealthy Mussulmans generally, one black eunuch at least; but the annual import is small and diminishing'. These African slaves came through Egypt and were shipped from Alexandria. In Bowring's opinion, the ones who ended up in households in Damascus were fortunate: 'They are well-treated and frequently comfortably settled by their masters, after a certain period of service.' At the time in Syria, there was a war going on in the Caucasus, the area from which the white slaves known as mamluks came, and this, he wrote, had pushed up their prices: 'I saw a Georgian Mamluke of about 10 years old, sold at Nablous for 7,000 piastres – £70.' Bowring was at pains to explain to his English readers that the distinction between the white slave and his owner, in the Middle East, was slight – so much so 'that the Mamlukes of a master are frequently more advanced than his own children'.

The railway to Mecca had opened in 1908, but in those days pilgrims embarked at Qadam Station in the suburbs (which today is a sort of elephants' graveyard of the grand old steam engines and wooden carriages that once chugged across the deserts to Medina). In 1912, a competition was organized to find a design for the new Hijaz Station to be built in the centre of the city. The architect who won, and whose elegant station is now a landmark in Damascus, was Fernando de Aranda, a Spaniard whose life was unusual, to say the least. Ferdou, as he was known, was brought up at the court of the Sultan of the Ottoman Empire in Istanbul, where his father was employed as music master to the Sultan's family, and as Director of the Imperial Military Band. In 1909, when the Sultan was deposed, the de Aranda family returned to Barcelona, but Ferdou, then nearly thirty, went to live in Damascus instead. He married

Left: The ticket office – for 1st-, 2nd- and 3rd-class passengers – at the Hijaz Railway Station.

Below left: Detail of the Hijaz Station façade.

Below right: An early photograph of the Hijaz Station, designed by Fernando de Aranda.

Opposite: Panels from an old Damascus house, re-used in the 1930s to decorate a small room in Bait 'Araqtanji.

two wives (one Christian and one Muslim), had two sons, and died in 1969 when he was ninety-one years old. He is buried in the Muslim cemetery at Bab al-Saghir. De Aranda had never actually qualified as an architect, so he could not sign his work officially, which has led to a great deal of confusion about which buildings he was involved with; but the railway station was undoubtedly his – and a triumph. The sad part is that the station was completed only just before the outbreak of the First World War and no trains have left it for Medina since Lawrence of Arabia and the Arab army blew up the tracks in the desert to cut the supply lines of the Turkish army. Today, the station is a ghost of the past, with ticket booths for 1st-, 2nd- and 3rd-class passengers, but every morning in summer a steam train leaves for Zabadani in the Anti-Lebanon mountains, and once a week there is a train to Amman in Jordan.

De Aranda also designed some private houses in Damascus – all outside the old city. The best known of these are two large villas in gardens, on the hill behind the French Embassy. During the First World War, the architect found himself the unpaid consul for most of the Allied powers, whose own consuls had left on the outbreak of hostilities. For his services, de Aranda was decorated with the *Légion d'Honneur* by the French Government, making him the second unlikely candidate (the first being 'Abd al-Qadir, the Algerian hero) to receive this honour in Damascus.

The idea of living in a house outside the city wall became even more desirable when motor cars became commonplace and, more and more, the grand old families and wealthy merchants began to move out to Salihiyya, Muhajirin and the growing new suburbs.

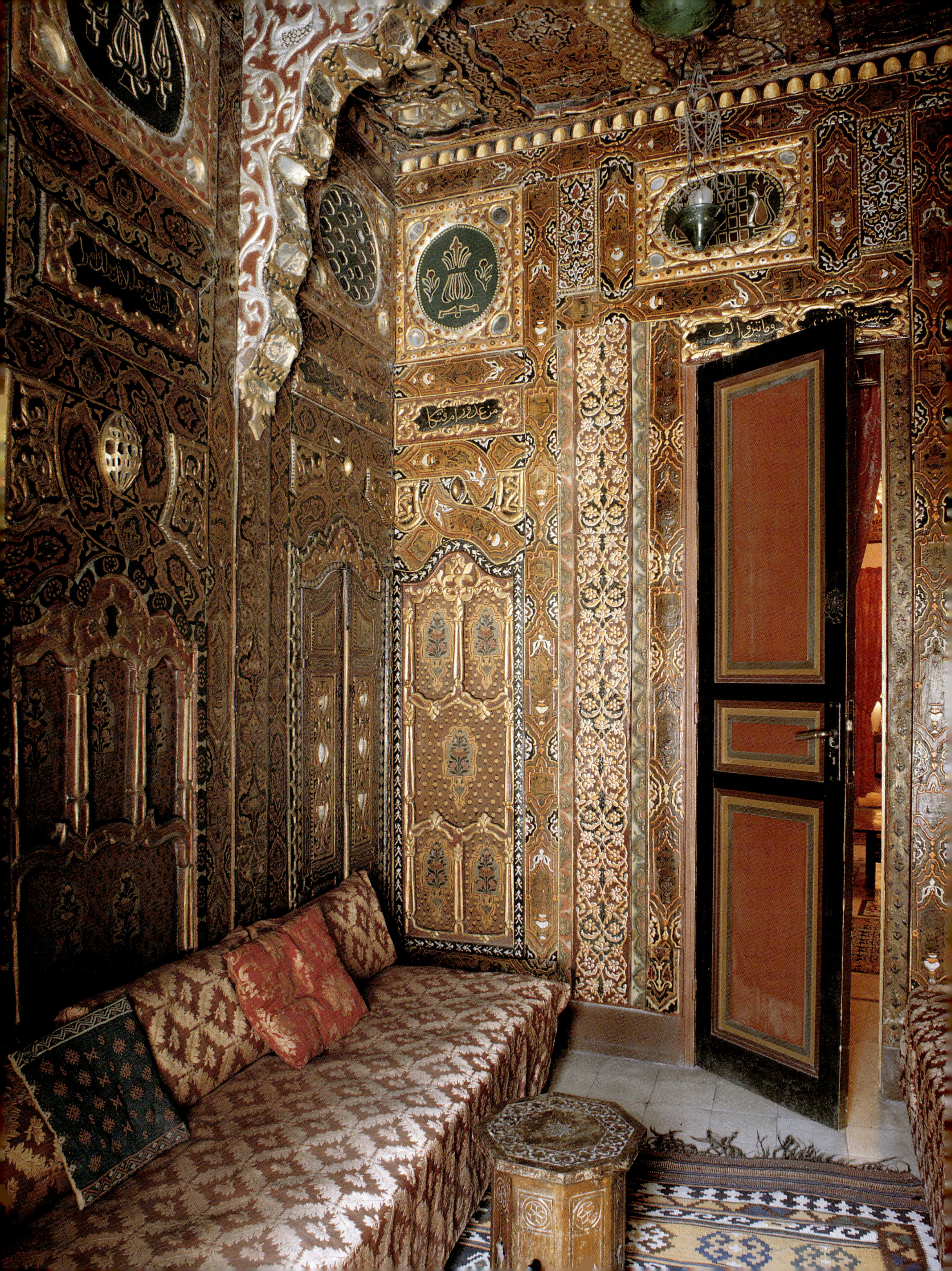

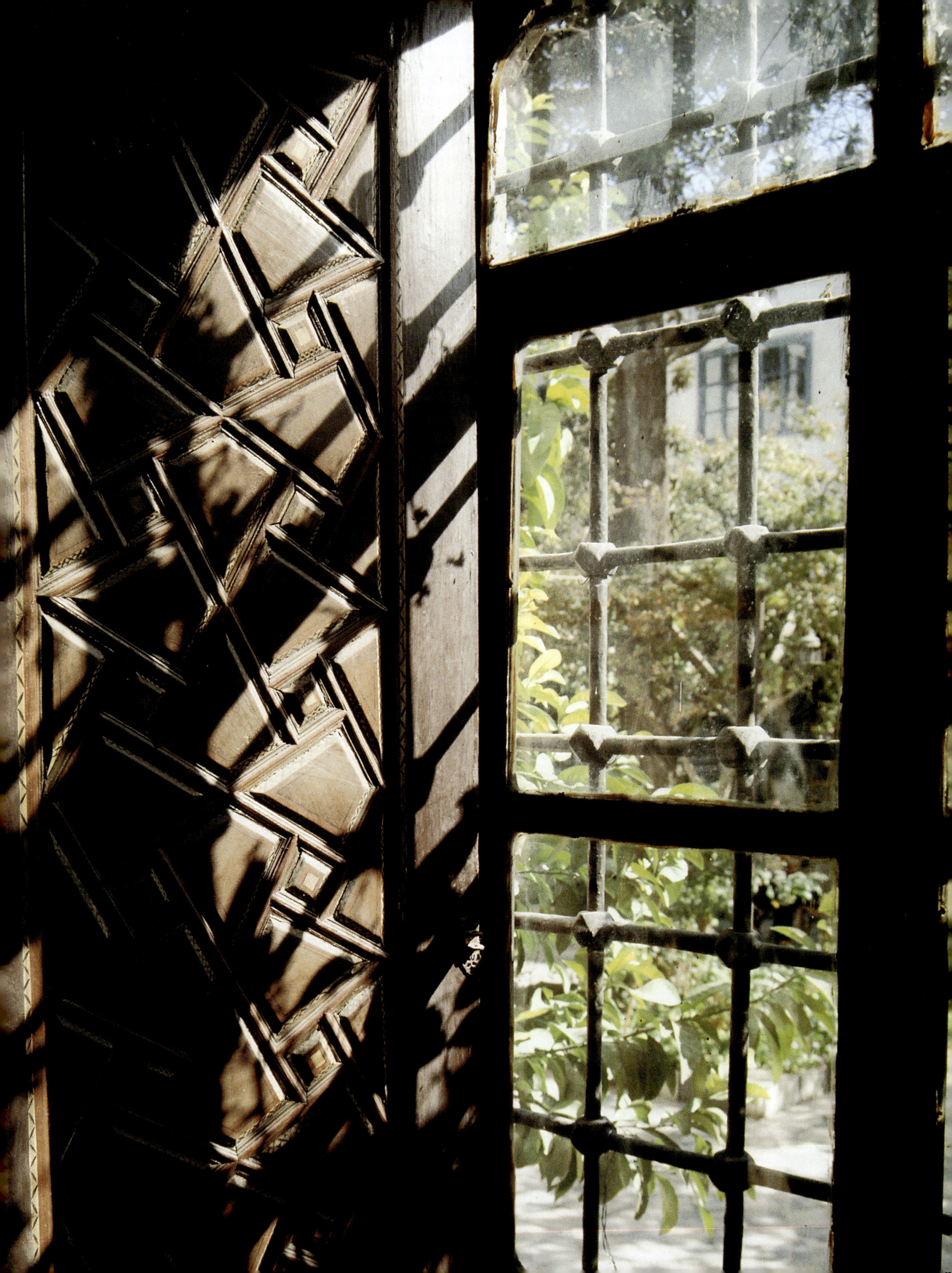

Windows

Opposite: Wooden window shutters in complex geometric design at the Historical Museum.

Left: The carved woodwork on the windows at Bait Barudi echoes the paintings above them.

Below: Slender pillars and delicate wood carving decorate a wall of windows at Bait Lisbona.

Traditionally, the windows of a Damascus house were simple, shallow-arched openings in the black-and-white striped walls of the courtyards, perhaps decorated on the lintel with coloured paste designs. Their protective ironwork was simple too. Later, in the 19th century, European influence inspired bigger, more ornate windows with lots of carved-wood decoration. The protective ironwork became fancier (sometimes even an integral part of the window design). More and more, windows were opened on the outside walls of the houses.

Windows

Corner of a spectacular room at Bait Barudi, where the walls are entirely taken up with carved niches, each with an oval window above.

198

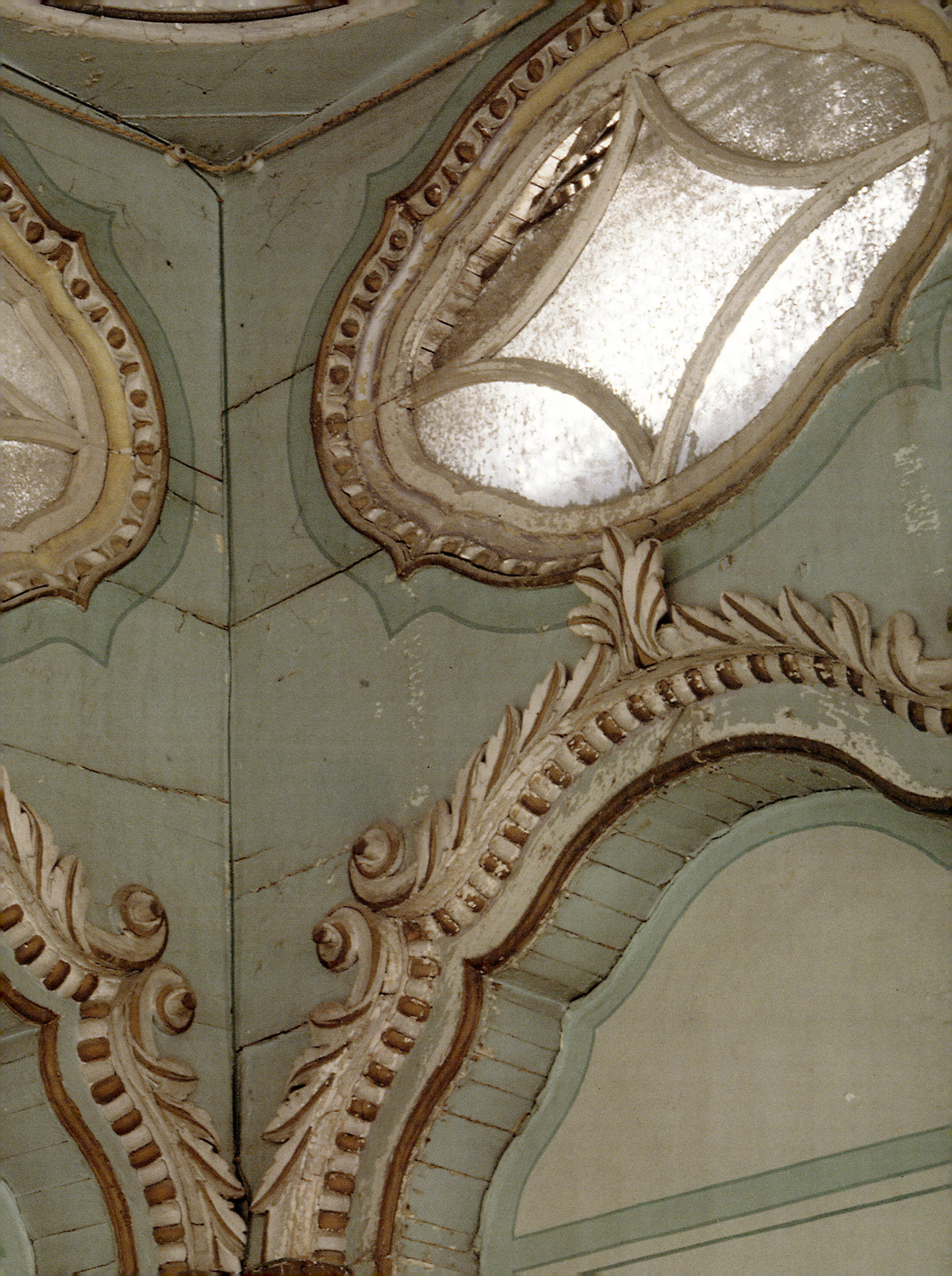

Windows

Above: The North African-style windows distinguish 'Abd al-Qadir's house from all others.

Opposite: Enormously tall French-style windows and door illuminate the sitting room at Bait Mardam Bey.

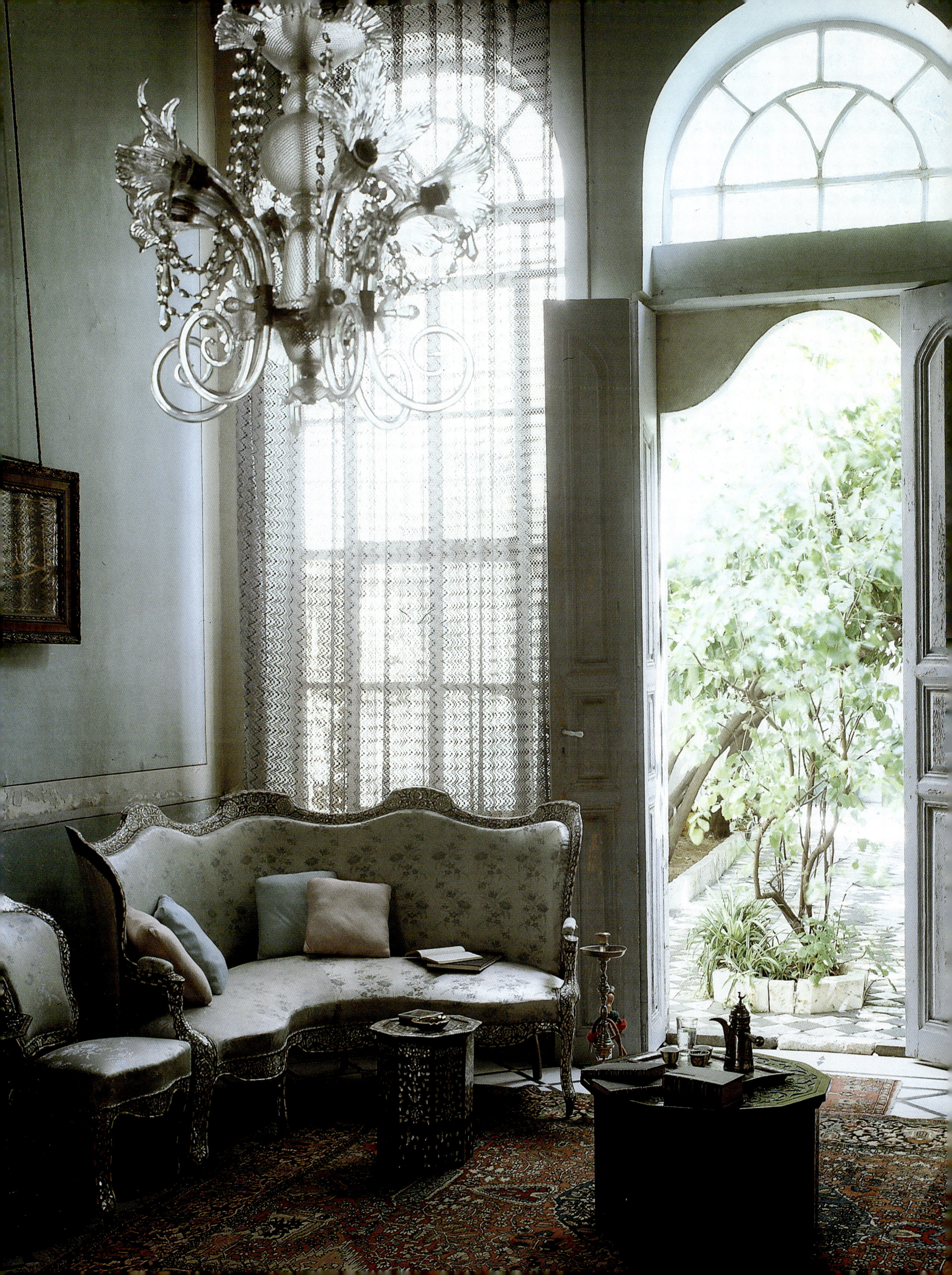

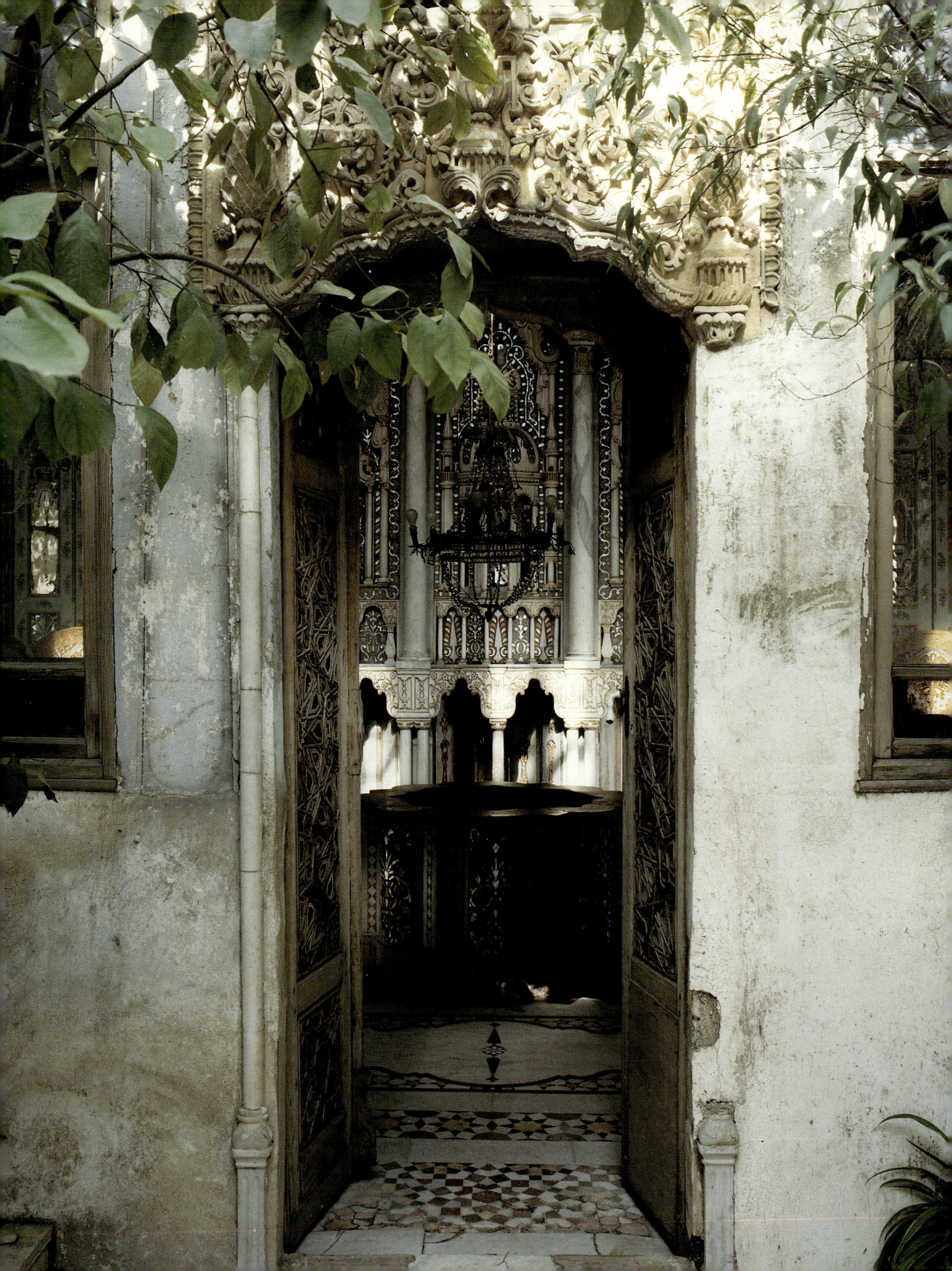

Doors

Opposite: Geometric wooden door inlaid with mother-of-pearl for the reception room at Bait Mujallid.

Left: Cupboard doors painted with little landscapes and arabesques at Bait Quwatli (a).

A house in Damascus may have many different types of door: entrance doors were traditionally quite simple; made in heavy wood studded with iron nails, they often had smaller doors set into them to make coming and going easier. Interior doors were altogether more elaborate: inlaid with mother-of-pearl or made out of a jigsaw of wooden geometrical shapes put together. Cupboard doors were painted and gilt. As with windows, doors and their surrounds became more ornate in the 19th century.

Doors

Above: Geometric wood for a window shutter (recently restored) at Bait Siba'i.

Opposite: Door surround with rococo carving and stone pastework at Bait Nizam.

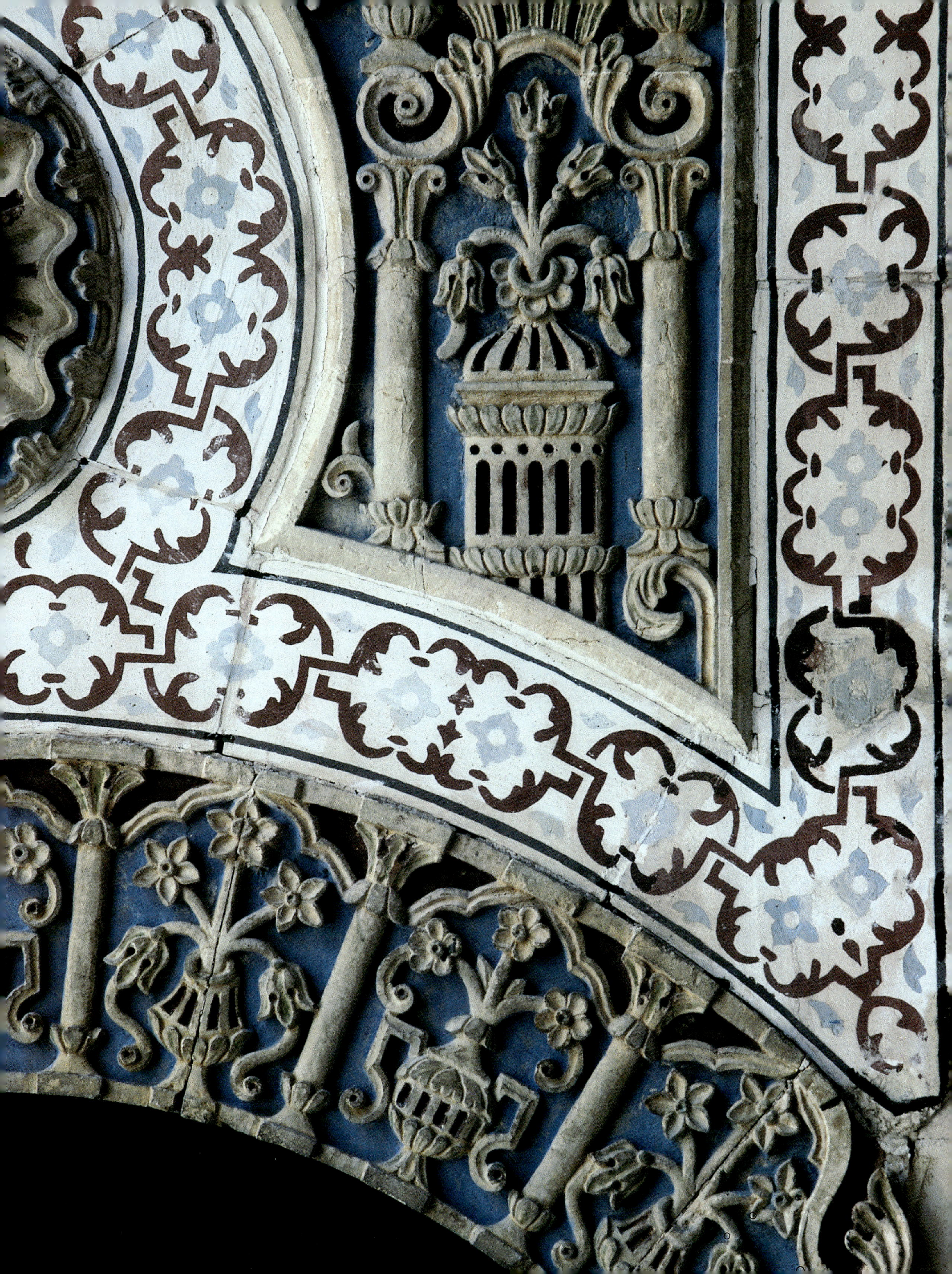

Doors

Many different designs are combined for this exquisitely worked marble and stone doorway in the courtyard at Bait Tibi.

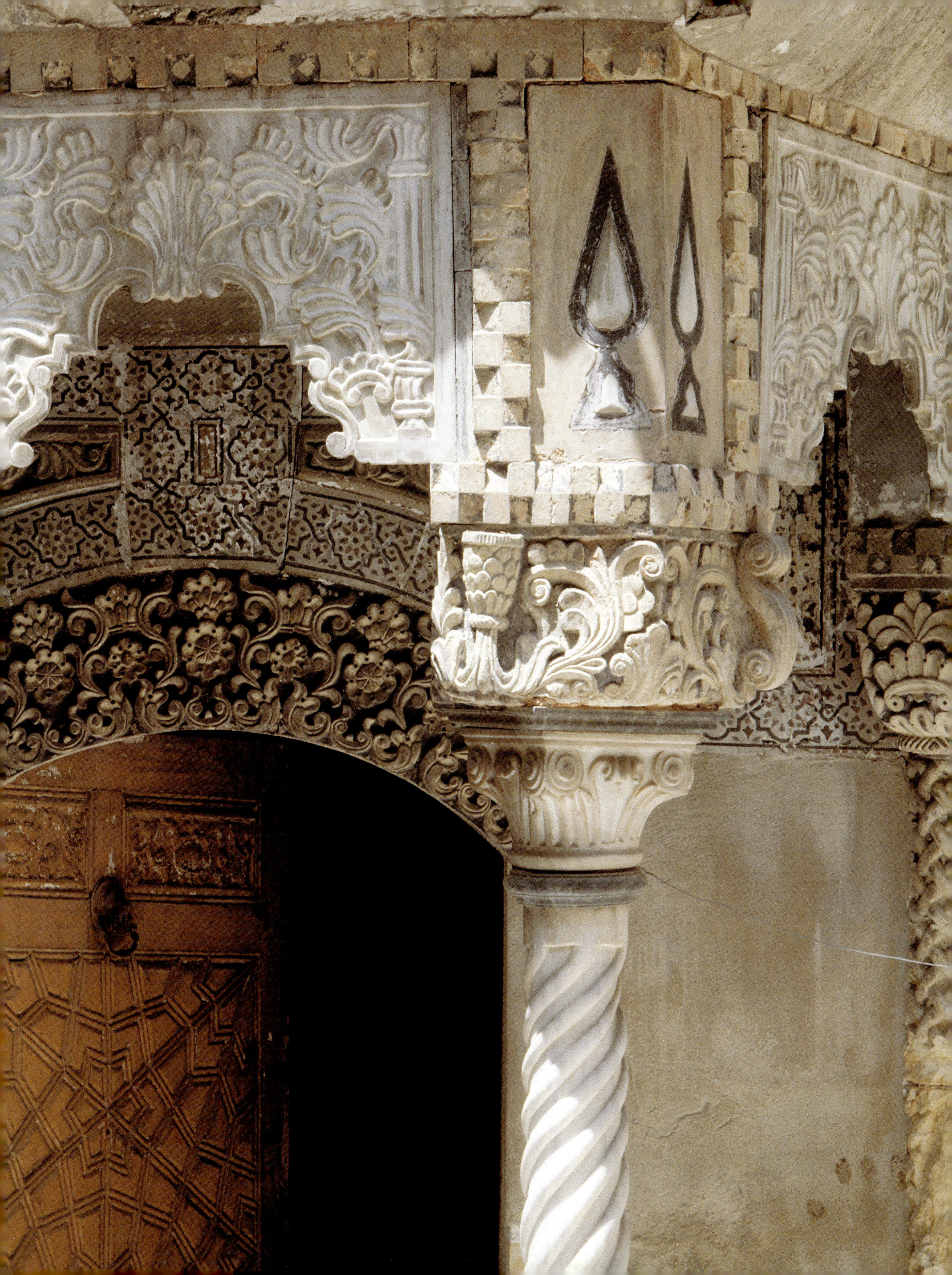

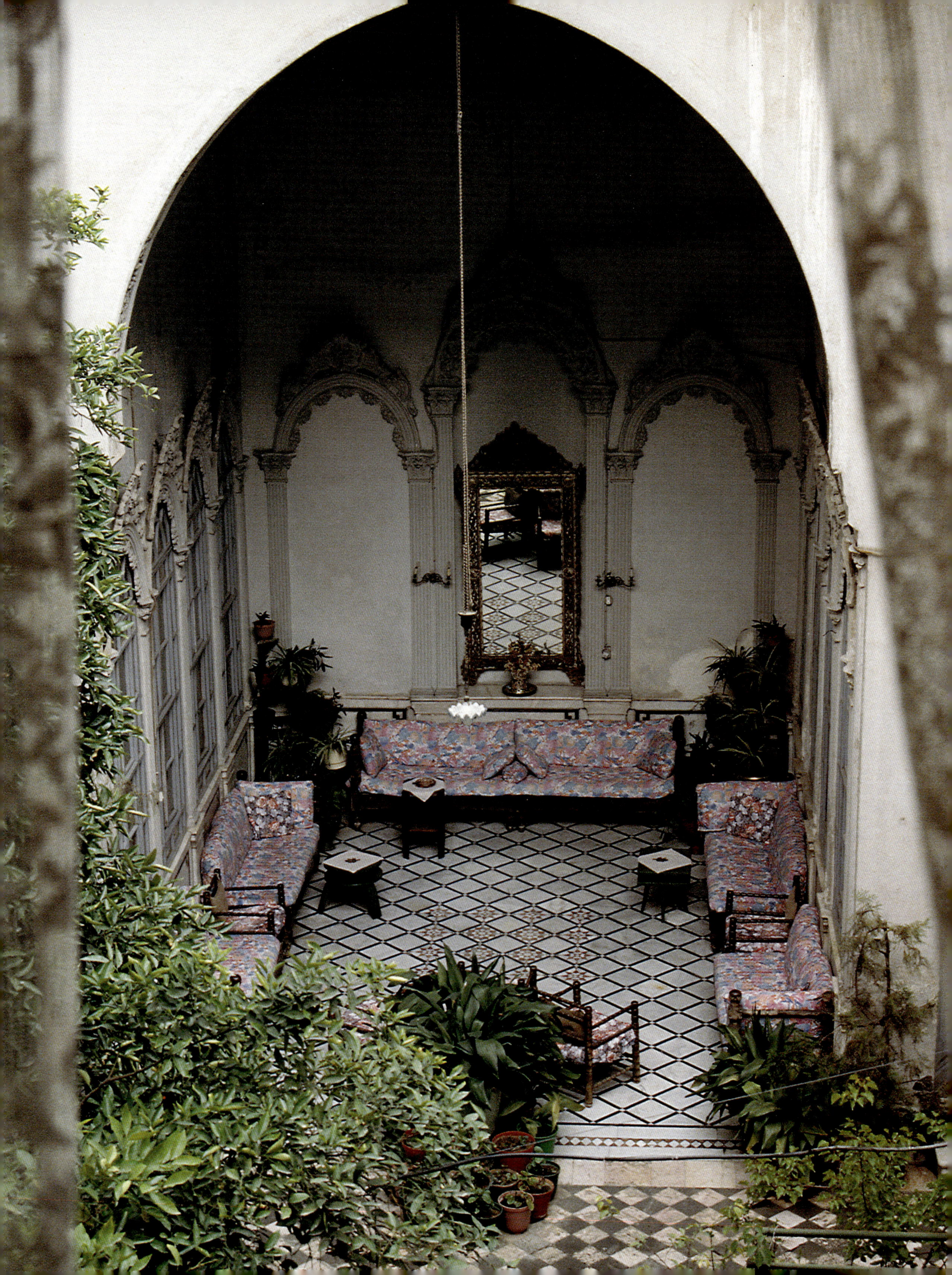

Opposite: The liwan of Bait Mardam Bey, one of the few houses still lived in by the family who built it. It was redecorated in its present style by the couple below: Ahmad Mukhtar Mardam Bey (1865–1911) and his wife Fatima, a greatly respected and cultured woman who was the daughter of the Mufti of Damascus. Among their descendants were three well-known poets, one of whom, Khalil, wrote the Syrian Anthem.

Their former homes in the old city were abandoned, the courtyards and rooms divided up and rented out as storehouses or small factories, or as accommodation for poor families and Palestinian refugees (of whom there are more than a quarter of a million in greater Damascus). As an architect remarked, there are villages in houses now, instead of the other way round. No one family any longer had the overall responsibility – or the money – to maintain the houses, and so, over the years, they have become semi-derelict or have collapsed altogether.

Some families felt nostalgic about the old city, and their new apartments incorporated a 'feature' such as panelling from an old house – perhaps even *their* old house – in the city. The most astounding example of this is Bait 'Araqtanji, built in the 1930s for Yusuf 'Araqtanji, a successful doctor; it later became the residence of the Spanish Embassy in Damascus. On the outside, the house is pure Art Deco style, but inside you are back in the world of the Arabian Nights with whole panelled rooms (dating back to 1765), stone and marble floors and fountains, painted ceilings, and old blue-and-white Damascus tiles. These were all collected from the old city in the twenties and thirties – a period when many houses were being cleared for new roads or new construction, or had been shell-damaged. At this time, too, painted wood panels (dated 1797) were used to decorate the first-floor reception room of the new Fija water-supply offices near the railway station.

In the carve-up of what had been the Ottoman Empire after the First World War, France was 'given' Syria. To sweeten the pill, France's rule over the country was

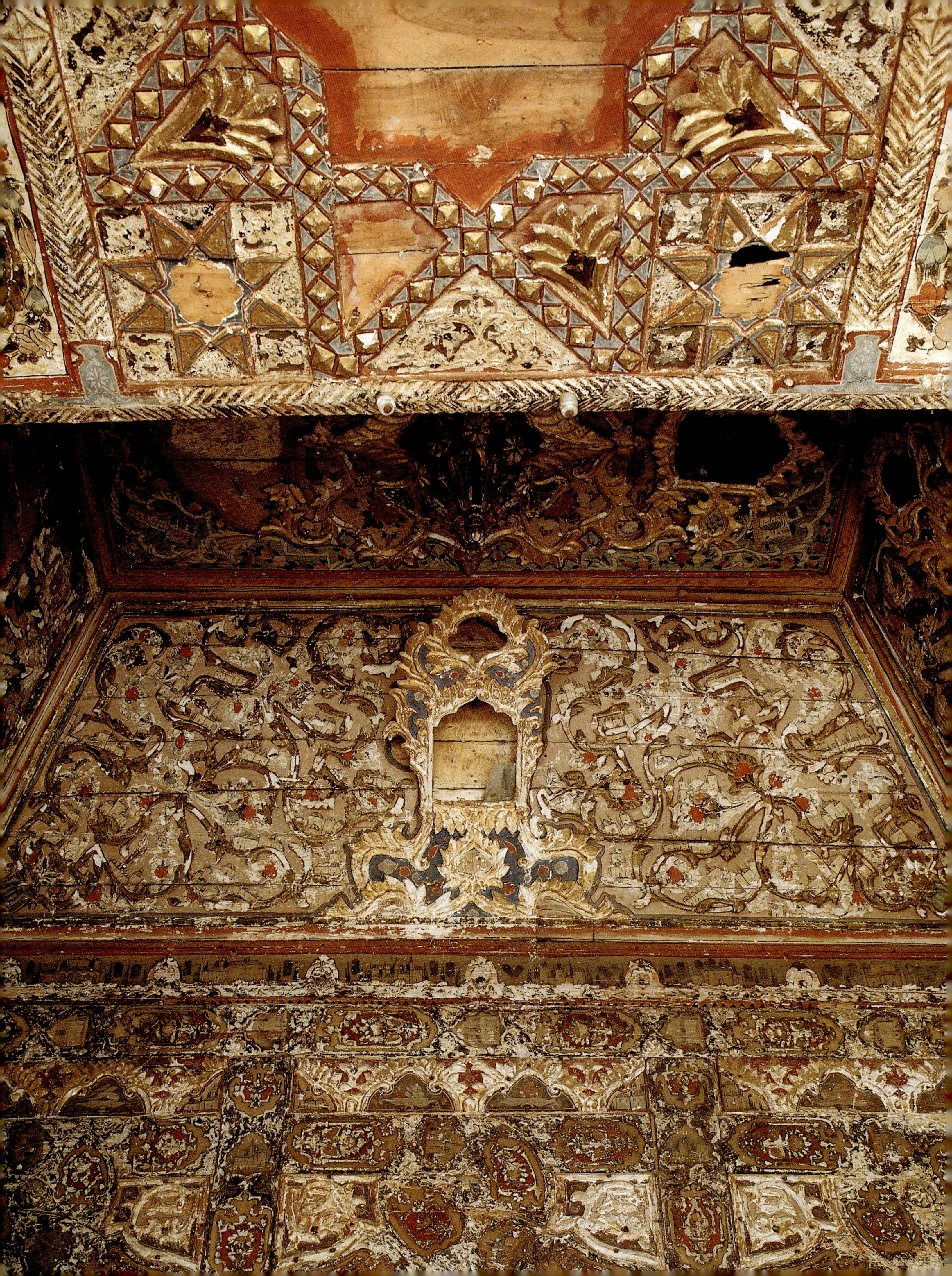

Opposite: The grand reception room at Bait Tibi is in need of restoration.

Below: The liwan at Bait Tibi with its elegant painted ceiling and stonework.

called a Mandate; it was to be only temporary, to help the nation develop and to prepare it for independence. But the Syrians opposed the French bitterly. A fierce uprising against their rule started in the Druze heartland in southern Syria in 1925 and spread to Damascus. In October that year (as mentioned earlier), the Azem Palace was burned and looted by the rebels and the whole city was in a ferment. The French authorities became alarmed and, in an attempt to subdue the rebels, attacked the old city with tanks and shells. The fighting lasted for three days, at the end of which a part of old Damascus was totally destroyed. (Rebuilt in ugly modern style, this area is today known as Hariqa, meaning 'Fire'.) It was another death-blow to the old city. In those three days of terror, 135 people were killed and 250 old houses destroyed, including Bait Murad Quwatli, supposedly one of the richest and most beautiful houses in Damascus (not to be confused with the Bait Quwatli which was the British Consulate).

A French woman, Alice Poulleau, who witnessed the drama, vividly described it: 'Between Hamidiye and Straight Street is an area of horror where nothing is

211

Below: Evening light on the houses and khans of the Saddle Souk (Suq Sarujiyya) overlooking the river.

Right: 19th-century drawing of the picturesque bridge in the Saddle Souk.

standing and where, in certain places where people are buried under the rubble of their houses, there is a sickening smell. Everywhere the poor delicate trees, which grew in the interior courtyards, are broken and burnt. In the smoking courtyards, the Bedouin are scavenging … electric wires are lying everywhere and the broken pipes are flooding the dead streets.… In the worst part, on the edge of Straight Street, it looks as though a volcano had erupted and is still smoking.'

The foreign consuls protested at the brutality of the repression, but in 1926, barely six months later, when the rebels began to stir again, the French shelled the Midan quarter. This was poignantly recorded by Alice Poulleau: 'I wonder what can be left of Midan. Today they burnt a mosque … and a great number of houses all around it. Nearly everything has been pillaged; the inhabitants of the quarter have fled.'

After the uprising, using money levied from the inhabitants of Damascus as a 'fine', the French put a barbed-wire fence around the old city and widened the surrounding streets into today's boulevards, to isolate Damascus from the Ghuta oasis (where rebels took refuge) and its suburbs. Alice Poulleau watched all this take place and warned: 'Damascenes, if you do nothing, in ten years your ancient Damascus will look like Lavallois-Perret' (an ugly industrial suburb of Paris).

In 1936 and again in 1968 (though the French had long gone by then), the architect and urban planner, Michel Écochard, was asked to propose schemes for the new Damascus. Écochard, according to the French writer

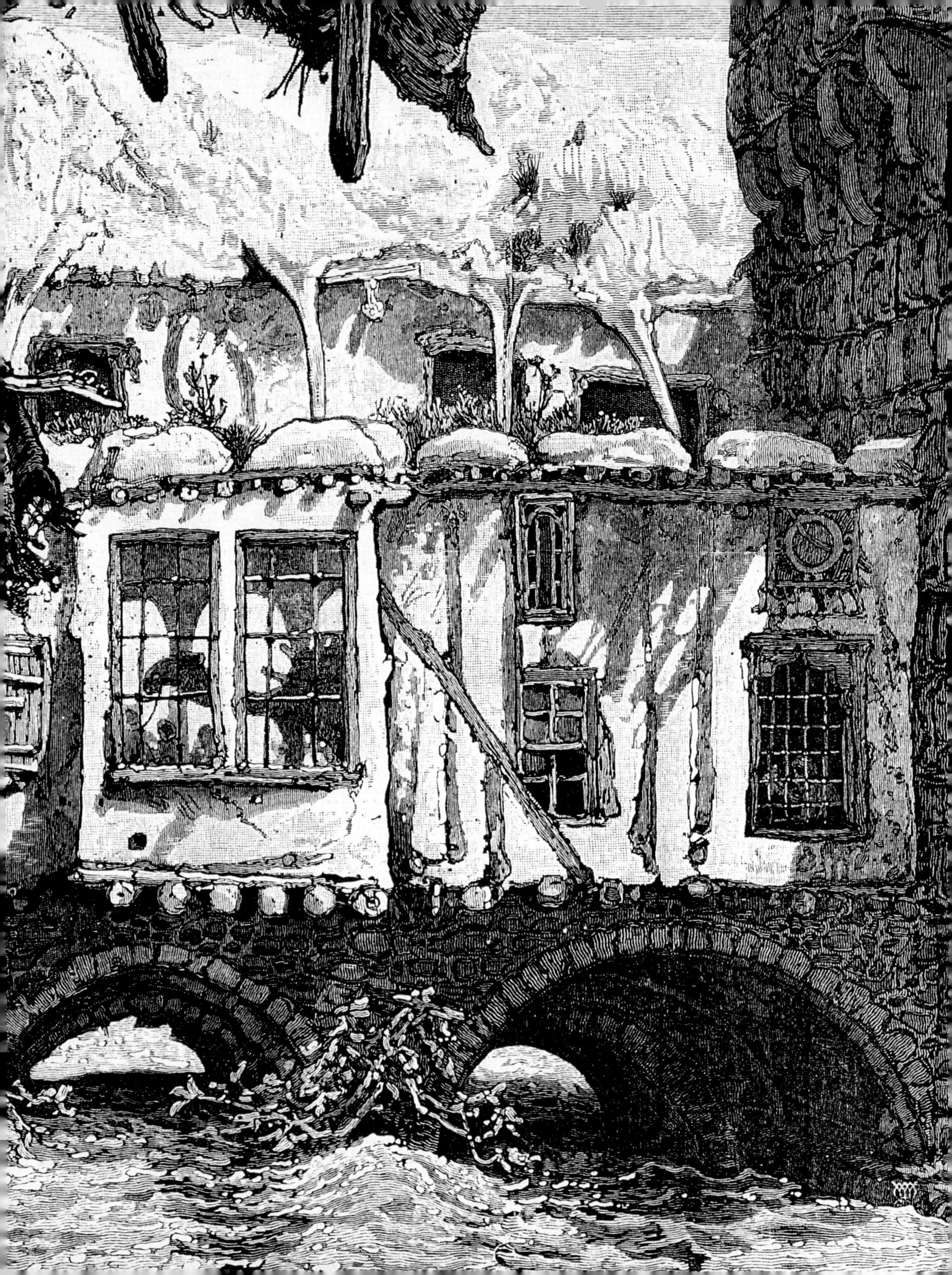

Gérard Degeorge, who is passionate about old Damascus, was not particularly sympathetic to those who felt the old city should be preserved as a whole: 'They do not take into account that houses crumble and melt in the rain every day and that to maintain just the character of the outside would be infinitely more costly than simply building a new house in modern materials.' Following Écochard's plan, the old souks clinging like barnacles to the Citadel and the city walls were cleared away, and redevelopment began in Midan and Suq Saruja and in the old city itself, where many fine houses were lost to new school buildings, street-widening schemes and the so-called 'enhancement' of monuments. A public outcry prevented the modernization plan from going ahead, and instead, in 1972, a law was brought in forbidding all demolition and rebuilding inside the old city wall. In 1979, the old city of Damascus was named as a world heritage site by UNESCO. Suq Saruja is now half-developed; happily, the picturesque narrow street with the Haramain and Rabi' backpacker hotels (both in little courtyard houses) is still untouched. In Midan, redevelopment continues, and in the Zuqaq al-Sakhr quarter, pretty houses are to be sacrificed for a big new hotel. Qanawat, luckily, remains more or less intact, though in a very poor state of repair.

Despite the new rules, in the 1980s a road was driven through the old city, past the Citadel to the Umayyad Mosque. The area all around was cleared of its limpet souks, and the mosque itself restored. Lots of houses were lost in the process, and more disappeared when the Iranians built a fancy new mosque over the tomb of Ruqayya, the great-granddaughter of the Prophet Mohammed. When the road to the Great Mosque was carved out, the newly exposed façades along it were painted in 'Mamluk' stripes and the new shops were decorated with flimsy wooden porches in an 'oriental' design, to make it all look more picturesque. A Syrian writer put many people's feelings into words: 'We *have* a genuine old Arab city, we don't need a Disney World version, we just need to look after the one we have.'

But the old city no longer has the powerful and the rich and the influential living within its walls to defend it. Only one of the grand old families still has its home there: the Mardam Beys, whose house (established by a powerful 'notable' ancestor, 'Uthman Mardam Bey, in the mid-19th century) is between the Suq al-Hamidiyya and Hariqa. Their public courtyard, the salamlik, was damaged in the French bombardment of the city (the handsome remains of it can be seen in the National Museum) and the family live in the attractive haramlik courtyard.

Modern Damascus now numbers around four million people and the old walled city is only a tiny part of the huge agglomeration that has grown up in the last fifty years, but it is the heart and the soul of the place – unique, unspoilt and endlessly fascinating. It is the old city that makes Damascus 'Damascus' and not just any other concrete city of the sort that can be found today anywhere on the globe. It is the old city, with its bread ovens, barbers, hammams and courtyard houses that visitors come to see.

'Damascus is not outstandingly rich in public buildings,' says Stefan Weber, 'but it has a treasure trove of wonderful houses.' Marwan Musselmani, a Syrian photographer, published a superb book of black-and-white pictures of some of the best Damascus houses in 1983. He is pessimistic about the future – some houses will be saved, he thinks, but most of the old city will be redeveloped. For this reason, he believes his book to be the most important thing he has done in his life. 'At least I have recorded the palaces of the old city before they all disappear', he says. About eight of the houses he photographed have already vanished; others, such as the precious Bait Tibi, are in a perilous state, and the picturesque houses of the old Saddle Souk (Suq Sarujiyya), along the river as you enter the old city, look as though they will collapse into the water at any time.

Old Damascus faces the biggest threat to its existence in thousands of years – not from war, nor earthquake, but simply from neglect and indifference.

Opposite: Roof cornice at Bait Niyadu with a wavy edge made out of wooden batons.

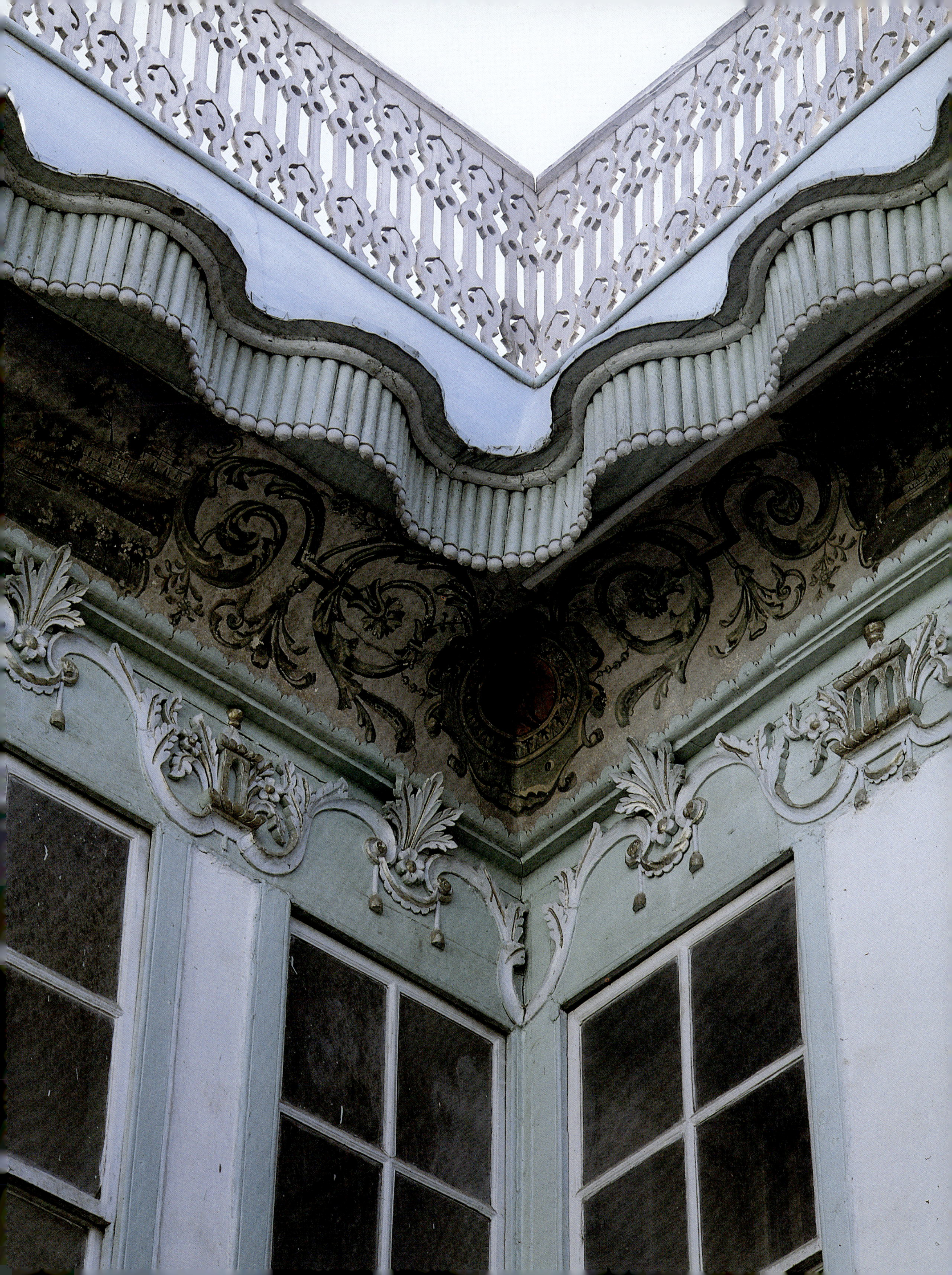

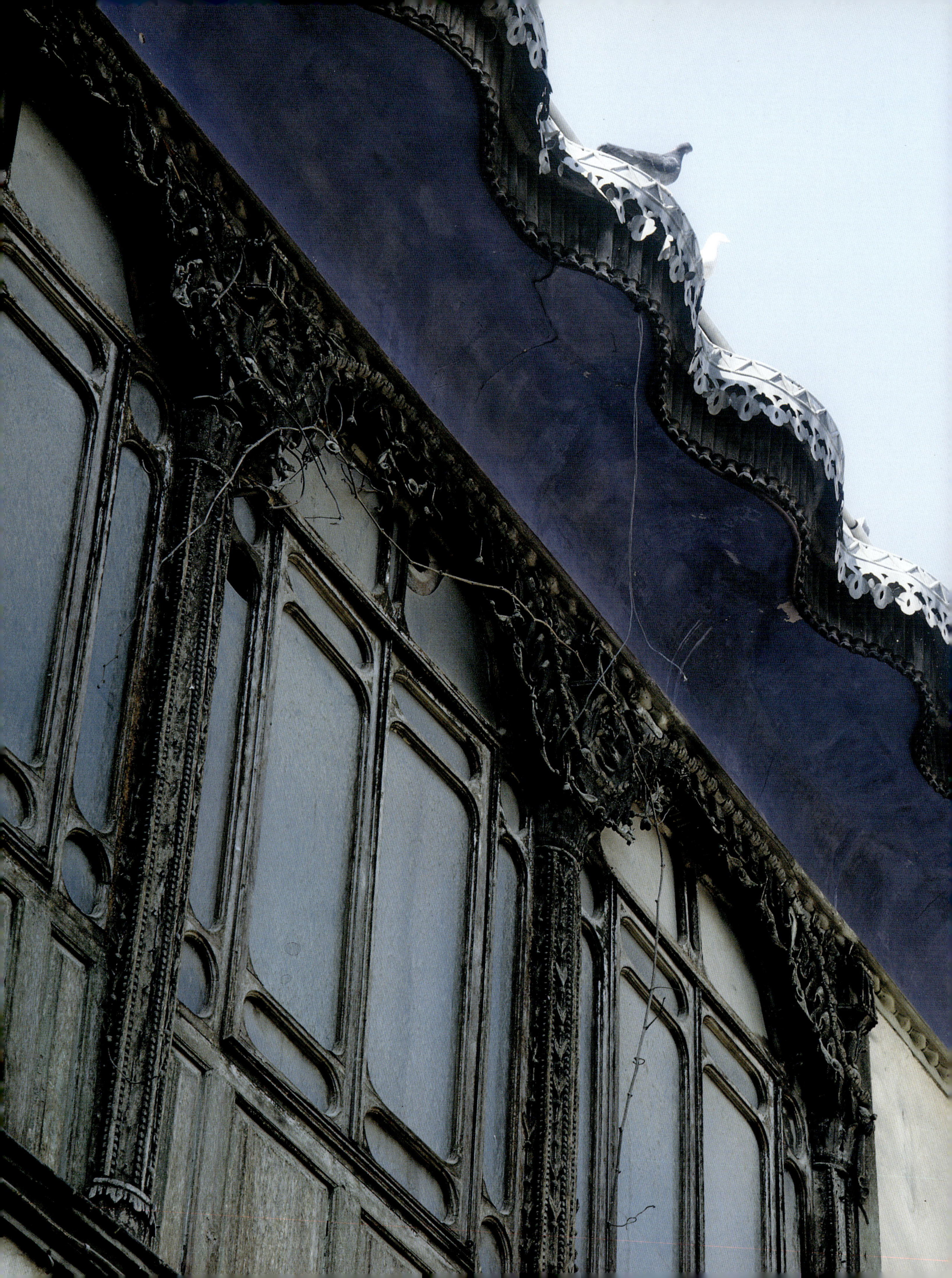

Epilogue

Opposite: Wavy roof edging at the House of the Spanish Crown with cut-out zinc protecting the wooden batons beneath.

There are glimpses of light at the end of the tunnel. In the 1990s, a number of restaurants opened in old courtyard houses – mostly in the Christian quarter, where you may drink alcohol. When the first one was announced, people in Damascus scoffed at the idea – 'Who on earth would ever want to go all the way to the old city in the evenings?' they asked; but the restaurants have been a resounding success.

A second beam of light is that, in the last few years, a handful of brave people have started a movement back to the city: Sheikha Hussah al-Sabah of Kuwait, who spent the Gulf War in Damascus and wished to say 'thank you' by doing something to help the old city, has bought three houses there, which are being restored (Arabs may buy property in Syria; foreigners have to have special permission). Then Nora Jumblatt, wife of the Druze leader in Lebanon, but herself a Damascene, bought Bait Mujallid, one of the most glorious houses in the old city. Until 1938, Bait Mujallid was the property of the Jabri family and it was Sa'id Agha Jabri, a Syrian tax-collector for the Ottoman administration, who rebuilt and restored the house between 1840 and 1877. He seems to have made a great deal of money, for he promised his wife that he would pave the floor of the qa'a with gold – but the religious authorities sensibly forbade any such thing. Another branch of the family still owns Bait Jabri, an equally beautiful – but very different – house, decorated at an earlier date (1744) with fine stone pastework.

Hikmat Shatta, an architect, and his brother have bought a charming house which was once lived in by Maryam 'Ajami, a poet and writer and friend of the intellectuals of her day (early 20th century), for whom she held a regular literary salon in the house. 'Ali 'Atassi, son of a former Syrian President, has bought a small house behind the Great Mosque, and many others are interested in acquiring something for themselves. At the same time (as mentioned earlier), the Danish Government has leased Bait al-'Aqqad, a magnificent palace in the Wool Souk off Straight Street, which has been painstakingly restored (with the Syrian Antiquities Department) by the archaeologist and museum curator Peder Mortensen, whose brainchild the project was, and which opened in 2000 as the Danish Institute in Damascus.

In order for others to be tempted to join these pioneers, it is necessary to improve the infrastructure of the city, so that it is an easier place to live in. This has been done in other historic old cities – from Fez to Vienna, from Tunis to Aix-en-Provence. Money need not be a problem; funds could be found for a project to rehabilitate Damascus. What is needed is the will and determination to do it: to create a sensitive master plan; to offer incentives to businesses or embassies to take over old houses and restore them; to have loan schemes for house improvements; to organize the parking and the traffic so that the inhabitants can come and go more easily, and – almost the most important – to improve the quality and taste of restoration work. (There are wonderful craftsmen in Damascus, but a terrible tendency to restore with inappropriate shiny marble and glitz. Indeed, some houses in the old city have been redone in such a flashy pseudo-oriental style that it might have been better if they had been allowed to fall down.)

In Europe in the 1950s and 1960s, developers recklessly destroyed many inner cities and old quarters in a new enthusiasm for everything modern – supermarkets, multistorey car parks and high-rise apartment buildings. This is bitterly regretted now, but the clock cannot be put back.

Damascus has the luxury of being able to learn from those mistakes; she does not have to make them herself.

A lovely small courtyard at Bait al-Haffar crowded with potted plants.

Key to the Maps

The houses photographed for this book are marked on the maps on pages 73–75. They are also among the principal houses in the old city, but there are many others, for every house in Damascus had its courtyard and its fountain and its reception room, large or small.

With few exceptions, all the houses are privately owned and not open to the public.

Damascus houses take the name of their owners, or their past owners, which can make things confusing; Bait Mujallid, for instance, was owned by the Mujallid family for a comparatively short time, and so it should in theory be called after the Jabri family who lived there and decorated it so splendidly in the 19th century, or after its present owner Nora Jumblatt, but somehow the name Mujallid has stuck, and so it goes on.

DAMASCUS
WEST OF THE WALLS

1. Historical Museum of Damascus
Also known as Bait Khalid al-Azem (Khalid al-Azem was President of Syria in 1962). Open to the public and well worth seeing, with many courtyards and some lovely decoration. Was the Prussian Consulate in the mid-19th century.

2. Bait al-Yusuf
One of the largest palaces in Damascus. It was flamboyantly decorated in the late 19th century by Yusuf Pasha, an important Damascus notable and the last Amir al-Hajj. Now lived in by many families.

3. Bait al-'Abd
The 'Abd family originally lived in Midan (where their huge house with several courtyards still stands, now divided up among many people). In the mid-19th century, the family built this house in fashionable Suq Saruja. It has two attractive courtyards and a third destroyed by fire. Ahmad 'Izzat al-Pasha al-'Abd rose to become one of the most powerful men in the Ottoman Empire.

4. The Rabi' and Haramain Hotels
These are the 'backpacker' hotels of Damascus in a street that retains its charm despite the modern high-rise buildings around. Both the hotels are in pretty courtyard houses with fountains.

5. Bait al-Ibish
This huge house once belonged to the Ibish family. It is now the restaurant of the Syrian Workers' Union, a pleasant place to eat. It still has its traditional painted reception room.

6. Bait 'Araqtanji
This house, built in 1933 for Dr Yusuf 'Araqtanji, is lavishly decorated inside with panels, stonework, tiles and treasures from houses in the old city. Some of the panels are dated 1765. For many years it was the residence of the Spanish Embassy.

7. Bait Barudi
This was the house of the well-known Damascene intellectual, patron and philanthropist Fakhri Barudi, and a centre for Damascene society. The beautiful stone-paved courtyard is traditional, but the many windows on the façade show Western influence and wall paintings in the reception room are of European cities. Now under restoration by the Architectural Faculty of Damascus University, it will be the centre for old city studies.

8. Bait Qatana
Difficult to visit, as it has been divided up into several houses. One has a beautifully painted reception room dated 1827. Older niches and stonework can be found in the alleyway that approaches the house.

9. Bait Bulad
A one-courtyard house with attractive panelled and painted reception room dated 1818. Parts of the house are probably earlier.

10. al-Ma'had al-Musiqi
This attractive house was at one time a music school. In traditional style, it has a painted reception room (kept under lock and key).

11. Bait Yaghmur
A huge house with a dramatic brown wood and white-painted façade along the main street in Qanawat.

12. Zawiyya Abu Shamat
This is a little oasis in the old city: a small garden surrounding a tomb and a mosque. The older parts of the building, such as the pastework decoration, probably date back to the 17th century, but the complex was revamped in the 19th century by Sheikh Abu Shamat.

13. Bait Sayrawan
A particularly lovely old house with a charming stone-paved courtyard and a beautifully painted 18th-century qa'a with muqarnas cornice.

WITHIN THE WALLS

1. Bait Shirazi
A large, beautifully decorated house with three seating areas in the main reception room and magnificent ceilings. It was the Persian Consulate until the 20th century and descendants of the consular family still live there. The stonework is dated 1765, but parts of the house may be older. Bait Shirazi has its own hammam and a 'maze' fountain in the courtyard. Some rooms have been adapted to make shops in the street outside.

2. Bait al-Amir al-Jaza'iri
'Abd al-Qadir al-Jaza'iri bought many houses in Damascus for his family and entourage. We photographed two of them (access to the others being impossible). His own residence was a classical Damascene house with 19th-century decoration. It is now an old people's home. Further along the river is a house lived in by one of his sons, which is decorated in North African style. There is a private bridge across the river at the back of this house.

3. Bait Mujallid
Was owned by the Jabri family until the 1930s when the Mujallid family bought it. It was Sa'id Agha Jabri who, from 1840, redecorated the house in its delicious Ottoman rococo style and constructed (or reconstructed from something else) the marvellous 'European' dining room and marble arcade. The house was bought in 1997 by Nora Jumblatt, who has painstakingly restored it.

4. Azem Palace
Now the Museum of Popular Arts and Traditions of Syria and open to the public. It was built in 1749/50 by As'ad Pasha al-Azem. The palace is famous for its large and beautiful haramlik, or family courtyard, and its hammam. It was damaged in the uprising of 1925, but restored.

5. Bait Jaza'iri
A pretty one-courtyard house 'modernized' in the late 19th century. Originally probably one of 'Abd al-Qadir's houses, it is still lived in by his distant relatives from Algeria.

6. Bait Saqqa' Amini
A large house, parts of which date back several centuries. It has been restored in places. Particularly beautiful is an arcade of pointed arches with a curious carved stone 'elbow' motif on the pillars, which can also be seen in other houses such as Bait Dahdah.

7. Bait Quwatli
There are, or were, four Bait Quwatlis in Damascus.
Bait Quwatli (a) is the one marked as the British Consulate on the Reverend Josias Porter's map of 1855. It is an enormous palace with several courtyards and lovely decoration in many of the rooms. The magnificent reception hall has distinctive oval 'bulls-eye' windows and stonework dated 1802 (though the house is older). Now divided up among many families and a paper store.
Bait Quwatli (b) is in the heart of the city, a huge house in a very poor state of preservation.
Bait Quwatli (c) is a beautiful rococo house with painted rooms dating from the 19th century (the house itself is probably older). Now owned by the Syrian authorities and to be restored.
Bait Quwatli (d) was destroyed in the French bombing of Damascus in 1925.

8. Bait Jabri
A lovely palace with a particularly beautiful courtyard and fountain. The house is decorated in fine coloured pastework – in some places painted over with the rococo designs of the 19th century. The Jabri family still own the house and have opened a simple restaurant in the courtyard.

9. Bait 'Ajlani
The courtyard of this house has become a public area with shops in it. Coloured pastework stones in the walls are 18th century or earlier. The rest of the house has become separate private apartments.

10. Bait Nabulsi
If in parts tumbledown, this is one of the most impressive houses in Damascus. The house has an entrance court and a kitchen court as well as haramlik and salamlik courtyards. The main reception room is painted and dated 1778 and is unusual in that it has windows looking over the second courtyard. Part of the main courtyard and some rooms have been separated off to make another house; this has a lovely painted reception room dated 1780.

11. Bait al-Sabah
There are three Bait al-Sabahs.
Bait al-Sabah (a) and *(b)* are attractive small courtyard houses restored by Sheikha Hussah al-Sabah, who discovered part of the outer temple wall running between the two houses.
Bait al-Sabah (c) is a larger house under restoration by Sheikha Hussah al-Sabah with a beautiful paved courtyard and simple cut-stone fountain. Parts of the house were 'modernized' in the 19th and early 20th centuries; other parts are 18th century or earlier. There are attractive indoor fountains.

12. Maktab 'Anbar
Now the offices of the Commission of the Old City, it has three lovely courtyards. The house was being built by Yusuf 'Anbar in 1870 at the time of Isabel Burton's stay in Damascus. It is possible to visit Maktab 'Anbar during office hours.

13. Bait al-Azem
One of the houses belonging to the Azem family, this was demolished for a development project which was never realized.

14. Bait Shawi
A house in Straight Street distinguishable by its unusual bow window with barley-sugar wood carving jutting over the street. Behind the façade it is an unexpectedly big house, partially restored. In the 19th century it was for a time the Austrian Consulate.

15. Bait Shatta
One of the most attractive smaller houses in Damascus with a particularly charming courtyard. Was once owned by Maryam 'Ajami, a poet and writer. It now belongs to the architect Hikmat Shatta and his brother.

16. House of the Spanish Crown
The Spanish coat of arms is carved above the front door, for this was the Spanish Consulate in the second part of the 19th century. It has a magnificent courtyard and two European-style reception rooms – one rather masculine, with 23 shell-shaped niches around the walls and huge paintings which have become obscured with layers of dust; the other, painted with delicate garden views, has an ornate white marble fountain. Other rooms are more traditional. The kitchen has its own courtyard. This is the house in which Wulzinger and Watzinger stayed early in the 20th century.

17. Bait Shamiyya
This house was once owned by a prosperous Christian merchant called Antun Shami. It was destroyed in the troubles of 1860 and then rebuilt in grander and more European style in 1863. It is now a convent.

18. Bait Fransa
A charming house with two courtyards, one derelict. Very prettily painted reception room and sitting room.

19. Madrasa Qunaitra (British Syrian School)
This house with two courtyards was a school run by Protestant missionaries from Britain in the second half of the 19th century. It is now a school for refugees from Qunaitra.

20. Bait Nassan
This is the house of a well-known merchant family famous for their brocade weaving. The courtyard, untypically, has pillars around it and was redesigned in the 20th century.

21. Bait Mishaqa
This was the US Consulate in the latter part of the 19th century. The house has 18th-century windows and an old kitchen, but was partially remodelled in the 19th century.

22. Bait Niyadu (Bait Stambuli)
This was a famous house, owned by Jews who came to Damascus from Istanbul (hence the original name). It is now owned by a Shi'a sheikh. The house was photographed by Bonfils in the 1870s and is still recognizable from those pictures, although the paving and the fountain in the courtyard have been changed since.

23. Bait Lisbona
This is the house that Isabel Burton liked second best in Damascus (her favourite was the Azem Palace). It was built by a Jewish family from Lisbon who fled Portugal during the Inquisition to live in Istanbul and then Damascus.

24. Bait Tuta
The Tuta family were well-known Jewish merchants. This is an attractive house with two styles – one side of the courtyard is late 19th century with big windows and Western-style reception rooms; the other has an earlier striped stone liwan with traditional rooms.

25. Bait Farhi
This was one of the grandest houses in Damascus at the beginning of the 19th century, when it impressed Lady Hester Stanhope and her doctor in 1812. It has four courtyards, but is now in a dilapidated state and is lived in by many families. This is the house that Sir Frederic Leighton, on a visit to Syria in 1873, depicted in his painting *Gathering Citrons*.

26. Bait Dahdah
A particularly beautiful house with an arched liwan (similar to the one in Bait Farhi) and a lovely courtyard.

27. Bait Shamaiyya
Once a grand house, photographed in the 1870s by Bonfils. Now almost a ruin, lived in by many families.

28. Bait Marie Qatash
A very pretty but sadly derelict house. It is famous for its extraordinary bay window on the outside façade.

29. Bait Nizam
A magnificent three-courtyard palace owned by 'Ali Agha, a mid-19th-century notable. The painted reception room (decorated in the 1830s) was described by Addison and Porter. The house itself is 18th century. Owned and restored by the Syrian authorities, it can usually be visited on working-day mornings. It is now used for receptions and weddings.

30. Bait Siba'i
A grand two-courtyard 18th-century house decorated in coloured pastework. Owned and restored by the Syrian authorities, it now houses the Ibish collection of hunting trophies. It can usually be visited on working-day mornings. (Enquire at Bait Nizam if no-one answers the door.)

31. Bait Qasim
Was used as a school for many years, but has recently been restored as a private house. Attractive 18th-century indoor fountain, painted ceilings and pretty courtyard.

32. Bait Tibi
A jewel of a house with an unusual upstairs reception room, exquisitely painted and gilt, as well as a beautifully decorated formal qa'a off the courtyard. On the ground floor are two ornate kiosks and the beautiful carved stone door that appears on the jacket of this book. Some inscriptions date the decoration to 1786/7 and to 1820.

33. Bait Kuzbari
A large two-courtyard house (one was destroyed in a fire). Remodelled in the late 19th century.

34. Bait Kabbani
Once the home of the Syrian poet Nizar Kabbani. Recently modernized by new owners, but has a lovely courtyard.

35. Bait al-Haffar
Charming small house with pretty stone-paved courtyard and fountain. Some 18th-century coloured pastework, but redecorated in the late 19th century.

36. Bait al-'Aqqad
A magnificent palace with 15th-century stonework and 18th- and 19th-century rooms, built on top of a Roman theatre. Leased from the Syrian Government by the Danish Government, the house has been painstakingly restored and is now the Danish Institute in Damascus.

37. Bait al-Istwani
A charming house with coloured pastework on the courtyard façades and unusual windows and arcade. Beautiful painted reception room. 18th century (possibly earlier in parts). Now used as a depot and offices.

38. Bait Mardam Bey
A grand old house still lived in by its original family. It once had two courtyards, but one was damaged in the uprising of 1925 and the stonework was removed and re-erected at the National Museum.

Glossary

agha	military commander, leader	madrasa	Qur'anic school
'ajami	raised lacquer work	mahmal	pilgrim mascot carried on camel on hajj to Mecca
alfiyya	legendary house snake		
amir	commander, prince	maktab	religious school (or office)
Amir al-Hajj	commander of the pilgrimage	maristan	hospital, hospice
ard al-diyar	courtyard	masabb	mihrab-shaped niche in a private house used for storing jugs of water
ashraf	descendants of the Prophet Mohammed		
'ataba	lower area, or threshold, of reception room	mihrab	prayer niche in a mosque
		muezzin	man who calls to prayer from the minaret of a mosque
bab	door, gate		
bait	house	muqarnas	'stalactite' design in wood or stone
Bedouin	nomads		
bey (beg)	title of honour	murabba'	sitting room
caliph	Muslim leader	naranj	type of bitter-orange tree
chador	Iranian enveloping garment	narghila	water pipe, hubble-bubble or hookah
daftardar	treasurer		
dervish	Muslim mystic	pasha	Turkish title of respect
dihliz	entrance courtyard	qa'a	reception room
divan	seat on raised area of reception room	qadi	judge
		salamlik	reception section of a house
dragoman	guide, translator		
Druze	member of an Islamic sect from the Mount Lebanon region	shahada	profession of faith in one God and in Mohammed as the Prophet of God
hajj	Muslim pilgrimage		
hakawati	story-teller	sheikh	religious man or elder
hammam	bath, bathhouse	Shi'a	the branch of Islam that regards 'Ali as Mohammed's rightful successor (from Shi'at 'Ali, the party of 'Ali)
hara	quarter, now used to indicate an alleyway		
haramlik	family section in house		
harem (haram)	private quarters of a house	simis	wooden cornice round courtyard roof
hijab	scarf worn by women as veil		
Hijaz	area of Arabian peninsula containing the cities of Mecca and Medina	sufi	Muslim mystic
		sultan	Muslim ruler
		sunduq	chest
'Id al-Adha	Muslim feast at the hajj	Sunni	the branch of Islam that acknowledges the orthodox tradition (the Sunna)
'Id al-Fitr	Muslim feast at the end of Ramadan		
'Id al-Kabir	Muslim feast at the hajj		
kabbad	type of lemon tree	suq (souk)	market
kashash hamam	pigeon fancier	takiyya	Muslim hostel
kavass	guard	tanzimat	Ottoman reforms
khadamlik	auxiliary courtyard for servants and services	tarbush	cap, similar to fez
		tayyara	room on roof of house
khan	caravanserai, hostel-cum-storage-cum-trading place for merchants	tell (tal)	hill, mound
		'ulama	Muslim scholars, religious élite
kohl	Arab eyeliner		
liwan (iwan)	traditional indoor/outdoor room that faces into the courtyard and has no front wall	vizier	adviser to ruler
		wali	governor
		waqf	system of Islamic trusts

Dates throughout the book are given according to the Christian calendar.
The date in the Muslim calendar, which is based on a lunar year, is reckoned from the beginning of the year of Mohammed's migration from Mecca to Medina (the Hijra; hence Anno Hegirae, or AH), equivalent to 16 July 622 in the Christian calendar (AD).

The following formulas may be used to calculate one date from the other:
Year AH × 0·97 + 621·6 = Year AD (thus, AH 487 = AD 1094)
Year AD − 621·6 ÷ 0·97 = Year AH (thus, AD 1549 = AH 956)

Bibliography

Books

ADDISON, CHARLES G. *Damascus and Palmyra: A Journey to the East.* 2 vols. London, 1838.

AVEZ, RENAUD. *L'Institut Français de Damas au Palais Azem, 1922–1946.* Institut Français des Études Arabes à Damas. Damascus, 1993.

BELL, GERTRUDE. *The Desert and the Sown.* London, 1907.

BÉRARD, VICTOR. *Le Sultan, l'Islam et les puissances.* Paris, 1907.

BLUNT, WILFRID. *Splendours of Islam.* London, 1976.

BOWRING, JOHN. *Report on the Commercial Statistics of Syria, Palestine and the Holy Land.* London, 1840.

BRODIE, FAWN M. *The Devil Drives: A Life of Sir Richard Burton.* New York, 1967.

BRUHNS, E. MAXINE. *The Nationality Rooms.* Pittsburgh, 1990.

BURNS, ROSS. *Monuments of Syria.* London, 1992.

BURTON, ISABEL. *The Inner Life of Syria, Palestine, and the Holy Land.* London, 1884.

CURTIS, GEORGE W. *The Howadji in Syria.* New York, 1857.

DALRYMPLE, WILLIAM. *From the Holy Mountain: A Journey in the Shadow of Byzantium.* London, 1997.

DEGEORGE, GÉRARD. *Damas, des Ottomans à nos jours.* Paris, 1994.

———. *Damas, des origines aux Mamluks.* Paris, 1997.

DOUGHTY, CHARLES M. *Travels in Arabia Deserta.* Cambridge, 1888.

DUDA, D. 'Painted and Lacquered Woodwork in Arab Houses of Damascus and Aleppo' in *Lacquerwork in Asia and Beyond*, ed. William Watson. SOAS, London, 1982.

ESTABLET, COLETTE, AND PASCUAL, JEAN-PAUL. *Familles et fortunes à Damas.* Institut Français des Études Arabes à Damas. Damascus, 1994.

———. *Ultime voyage pour la Mecque.* Institut Français des Études Arabes à Damas. Damascus, 1998.

FEDDEN, ROBIN. *Syria: An Historical Appreciation.* London, 1955.

FRANKEL, JONATHAN. *The Damascus Affair.* Cambridge, 1997.

GLASS, CHARLES. *Tribes with Flags: A Journey Curtailed.* London, 1990.

GONNELLA, JULIA. *Das Aleppo-Zimmer.* Museum für Islamische Kunst, Mainz, 1996.

GOODWIN, GODFREY. *Islamic Spain.* London, 1990.

GOODWIN, JASON. *Lords of the Horizons.* London, 1998.

GRANT, CHRISTINA P. *The Syrian Desert: Caravans, Travel and Exploration.* London, 1937.

GREEN, JOHN. *A Journey from Aleppo to Damascus.* London, 1736.

HASLIP, JOAN. *Lady Hester Stanhope: A Biography.* London, 1934.

HOURANI, ALBERT. *A History of the Arab Peoples.* London, 1991.

IBN-MUNQIDH, USAMAH. *An Arab-Syrian Gentleman and Warrior in the Period of the Crusades.* London, 1987.

IDILBI, ULFAT. *Sabriya, Damascus Bitter Sweet.* Translated by Peter Clark. London, 1995.

JESSUP, HENRY. *Fifty-Three Years in Syria.* New York, 1856.

KALTER, JOHANNES, ET AL. *The Arts and Crafts of Syria.* Collection Antoine Touma and Linden Museum, Stuttgart. London, 1992.

KELMAN, JOHN, *From Damascus to Palmyra.* London, 1908.

KINGLAKE, ALEXANDER. *Eothen.* London, 1844.

LABEYRIE, IRÈNE. 'Quartiers et paysages' in *Damas, miroir brisé d'un Orient arabe,* ed. Anne-Marie Bianquis. Paris, 1993.

LAMARTINE, ALPHONSE DE. *Souvenirs, impressions, pensées et paysages pendant un voyage en Orient, 1832–1833.* Paris, 1856.

LANE-POOLE, STANLEY. *The Mohammadan Dynasties.* London, 1894.

LAWRENCE, T. E. *Seven Pillars of Wisdom.* London, 1935.

LE STRANGE, GUY, *Palestine under the Moslems.* London, 1890.

LORTET, L.-C. *La Syrie d'aujourd'hui.* Paris, 1884.

LOVELL, MARY S. *A Scandalous Life: The Biography of Jane Digby el Mezrab.* London, 1995.

———. *A Rage to Live: A Biography of Richard and Isabel Burton.* London, 1998.

MAALOUF, AMIN. *The Crusades through Arab Eyes.* London, 1984.

MAITLAND-KIRWAN, J. D. *Sunrise in Syria: A Short History of the British Syria Mission.* London, 1930.

MAUNDRELL, HENRY. *A Journey from Aleppo to Jerusalem at Easter, AD 1697.* Oxford, 1703.

MAURY, BERNARD. 'La Maison damascène au XVIIIe siècle et au début du XIXe siècle' in *L'Habitat traditionnel dans les pays musulmans autour de la Méditerranée.* Aix-en-Provence, 1988.

MISHAQA, MIKHAYIL. *Murder, Mayhem, Pillage, and Plunder: The History of the Lebanon in the 18th and 19th Centuries.* Translated by W. M. Thackston, Jr. New York, 1988.

MITCHELL, CRAWFORD. *The Syria-Lebanon Classroom in the Cathedral of Learning.* Pittsburgh, 1943.

MORTON, H. V. *In the Steps of St Paul.* London, 1937.

MOSS, ROBERT TEWDWR. *Cleopatra's Wedding Present: Travels through Syria.* London, 1997.

MUSSELMANI, MARWAN. *Damascene Homes.* Damascus, 1983.

PECK, AMELIA, ET AL. *Period Rooms in the Metropolitan Museum of Art.* New York, 1996.

PEÑA, IGNACIO. *The Christian Art of Byzantine Syria.* Reading, 1997.

PETRAN, TABITHA. *Syria.* London, 1972.

PORTER, JOSIAS L. *Five Years in Damascus.* London, 1855.

POULLEAU, ALICE. *À Damas sous les bombes. Journal d'une Française pendant la révolte syrienne.* Yvetot, 1925.

RAFEQ, ABDUL-KARIM. *The Province of Damascus 1723–1783.* Beirut, 1970.

ROBINE, GÉRARD. *Palais et demeures de Damas au XVIII.* Damascus, 1990.

ROUJON, YVES, ET AL. *Le Midan: Actualité d'un faubourg ancien de Damas.* Damascus, 1997.

SACK, DOROTHÉE. *Damaskus – Entwicklung und Struktur einer orientalisch-islamischen Stadt.* Mainz, 1989.

SAUVAGET, JEAN. *Les Monuments historiques de Damas.* Beirut, 1932.

SCHATKOWSKI SCHILCHER, LINDA. *Families in Politics: Damascene Factions and Estates of the 18th and 19th Centuries.* Stuttgart, 1985.

SEABROOK, WILLIAM. *Adventures in Arabia.* London, 1928.

STEWART, FREDERICK, VISCOUNT CASTLEREAGH. *A Journey to Damascus.* 2 vols. London, 1847.

TERGEMAN, SIHAM. *Daughter of Damascus.* English version and introduction by Andrea Rugh. Austin, Texas, 1994.

THUBRON, COLIN. *Mirror to Damascus.* London, 1967.

TUǦLACI, PARS. *The Role of the Balian Family in Ottoman Architecture.* Istanbul, 1990.

TWAIN, MARK. *The Innocents Abroad or The New Pilgrim's Progress.* New York and London, 1869.

UNESCO. *L'Architecture libanaise du XV au XIX.* Beirut, 1985.

WARNER, CHARLES D. *In the Levant.* Boston, 1886.

WEBER, STEFAN. 'Ottoman Damascus of the 19th Century: Artistic and Urban Development as an Expression of Changing Times' in *Art Turc/Turkish Art* (10th International Congress of Turkish Art, 17–23 September 1995). Geneva, 1999.

WILSON, CHARLES W., ED. *Picturesque Palestine.* 4 vols. London, 1880.

WULZINGER, KARL, AND WATZINGER, CARL. *Damaskus: Die islamische Stadt.* Berlin and Leipzig, 1924.

Guidebooks

BEATTIE, ANDREW, AND PEPPER, TIMOTHY. *Syria: The Rough Guide.* London, 1998.

CHAUVET, A. D., AND ISAMBERT, É. *Itinéraire descriptif, historique et archéologique de l'Orient.* Vol. 3: *Orient, Syrie, Palestine* [Librairie Hachette guide]. Paris, 1890.

GRIMES, CLAIRE E. *A Guide to Damascus.* Syria, 1997.

LONELY PLANET. *Syria.* London, 1999.

MACMILLAN & CO. *Guide to Palestine and Syria.* 3rd edn. London, 1905.

[PORTER, JOSIAS L.] *A Handbook for Travellers in Syria and Palestine* [Murray's *Handbook*]. 2 vols. London, 1858.

Journal and Magazine Articles

ABU AL FARAJ AL 'USH. 'Al Dar al Athariyya al Khasa fi Dimashq.' *Annales Archéologiques de Syrie* III, 8/9 (1953).

DEGEORGE, GÉRARD. 'Sight of All Ages – The Umayyad Mosque.' *FMR* no. 58 [English edition] (October, 1992).

———. 'Le mille e una dimora – Le case di Damasco.' *FMR* no. 97 (April, 1993).

DE MAUSSION DE FAVIÈRES, JACQUES. 'Note sur les bains de Damas.' *Bulletin d'Études* XVII (1961–62).

ÉCOCHARD, MICHEL. 'Le Palais Azem de Damas.' *Gazette des Beaux-Arts* (April 1935).

ELISSÉEFF, NIKITA. 'Les Monuments de Nur ad-Din.' *Bulletin d'Études* XIII (1949–50).

GASCÓN, EUGENIO GARCÍA. 'El arquitecto español Fernando de Aranda (1878–1969) en Damasco.' *Awrāq. Estudios sobre el Mundo Árabe e islámico contemporáneo* IX (1988).

'LES ARTS EN SYRIE.' *L'Œil* 337 (August 1983). [Whole issue dedicated to articles on Syria.]

MARKOE, GLEN. 'Asian Art in the Cincinnati Art Museum.' *Arts of Asia* (March–April, 1993).

PHILIPP, T. 'The Farhi Family and the Changing Position of the Jews in Syria 1750–1860.' *Middle East Studies* 20, no. 4 (October 1984).

ROUANET, ANNE, AND PIPONNIER, DENIS. Étude iconographique et technique d'un ensemble décoratif: la maison Nizam à Damas.' *Bulletin des Études Orientales* 37–38 (1985–86).

SOURDEL-THOMINE, J. 'Les Anciens Lieux de pèlerinage damascains d'après les sources arabes.' *Bulletin d'Études* XIV (1952–54).

WEBER, STEFAN. 'The Creation of Ottoman Damascus. Architecture and Urban Development of Damascus in the 16th and 17th Centuries.' *ARAM* 10 (1998).

Illustration Credits

All photographs by Tim Beddow unless otherwise stated.

Endpaper design of blue-and-white tiles in the Tayruzi Mosque from a photograph by Stefan Weber.

The following references (to page numbers) give the sources of the illustrations, together with some additional information not included in the captions. The author and publisher extend their gratitude to the individuals and organizations named.

14–15 Dutch engraving, courtesy of Professor Akili; 15 (above) Courtesy of Antoine Touma; 16 (above and below) Courtesy of Professor Akili; 16–17 Courtesy of Antoine Touma; 20–21 and 23 Courtesy of Professor Akili; 34 Photograph by Bonfils, courtesy of Harvard Semitic Museum Photographic Archives, Fine Arts Library, Harvard University; 36–37 From Girault de Prangey, *Monuments arabes et moresques, c.* 1832; 40 Courtesy of the Harvard Semitic Museum Photographic Archives, Fine Arts Library, Harvard University; 42 Courtesy of Professor Akili; 49 Courtesy of Stefan Weber; 60 Courtesy of Professor Akili; 61 (below) From Karl Wulzinger and Carl Watzinger, *Damaskus: Die islamische Stadt,* 1924; 64 Courtesy of Professor Akili; 66–67 Courtesy of the Institut Français d'Études Arabes de Damas; 69 Photograph by the author; 70 Courtesy of the Imperial War Museum, London; 71 Courtesy of the Trustees of the Liddell Hart Centre for Military Archives, King's College, London; 73–75 Maps drawn by Ross Burns; 81 Courtesy of Mary S. Lovell; 86 (above) Courtesy of the Institut Français d'Études Arabes de Damas; 86 (below) Courtesy of Professor Akili; 91 (below left) Courtesy of Na'im Zabita; 95 Courtesy of Michael F. Price and the Royal Academy of Arts, London; 96 (below) Courtesy of Harvard Semitic Museum Photographic Archives, Fine Arts Library, Harvard University; 101 Courtesy of Peder Mortensen and the Danish Institute, Damascus; 108 (all) Courtesy of Na'im Zabita; 135 Courtesy of the Cincinnati Art Museum; 154 Courtesy of Professor Akili; 157 Courtesy of Dr Sabah Kabbani; 158 (below left) Courtesy of Marwan Musselmani; 163 Courtesy of Mary S. Lovell; 165 Courtesy of Na'im Zabita; 169 Courtesy of the Tareq Rajab Museum, Kuwait; 170 Courtesy of Harvard Semitic Museum Photographic Archives, Fine Arts Library, Harvard University; 172 Courtesy of Mary S. Lovell; 176 Photograph by Bonfils, courtesy of Harvard Semitic Museum Photographic Archives, Fine Arts Library, Harvard University; 182 (above) From Josias L. Porter, *Five Years in Damascus,* 1855; 182 (below), 183 and 184 (above left) Courtesy of Harvard Semitic Museum Photographic Archives, Fine Arts Library, Harvard University; 184 (above right) Courtesy of the Institut Français d'Études Arabes de Damas; 185 Courtesy of Dr Sabah Kabbani; 189 Courtesy of Na'im Zabita; 192, 193 and 194 (below right) Courtesy of Professor Akili; 209 (left and right) Courtesy of Hassana Mardam Bey and her family; 212–13 Courtesy of Professor Akili.

Index

Numerals in *italics* refer to the captions to illustrations.

'Abbas (uncle of Mohammed) 37
Abbasids 37, 39, 40
'Abd al-Ghani 68
'Abd al-Qadir al-Jaza'iri 161–62, 165, 167, 168, 179, 192, 194, 219; *163, 165, 166, 200*
'Abd family 146, 154, 185, 219
'Ablaq Palace 44–47, 59, 99
Abu Shamat, Sheikh 219
Addison, Charles 64, 133, 158, 219; *132*
Ahmet III, Sultan 133
'Ain al-Fija 114, 192
'Ajami, Maryam 217, 219
'Ajlani family 146
Akrad district 155
al-'Abd, Ahmad 'Izzat al-Pasha 185, 219; *185*
al-'Adil, al-Malik 43
al-Azem, 'Abdullah Pasha 68
al-Azem, As'ad Pasha 39, 59, 60–64, 68, 144, 146, 219
al-Azem, Isma'il 60, 154
al-Azem, Khalid 114, 154–55, 219
al-Azem, Mohammed Fawzi Pasha 154
al-Azem, Sulaiman Pasha 59, 60
al-Azem, Ziyad 144, 146
al-'Aziz (son of Saladin) 42
al-Bahri, Hanna 94
Al-Baris, palace 99
al-Budairi (barber and diarist) 144
al-Ibish, Husain 157
al-Idrisi, Ibn Mohammed 40, 114
al-Istwani, 'Abdullah 93
al-Jaza'iri, Amira Amal 162
al-Jazzar, 'Butcher' 94
al-Ma'had al-Musiqi 219; *112*
al-Maqdisi (geographer) 15, 27
al-Nabulsi, Yusuf 68
al-Quwatli, Mohammed Sa'id 93
al-Sabah, Sheikha Hussah 217, 219
al-Walid, Caliph 25, 27
al-Yusuf, 'Abd al-Rahman Pasha 155, 219; *157*
Aleppo 40, 44, 112, 120, 184
'Ali, Caliph 22
'Ali Agha 133, 158, 161, 179, 219; *132, 158*
Amir al-Hajj 65, 68, 155, 219; *157*
'Anbar, Yusuf 98, 219
Anderson, Gayer 135
Ansari Mosque 69
Anti-Lebanon mountains 13, 15, 194; *16*
'Aqqad family 93
Arab Revolt 72, 185
Arameans 21, 72, 99
Aranda, Fernando de 193–94; *194*
'Araqtanji, Yusuf 209, 219
Armenia/Armenians 40, 96, 134, 135
Arvieux, Chevalier d' 40

Assyrians 72, 99
'Atassi, 'Ali 217
Ayyubids 43–44, 47
Azem family 60, 135, 144, 146, 154, 158, 161
Azem Palace (Museum of Popular Arts and Traditions) 47, 64, 98, 112, 144, 146, 154, 211, 219; *144, 147*
Bab al-Faradis 161, 162
Bab al-Saghir 22, 158, 194
Bab Musalla 69
Bab Tuma (Christian quarter) 27, 72, 93, 94, 96, 98, 177, 179, 217; *98*
Baghdad 39, 44, 98, 112
Bahsa district 40
Baibars, Sultan 44–47, 59, 101
  tomb of 47; *79*
Bait 'Ajlani 113, 219
Bait al-'Abd 119, 219; *184*
Bait al-Amir al-Jaza'iri 219
Bait al-'Aqqad 93, 99, 217, 219; *101*
Bait al-Azem 219
Bait al-Basha 158; *158*
Bait al-Haffar 219; *218*
Bait al-Ibish
  see Syrian Workers' Union
Bait al-Istwani 93, 113, 219; *76, 153*
Bait al-Sabah 219
Bait al-Yusuf 154–55, 219; *13, 114, 154, 157*
Bait 'Araqtanji 209, 219; *53, 133, 194*
Bait Barudi 99, 134, 219; *79, 84, 108, 139, 186, 197, 198*
Bait Bulad 219; *76*
Bait Dahdah 113, 219; *103, 120, 148*
Bait Farhi 96, 98, 219; *76, 94*
Bait Fransa 96, 98, 219; *98*
Bait Jabri 113, 119, 217, 219; *112*
Bait Jaza'iri 219
Bait Kabbani 219
Bait Khalid al-Azem
  see Historical Museum of Damascus
Bait Kuzbari 219; *120*
Bait Lisbona 96, 98, 219; *91, 93, 130, 189, 191, 197*
Bait Mardam Bey 114, 219; *84, 200, 209*
Bait Marie Qatash 134, 219
Bait Mishaqa 219
Bait Mujallid 8, 99, 112, 119, 134, 217, 219; *6, 8, 117, 122, 137, 140, 203*
Bait Murad Quwatli 211
Bait Nabulsi 219
Bait Nassan 219
Bait Niyadu (Bait Stambuli) 98, 219; *32, 96, 214*
Bait Nizam 133, 161, 179, 219; *79, 107, 132, 158, 161, 182, 191, 204*
Bait Qasim 219; *32, 120*
Bait Qatana 219
Bait Quwatli 93, 114, 135, 179, 211, 219; *81, 122, 133, 179, 203*
Bait Saqqa' Amini 219

Bait Sayrawan 219; *153*
Bait Shamaiyya 219; *34*
Bait Shamiyya 96, 98, 179, 219; *96, 137, 184*
Bait Shatta 219; *88, 119*
Bait Shawi 179, 219
Bait Shirazi 114, 119, 132, 177, 219; *79, 81, 127, 130, 179*
Bait Siba'i 113, 114, 119, 158, 161, 219; *108, 111, 114, 148, 153, 204*
Bait Stambuli *see* Bait Niyadu
Bait Tibi 132, 214, 219; *107, 127, 206, 211*
Bait Tuta 134, 219; *134*
Bait Wakil (Aleppo) 120
Bait Yaghmur 219; *184*
Barada river 15, 18, 40, 44, 59, 60, 114, 161; *15, 61, 165*
Barudi, Fakhri 134, 192, 219
Basha family 158
Beaumont, Sir Richard 179
Bedouin 65, 68, 167, 171, 212
Beirut 42, 144, 161, 162, 171, 177, 179, 182
Beiteddine (Lebanon) 144
Bell, Gertrude 56, 154, 167, 185, 192; *192*
Bludan 177
Bonfils (photographers) 179, 182, 219; *21, 40, 96, 171, 182, 184*
Bowring, John 91, 93, 193
  Report 40, 69, 91, 93, 193
British Syrian School (Madrasa Qunaitra) 177, 219; *179*
Burchardt, Hermann 135
Burns, Ross 13
Burton, Isabel 8, 59, 60, 68, 81, 84, 93, 94, 98, 112, 161, 162, 167, 168, 171, 173–77, 179, 184, 219; *81, 174*
Burton, Richard 8, 84, 161, 171, 173, 177, 184; *81, 172*
Busch, Moritz 99
Byzantine Empire/Byzantines 22, 25, 40, 72, 99, 101
cadastral plan of Damascus 88; *86*
Cairo 21, 98, 135, 144, 157
carpet market 69; *68*
Castelli, Signor and Signora 167, 177
Caucasus 44, 69, 193; *68*
Charles V, Holy Roman Emperor 37
Christian quarter *see* Bab Tuma
Christians 18, 22, 25, 27, 59, 69, 72, 93, 94, 96, 98, 120, 154, 162, 177, 179, 182, 184, 194; *96, 98, 176, 184*
Citadel, Damascus 42, 43, 162, 214; *42*
coffee houses 60; *61*
Constantinople 25, 47, 56, 59
  see also Istanbul
Córdoba, Great Mosque 37; *37*
Curtis, George William 91
Crusaders 40, 42, 43, 44, 72, 184
'Customs House' *see* Khan al-Jumruk
Damascus rooms abroad 135, 144; *134*

Darwish, Fatie 168–71
Darwish Pasha 59
  mosque of *50, 54*
Degeorge, Gérard 44, 214
Digby, Jane 161, 167–68, 171, 173; *166, 168*
Dimitri's Hotel 171, 173
Dome of the Rock (Jerusalem) 27; *48*
Doughty, Charles 68
Druze 144, 171, 211, 217
Écochard, Michel 212–14
Egypt/Egyptians 40, 42, 44, 69, 72, 94, 133, 135, 144, 157, 158, 171, 193
Faisal, Amir (King) 42, 72, 192; *70*
Farhi, Haim 94
Farlan (daughter of 'Ali Agha) 144, 158
Farren, John 171
Fathi Falaqinsi 59; *59*
Fatimids 40, 42
Flaubert, Gustave 135
Floyd, Rolla 179
French Mandate period 72, 88, 134, 135, 146, 155, 192, 209–11
Friday Market 56
Furukhshah (nephew of Saladin) 43
Gautier, Théophile 134
German Consulate 154
German Institute of Archaeology 42, 161
Ghaybi workshop 48
Ghazzi family 146
Ghuta oasis 15, 99, 212
Gold Souk 13, 22
Great Mosque *see* Umayyad Mosque
Green, John 40, 59, 88
Green, Kirby 179
Green Palace 99
Haag, Carl 168
hajj 21, 56, 59, 64–69, 155; *65, 68*
  see also Amir al-Hajj
Halbuni district 179
Hama 144
Hamid, Sultan Abdul 185
Hammam Nur al-Din 42
Hamza family 146, 161
Hanbali Mosque 44
Haramain Hotel 214, 219
Harat al-Yahud (Jewish quarter) 93, 94, 98, 134, 146
Hariqa district 101, 211, 214
Hijaz 69
Hijaz Station 193–94; *194*
Hinnawi, Hussein 168
Historical Museum of Damascus (Bait Khalid al-Azem) 114, 154–55, 219; *31, 32, 34, 39, 147, 148, 197*
House of the Spanish Crown 112, 119, 179, 219; *103, 217*
Husain (grandson of Mohammed) 21, 22
Ibish family 155–57, 161, 219
Ibn 'Arabi *see* Muhi al-Din
Ibn Batuta (traveller) 27, 65

Ibn Hawqal (traveller) 39
Ibn Jubair (traveller) 25, 65
Ibn Munqidh (writer) 40
'Id al-Kabir 68, 69
Idilbi, Ulfat 86
Imperial War Museum (London) 42
Institut Français d'Archéologie et d'Art Musulman 146
Iran/Iranians 21, 120, 214; *22, 48*
 see also Persia/Persians
Istanbul 39, 64, 98, 133, 134, 154, 192, 193, 219; *137, 192*
 see also Constantinople
Istwani family 93
Jabri, Sa'id Agha 217, 219
Jabri family 217, 219
Jamal Pasha 72, 119
Jergens, Andrew 135
Jerusalem 21, 27, 42, 43, 184
Jessup, Henry 42, 72, 162, 177
Jesus 27, 94
Jewish quarter see Harat al-Yahud
Jews 18, 59, 69, 91, 93, 94, 96, 98, 134, 146, 171, 177, 184, 219
Jobar district 98
John the Baptist, Saint 22, 27
Julian 'the Apostate', Emperor 22
Jumblatt, Nora 217, 219
Kabbani, Nizar 84, 219; *84*
Kamal, Prince Yusuf 157
Kelman, John 192
Kevorkian, Hagop 135
Khan al-Harir (Silk Khan) 59
Khan al-Jumruk ('Customs House') 193
Khan As'ad Pasha 64, 146; *61, 65*
Khan Sulaiman Pasha 65
Khost, Nadia 155
King Faisal Street 168
Kinglake, Alexander 15, 119
Kissinger, Henry 182
Koran see Qur'an
Kukabaye, mausoleum of 47
Kurds 42, 155, 171
Lady of Damascus see Sitt al-Sham
Lamartine, Alphonse de 18, 64, 91, 171
Lawrence, T. E. (of Arabia) 42, 72, 171, 194; *70*
Lebanon 144
Leighton, Sir Frederic 219; *94*
le Strange, Guy 65
Librairie Hachette guide 18, 179
Lorey, M. de 146
Lortet, Dr L.-C. 168
Loti, Pierre 135
Lovell, Mary 168
Ludwig I, King of Bavaria 167
Lütticke, Ernst 154
Lyon, Prof. David 182
Ma'arat al-Nu'man 60
McCabe, Joseph 37
Madrasa 'Abdullah al-Azem 68, 154
Madrasa al-'Adiliyya 43
Madrasa al-Fathiyya 59; *59*
Madrasa al-Nuriyya 42
Madrasa al-Qilijiyya 43, 47

Madrasa al-Zahiriyya 47
Madrasa Qunaitra see British Syrian School
Maktab 'Anbar 98, 99, 113, 219; *88, 91, 108, 186*
Mamluks 44, 47, 72, 99, 113, 132, 133, 144, 184, 214; *44, 48, 79, 101, 125, 148, 186*
Manial Palace (Cairo) 135, 157
Mardam Bey, Ahmad Mukhtar 209
Mardam Bey, Fatima 209
Mardam Bey, Hassana 112
Mardam Bey, Khalil 209
Mardam Bey, 'Uthman 214
Mardam Bey family 146, 214, 219
Maristan Nur al-Din 42
Marja Square 47, 72, 171, 179, 185, 192; *192*
Mary, the Virgin 18, 94
Maundrell, Henry 60, 99, 177
Mecca 21, 47, 56, 64–69, 184, 192, 193; *76, 192*
Medina 21, 22, 56, 69, 193, 194
Meryon, Dr 96, 98, 219
Mezze (suburb) 37, 72, 113
Midan 47, 59, 68, 184, 185, 212, 214, 219; *59*
Midhat Pasha 185
Minaret of Jesus
 see Umayyad Mosque
Minaret of the Bride
 see Umayyad Mosque
Mirna (visionary) 18
Mishaqa, Dr Mikhayil 162, 177–79; *176*
Mishaqa, Nasif 179
Mohammed, the Prophet 16, 18, 21, 22, 37, 93, 112, 214
Mongols 44, 47
Mortensen, Peder 217
Morton, H. V. 81
Mott, Mr and Mrs 177
Mu'awiyya, Caliph 22, 25
Muhajirin district 192, 194
Muhi al-Din (Ibn 'Arabi) 56
 tomb of 162; *50*
Murray's *Handbook* 59, 68, 72, 94–96, 98, 158, 171
Museum of Popular Arts and Traditions
 see Azem Palace
Musselmani, Marwan 214
Napoleon III, Emperor 162
National Museum 21, 43, 47, 214; *44*
Natural History Museum of Damascus 64
Nawfara café 60; *61*
Nazim Pasha 192; *192*
Nur al-Din see Nureddin
Nureddin, Sultan 39, 40, 42
Ottomans 39, 47, 56–59, 60, 65, 69, 72, 98, 99, 133, 134, 144, 155, 171, 184, 185, 193, 209, 217; *137, 154, 186*
Palace of Gold 47, 99, 144
Palmyra 21, 96, 167; *168*

Paul, Saint 18, 81
Persia/Persians 40, 68, 72, 171, 177
 see also Iran/Iranians
Pharaon, Henri 144
Porter, Rev. Josias Leslie 22, 42, 59, 81, 94, 133, 146, 158, 171, 179, 193, 219; *132, 182*
Poulleau, Alice 211–12
Qadam (suburb) 18
Qadam Station 193
Qaimariyya district 43, 59; *31, 59*
Qanawat district 184, 214, 219; *112, 184*
Qasyun mountain 8, 21, 173, 192
Qur'an 119; *25*
Quwatli, Shukri 93
Quwatli family 93
Rabi' Hotel 214, 219
Rabwa valley 94
Richard I (the Lionheart), King 42
Rogers, Miss M. E. 18, 113
Roman remains 13, 21, 22, 25, 44, 93, 99, 144, 184, 219; *22, 25*
Runciman, Sir Steven 72
Ruqayya (great-granddaughter of Mohammed) 21, 214; *22*
Sack, Dorothée 99
Saddle Souk see Suq Sarujiyya
Saladin, Sultan 42–43, 44, 47; *42*
 tomb of 42; *39, 42, 53*
Salah al-Din see Saladin
Salihiyya district 44, 47, 56, 84, 168, 173, 177, 184, 185, 194
Samarkand 47
Sanjaqdar Mosque 18
Sarrail, General Maurice 146
Sau, Marquis Louis de 161
Sauvaget, Jean 42
Seabrook, William 65
Selim I, Sultan 56–59
Selim II, Sultan 59
Seljuks 40
Shamdin family 155
Shami, Antun 219
Sharif Pasha 144, 158
Shatta, Hikmat 217, 219
Shi'a 22, 40, 68, 98, 120
Siba'i, Governor 47
Silk Khan see Khan al-Harir
Sinan (architect) 59; *56*
Sinan Pasha 59
 mosque of *48, 56*
Sitt al-Sham (Lady of Damascus) 43, 144
slave-market 44, 192–93
Spice Souk see Suq al-Buzuriyya
Stanhope, Lady Hester 96, 219
Straight Street 13, 18, 40, 42, 47, 59, 60, 93, 99, 158, 179, 185, 211–12, 217, 219; *40, 65*
Suez Canal 68
Sufaniyya district 18
Sulaiman 'The Magnificent', Sultan 59; *48*
Sunni 22, 68, 120

Suq al-Buzuriyya (Spice Souk) 42, 43, 64, 185
Suq al-Hamidiyya 42, 154, 185, 214; *154*
Suq al-Khayyatin (Tailors' Souk) 42, 47, 60; *174*
Suq Saruja district 43, 154–55, 158, 184, 185, 214, 219; *184*
Suq Sarujiyya (Saddle Souk) 214; *18, 212*
Syrian Workers' Union (Bait al-Ibish) 155, 157, 219
Tailors' Souk see Suq al-Khayyatin
Takiyya al-Sulaimaniyya 44, 59, 68; *48, 56, 65*
Tamerlane 27, 47, 59, 120
Tayruzi Mosque 47; *48*
 hammam 47; *186*
Tengiz, Governor 47, 144
Tergeman, Siham 86
Thompson, Mrs Bowen 177
Thubron, Colin 162
Tibi family 132
Topkapi Palace (Istanbul) 39, 133
Turkey/Turks 47, 60, 72, 119, 158, 171, 177, 185, 194
Tuta family 219
Twain, Mark 13, 15
'Umar, Caliph 27
Umayyad Mosque (Great Mosque) 21, 25, 27, 37, 42, 43, 47, 56, 59, 60, 86, 93, 99, 214, 217; *13, 21, 25, 27, 61, 182*
 Minaret of Jesus 25, 27
 Minaret of the Bride *13, 21*
 Treasury *13*
Umayyads 22, 25, 37, 39, 99; *37*
'Uthman, Caliph 47
'Uthman Nuri Pasha 185, 192
Victoria Hotel 65, 171; *70*
Villamont, Jacques de 40
Vogüé, Eugène-Melchior de 91, 135
Wakil family 120
Wales, (Edward) Prince of 167
Warner, Charles Dudley 167
Watzinger, Carl 119, 134, 179, 219
Weber, Stefan 42, 113, 161, 214
Wetzstein, Johann Gottfried 154
Wiegand, Theodor 119
Wilhelm II, Kaiser 42, 135
Wool Souk 93, 113, 217
World War, First 72, 119, 179, 185, 194, 209
 Second 72, 144, 182
Wulzinger, Karl 119, 134, 179, 219
Yalbogha Mosque 47; *44*
Ya'qubi (historian) 27
Yaqut (geographer) 27
Yazid, Caliph 22
Yusuf family 146, 155
Zainab (granddaughter of Mohammed) 21
Zangi (Seljuk ruler) 40
Zangids 40
Zawiyya Abu Shamat 219; *44*
Zuqaq al-Sakhr district 43, 214